EVANGELICAL PREACHING

EVANGELICAL PREACHING

By Charles Simeon

Introduction by John R. W. Stott

MULTNOMAH · PRESS

Portland, Oregon 97266

Other *Classics of Faith and Devotion:*
  Real Christianity by William Wilberforce
  The Reformed Pastor by Richard Baxter
  Sin & Temptation by John Owen
  The Love of God by Bernard of Clairvaux
  A Life of Prayer by St. Teresa of Avila
  The Benefit of Christ by Juan de Valdés and Don
    Benedetto
  Religious Affections by Jonathan Edwards
  Toward a Perfect Love by Walter Hilton

All author royalties received from the sale of this book are being used to support the ministry of the London Institute of Contemporary Christianity.

Scripture references in this volume are a paraphrase by the original author.

Pen and ink drawing of Charles Simeon: Sarah Chamberlain

EVANGELICAL PREACHING
This abridged edition
© 1986 by Multnomah Press
Portland, Oregon 97266

Printed in the United States of America

Library of Congress Cataloging-in-Publication Data

Simeon, Charles, 1759-1836.
  Evangelical preaching.

  (Classics of faith and devotion)
  Bibliography: p.
  Includes index.
  1. Church of England—Sermons. 2. Anglican Communion—Sermons. 3. Sermons,
English. I. Title. II. Series.
BX5133.S53E93   1985   252'.03   85-28389
ISBN 0-88070-120-X

85   86   87   88   89   90   –   10   9   8   7   6   5   4   3   2   1

CONTENTS

Part II: The Nature of the Gospel

Part III: Warnings

Part IV: Repentance

Part V: Practical Christianity

Part VI: Worship

Part VII: Prayer

Part VIII: The Holy Scriptures

PREFACE TO THE CLASSICS OF FAITH AND DEVOTION

With the profusion of books now being published, most Christian readers require some guidance for a basic collection of spiritual works that will remain lifelong companions. This new series of Christian classics of devotion is being edited to provide just such a basic library for the home. Those selected may not all be commonly known today, but each has a central concern of relevance for the contemporary Christian.

Another goal for this collection of books is a reawakening. It is a reawakening to the spiritual thoughts and meditations of the forgotten centuries. Many Christians today have no sense of the past. If the Reformation is important to them, they jump from the apostolic Church to the sixteenth century, forgetting some fourteen centuries of the work of the Holy Spirit among many devoted to Christ. These classics will remove that gap and enrich their readers by the faith and devotion of God's saints through all history.

And so we turn to the books, and to their purpose. Some books have changed the lives of their readers. Notice how Athanasius's *Life of Antony* affected Augustine or William Law's *A Serious Call to a Devout and Holy Life* influenced John Wesley. Others, such as Augustine's *Confessions* or Thomas à Kempis's *Imitation of Christ*, have remained perennial sources of inspiration throughout the ages. We sincerely hope those selected in this series will have a like effect on our readers.

Each one of the classics chosen for this series is deeply significant to a contemporary Christian leader. In some cases, the thoughts and reflections of the classic writer are mirrored in the leader's genuine ambitions and desires today, an unusual pairing of hearts and minds across the centuries. And thus these individuals have been asked to write the introduction on the book that has been so meaningful to his or her own life.

PURPOSE FOR THE CLASSICS: SPIRITUAL READING

Since our sensate and impatient culture makes spiritual reading strange and difficult for us, the reader should be cautioned to read these books slowly, meditatively, and reflectively. One cannot rush through them like a detective story. In place of novelty, they focus on remembrance, reminding us of values that remain of eternal consequence. We may enjoy many new things, but values are as old as God's creation.

The goal for the reader of these books is not to seek information. Instead, these volumes teach one about living wisely. That takes obedience, submission of will, change of heart, and a tender, docile spirit. When John the Baptist saw Jesus, he reacted, "He must increase, and I must decrease." Likewise, spiritual reading decreases our natural instincts, to allow His love to increase within us.

Nor are these books "how-to" kits or texts. They take us as we are—that is, as persons, and not as functionaries. They guide us to "be" authentic, and not necessarily to help us to promote more professional activities. Such books require us to make time for their slow digestion, space to let their thoughts enter into our hearts, and discipline to let new insights "stick" and become part of our Christian character.

James M. Houston

EDITOR'S NOTE ABOUT CHARLES SIMEON (1758-1836) AND THE PRINCIPLES OF HOMILETICS EXEMPLIFIED IN THIS ANTHOLOGY OF HIS SERMONS

Apart from the re-publication in 1959 of ten of Simeon's University Sermons which he wrote out in full (and seven sermon outlines),[1] this anthology is the first attempt to provide a wide arrangement of his sermons since 1832. Only one University Sermon is included here in full. This is "Christ Crucified, or Evangelical Religion Described" (Sermon 1933). Most of the others are sermon outlines which he gradually developed during his lifetime. Apart from minor changes of the English, these are reproduced as he wrote them. In 1796, he published one hundred Skeletons. In 1801, he published five hundred sermon outlines, entitled *Helps to Composition*. In 1819, these grew to seventeen volumes, and the whole in twenty-one volumes was completed in 1832 as the *Horae Homileticae*.[2] This labor of love he completed for his fellow clergy "to render their entrance on their holy and honorable calling more easy and their prosecution of it more useful." It is a further labor of love today to read through the 2,536 sermons that he published, and to select those that communicate effectively the elements he deemed characteristic of the preaching of Evangelical Christianity.

There have been notable preachers in the English pulpit, from Wycliffe in the fifteenth century to C. H. Spurgeon in the last. But Charles Simeon was the first preacher of the Church of England to appreciate that it is necessary and possible to teach other pastors how to preach well. He himself had no instruction in homiletics, for it was not taught in the theological schools (although preaching was still an important aspect of English public

life in the late eighteenth century). He later confessed that for the
first seven years of his ministry, he "did not know the head from
the tail of a sermon." After the first year of his ministry he gave up
writing his sermons, but "so stammered and stumbled, that I felt
this was worse than before—and so I was obliged to take to a written sermon again. At last, however, the reading of a sermon appeared so heavy and dull that I once more made an attempt with
notes, and determined if I did not succeed now, to give up preaching."[3]

What saved his ministry was the discovery of Jean Claude's
Essay in the Composition of a Sermon, which his Baptist neighbor,
Robert Robinson, translated in 1788 from the French. It was like
a gift from heaven to the young preacher, having a system of
preaching outlined by this seventeenth-century Huguenot.

He was encouraged to see that he had discovered many of
Claude's principles of preaching for himself. Other ideas of
homiletics he modified to suit his own style. Then he began
weekly to teach a group of young ordinands the principles of
homiletics. Eventually some eleven hundred Anglican clergy had
come under his teaching, filling pulpits of parish churches
throughout the length and breadth of England.[4] Some, like Henry
Martyn, became chaplains in the East India Company. To them
all, he taught the need to write out perhaps the first 300 to 600
sermons, and then to speak extempore after the first three or four
years of preaching. Simeon himself labored at his sermons—at
least twelve hours for each one, and often double that.

In these ways he both set a new standard for the English pulpit
and recovered a new clarity of evangelical, biblical exposition. In
1827 he said, "I think the tone in general is rising," referring to
the quality of biblical preaching throughout England, and "not to
follow the humdrum mode, but to bring out the richness of Scripture." Along with his Bible, his one indispensable tool was John
Brown's *Self-Interpreting Bible* which he obtained in 1785 and
which remained with him all his life. But it was Simeon's indomi-
table spirit, like that of his young protege, Henry Martyn, which
spurred him on. Henry Martyn died at age twenty-nine, having
already served as Simeon's curate, then as a missionary in India,
and having translated the Scriptures into Hindi, Persian, and
Arabic. Whenever Simeon gazed at the face of Martyn's portrait

in his study years later, it seemed to tell him, "Be in earnest." Earnest preaching characterized all who fell under Simeon's spell.

Since it is as a preacher that Charles Simeon is best known, the best tribute one can give him is to summarize his own insights on this ministry.

The Aims of Preaching

It is helpful to read Simeon's sermons alongside of two seventeenth-century books that describe the moral standards required of the pastor-preacher. In *The Reformed Pastor* (ch. 6, VI), Richard Baxter emphasizes the great "skill necessary, to make plain the truth, to convince the hearers, to let in the irresistible light into their consciences, and to keep it there and drive all home; to screw the truth into their minds and work Christ into their affections. . . . This should surely be done with a great deal of holy skill." In one of his sermon classes for young ordinands, Simeon added that "in my sermons, the application is always another turn of the screw." So he emphasized the need to make sure every point hit home.

Perhaps Simeon also knew of George Herbert's *The Country Parson*, who said there were "two things in sermons—the one informing, and the other inflaming" his audience (XXI). This Simeon did with volcanic ardor, "acquiring, imparting, expounding, entreating, imploring, concluding" with the full use of his hands and eyes, as well as tongue, in order to drive home his message. For as William Carus, his curate and successor at Holy Trinity, explains in his memoir of Simeon: "his whole soul was in his subject and he spoke and acted exactly as he felt."[5]

Perhaps it was such fervor in stirring up his audience that aroused opposition against him in his early days. Audiences were not used to evangelical preaching that aroused them from the general torpor of eighteenth-century churchgoers. For Simeon, as for Jeremiah the prophet, God's "word was in mine heart as a burning fire shut up in my bones" (Jeremiah 20:9), a verse he noted specially in his Bible.

Simeon had, however, not two but three aims in his preaching: to instruct, to please, and to affect his audience. The aim of the preacher should first be to *instruct* by solving difficulties of the text, by unfolding mysteries of doctrine, to penetrate into the ways of divine wisdom, to establish truth and refute error. By *pleasing* the audience, Simeon meant the need to comfort his hearers, to fill them with admiration for the wonderful ways and works of God. The preacher should also *affect* his audience, inflaming their souls with zeal and thus powerfully inclining them to practice piety and to love holiness. This Simeon did as he emphasized three things which he prints in capital letters in the preface to his works:

> The Author . . . would wish his work to be brought to this test—Does it uniformly tend
>
> ## TO HUMBLE THE SINNER?
> ## TO EXALT THE SAVIOR?
> ## TO PROMOTE HOLINESS?
>
> If in any one instance it loses sight of any of these points, let it be condemned without mercy.[6]

Simeon himself saw he was but a creature, a mere worm who was a sinner, "whose guilt exceeds all that can be expressed, or conceived." He was wholly Christ-centered in all his ministry. His only ambition when preaching was to proclaim "the great doctrines of salvation by grace through faith in Christ".[7] On March 17, 1811, he preached a powerful sermon on 1 Corinthians 2:2, entitled "Evangelical Religion Described." It was designed "as a brief summary of all that I had preached to [his parishioners] for thirty years." In the codicil of his will he ensured that after his death, a copy of this sermon would be printed and presented to every family in his parish "as a voice to them from the dead." Simeon also emphasized the need of Christians to live lives of holiness. This, he said, "is a conformity of heart and life to the revealed will of God," a progressive work of sanctification that the child of God only gradually develops and matures. Since Simeon personally embodied all he taught, he exemplifies for us a famous definition of great preaching, given by Bishop Phillips Brooks: *Truth* through *personality*.

The Choice of Texts

Simeon, like the French preacher Jean Claude (whose discourse on *The Composition of a Sermon* he used), saw that a sermon should clearly and purely explain a text, recovering the sense it had for the biblical author. He therefore followed six rules laid down by Claude:

1. A preacher should never choose texts which he himself does not well understand. That is to say, do not isolate one or two words, or phrases, which do not reveal the whole context of the biblical passage. Remember—you want to preach the intent of the biblical writer, not your own ideas.

2. Exposition must include the complete sense of the writer. It is his language and his sentiments which you ought to explain.

3. Be selective in what text you choose, for you can take too much. By not being selective of those aspects of theology you wish to give your audience, you may lose them.

4. Pay due regard to the context—that is, to the times, places, and persons associated with the text.

5. Do not choose an unusual text out of personal vanity, simply to show yourself off as being original or clever. Rather, choose a text that is straightforward in expressing some aspect of the truth.

6. Do not censure your audience with a text. But if you do judge your audience, let it be done with wisdom, tempered with sweetness of spirit.[8]

General Rules for Sermon Composition

Much of what Claude taught Simeon is now common homiletical practice; it is still valuable advice.

1. A sermon should clearly and specifically explain a text, as the majority of the congregation is likely to be simple folk. Even if the audience is well-educated, members will still prefer a clear sermon.

2. The entire sense of the passage should be delivered. Avoid a boring or fruitless explanation. In matters of devotion, to be unedifying is destructive. One

cold and poorly delivered sermon will do more damage than a hundred good sermons can ever redeem.

3. A sermon should be wise, sober, and purely motivated. It should not be frivolous nor speculative. Avoid your own speculations, and do not stretch metaphorical language too far. Also, do not shock the audience with immodest allusions.

4. A preacher should be simple and not given to abstract theorizing. He should avoid slang expressions, but be polite and courteous.

5. The sermon should make a profound and heart-felt impact upon the audience, so that the hearers repent and are led to deepen their spiritual lives in a renewed desire for godly living. Constantly apply what you preach.

6. Above all, avoid all excess, whether it be academic brilliance that shows off the preacher rather than honoring the Spirit of God, or whether an overload of doctrine which cannot be digested properly. Be careful also never to overstress a particular point, or to rationalize it away. By all means, make all the critical observations you need for your own private study; but do not load it all upon the congregation, whether it be about grammatical observations, or critical readings of the text, or citing too many authorities for what you have been persuaded to accept. Yet an apt quotation can be effective, if chosen relevantly and not too frequently.

To his students, Simeon taught three other rules.

1. Take as your subject what you believe to be the mind of the Lord. Be careful to understand what may be the mind of God in the passage before you.

2. Mark the character of the passage. It may be a simple statement, a precept or promise, a threat, an invitation, or an appeal. Or it may be more complex, as in arguments of cause and effect.

3. Note the spirit of the passage. It may be tender and compassionate, or indignant—but let the preacher express it consistently. For God himself should be heard in us, and through us, as he spoke to us.

The true *meaning* of the text should be like the warp, which provides the whole texture of the composition; the *words* spoken should be the woof, so interwoven as to form one connected and continued whole. The spirit of the words should pervade the whole discourse.

Ways of Handling a Text

In his long and somewhat repetitious essay, Claude cited twenty-seven different ways of treating the topic for preaching a sermon. These can be reduced to the following points:

1. Go from the particular to the general principle, so that you see what is of significance.

2. Recognize the essential character of good or evil as you describe their traits.

3. Identify assumptions that are not explicit in the text itself.

4. Note the character or conditions of the person quoted or described in the text.

5. Note the time and place of the word or action in the text.

6. Consider the consequences noted in the text.

7. Examine anything remarkable in the manner of speech or action described.

8. Compare the words and actions of one text with another.

9. Guard against objections to your interpretation of the text.

10. Distinguish between the explanation and the application of a text.

The Composition of the Sermon

Having thoroughly understood the text by private study, the preacher should divide it up into its several aspects. He should make at least two, but not more than four points, argued Simeon. These should interrelate and be mutually dependent. Arrange your major points effectively, starting with the most general one. Follow in sequence the unfolding of your knowledge on the subject, so that the first proposition serves as a step toward the second, then the third, and so on. Think clearly and nobly, so that your observations are full of beauty and dignity, under the control of the text itself.

The flow of a sermon should commence with the introduction; then a number of observations should be made; and conclude with practical applications. Thus, four distinct aspects of the sermon should be drawn up: the explanations, observations, applications, and propositions. Each needs special handling, and the sermon itself may be colored by any one of these approaches as the prevailing feature of its composition.

The *Introduction* is made primarily to prepare the audience for what you are going to discuss, and so lead into the subject. But this is difficult to do well; aptly it has been described as "the cross of the preacher." The introduction must be stimulating to get the attention of the audience and to prepare them for the course of the address. It is also important to move your audience to conform with the nature of your sermon, whether it be to move them to sorrow or compassion, awe or reverence. So the introduction should always be identified with the nature of the subject to follow. We may sum up the needs of the introduction as follows:

1. It must be brief, so the hearer is prepared (not bored) for what follows.

2. It must be clear, free of all abstract thought. Let it come naturally and easily.

3. It must be gently and seriously introduced, neither too dramatic nor too dull.

4. It should be attractively and enjoyably presented, so that a negative atmosphere is avoided.

5. The introduction should integrate the whole of the sermon.

6. It must be simple, avoiding all bombast and over-strained language.

7. It must not trivialize or cheapen with jargon and superficial talk.

To convey all of these effects, you may have to prepare several forms of introduction before you settle finally on what is the most helpful and suitable (once you have made your completed outline for the sermon).

The *Conclusion* must be lively and stimulating, full of challenging and apt ideas that help to stir the affections of the Christian toward God. These may be zeal, love, hope, repentance, self-condemnation, desire for self-correction, comfort, a longing for eternal blessings, joy, courage, constancy, resistance to temptation, gratitude to God, recourse to prayer, and many others. Some of these are strong; others are gentle or ecstatic and worshipful, as we find at the end of Romans 8. The conclusion should be diversified, ranging over numerous Christian passions. It should also be imaginative, free to touch upon a range of suggestions, symbols, and insights.

The Spirit of Charles Simeon

To these and other insights of Claude, Simeon himself communicated his whole personality as he sought to express it in Christ. Never a friend of systematized theology, he endeavored to live practically by the Scriptures. He never believed one theological system had a monopoly on truth. He rejected all partisan teaching. Instead, Simeon sought to "give every text its just meaning, its natural bearing, and its legitimate use." He urged his hearers not to be sectarian, but to cultivate a devout and ecumenical spirit that focused upon the authority of the Bible in daily living. His aim was to make "Bible Christians" out of his hearers so that they lived out the reality of the gospel as revealed in the Holy Scriptures. He was remarkably understanding of people, and saw the danger of many preachers who lost touch with their congregations. Instead, he got closely in touch, through personal counseling as well as by soul-winning. In turn, he inspired some 1,100 clergy throughout the parishes of England to do likewise.

After his death in 1836, his friend Daniel Wilson, Bishop of Calcutta, listed ten traits of Simeon's life.[9] Among them: Simeon remained faithful to only one charge all his life, as the Vicar of Holy Trinity Church, Cambridge. He remained unmoved by numerous attractive offers of other ministry through fifty-four years of public ministry. He was bold in character, with decisive sincerity and consistency. In matters of secondary theological debate, he remained moderate and open-minded. He had a devout and godly spirit. His passionate concern was to help theological students, nurturing them to be faithful preachers of the Word. He worked hard and conscientiously on every sermon that he preached. He had broad interests in strategic religious institutions, such as the Church Missionary Society, the British and Foreign Bible Society, the Jews Conversion Society, the Prayer Book and Homily Society, and others. He communicated a balanced understanding of Protestant Episcopal Christianity. He lived a highly disciplined life. He was a great force for evangelical truth and holiness for over half a century.

The topical arrangement of this anthology of his sermons is intended to suggest the range of scriptural texts he used, the major foci of his convictions, and the heart of his message on evangelical preaching. The prayer book of *The Lesser Feasts and Fasts* has honored him with a prayer that we, too, can recite as we are inspired by his ministry:

> O loving God, we know that all things are ordered by Thine unswerving wisdom and unbounded love. Grant us in all things to see Thy hand; that following the example of Charles Simeon, we may walk with Christ in all simplicity, and serve Thee with a quiet and contented mind, through Jesus Christ our Lord, who liveth and reigneth with Thee, and with the Holy Spirit, one God, for ever and ever, Amen.[10]

We are grateful to my good friend, Dr. John Stott, who as Rector and now Rector Emeritus of All Souls Langham Place Church in London, England, has for long exemplified the qualities of evangelical preaching that Charles Simeon expressed. His introductory essay on Charles Simeon is therefore appropriate and helpful. We are also indebted to Mrs. Jean Nordlund and Miss Kathy Knight for their assistance in typing the manuscript.

James M. Houston

[1] Arthur Pollard, *Let Wisdom Judge* (London: Inter-Varsity Fellowship, 1959).

[2] The enumeration of sermons in this anthology is based upon the final collection of the *Horae Homileticae.* (London: Holdsworth & Ball, 1832).

[3] William Carus, *Memoirs of the Life of the Rev. Charles Simeon* (New York: Robert Carter, 1848), p. 37.

[4] Hugh Evan Hopkins, *Charles Simeon, Preacher Extraordinary* (Bramcote, Notts.: Grove Books, 1979), p. 33.

[5] Ibid., p. 15.

[6] Preface to the *Horae Homileticae*, vol.1 (1832), p. xxi.

[7] Ibid., p. xxii.

[8] Ibid., vol. 21, pp. 291-410.

[9] Carus, op. cit., pp. 485-491.

[10] *The Lesser Feasts and Fasts*, 3d edition (New York: Church Hymnal Corporation), p. 375.

Two standard biographies of Charles Simeon are:

Hopkins, Hugh Evan. *Charles Simeon of Cambridge*. London: Hodder & Stoughton, 1977.

Moule, Handley C. G. *Charles Simeon*. London, I.V.P., 1968, 1982.

INTRODUCTION
CHARLES SIMEON:
A PERSONAL APPRECIATION

It was during my undergraduate days at Cambridge University that I was introduced to Charles Simeon. I owe the introduction to Dr. Douglas Johnson, the first General Secretary of the British Inter-Varsity Fellowship (now the Universities and Colleges Christian Fellowship), whose vision for the recovery of biblical scholarship (and in particular for the Tyndale Fellowship for Biblical Research) has never been adequately acknowledged by the church. Simeon's uncompromising commitment to Scripture, as the Word of God to be obeyed and expounded, captured my admiration and has held it ever since. On many occasions I have had the privilege of preaching from his pulpit in Holy Trinity Church, Cambridge, and standing where he stood, have prayed for a measure of his outstanding faithfulness.

Charles Simeon was one of the greatest and most persuasive preachers the Church of England has ever known. His collected sermons, published in twenty-one volumes under the title *Horae Homileticae*, number about 2,500. If one were to read a single sermon a day, it would take seven years to get through them all. So widespread was his influence throughout the country that, in the opinion of Lord Macaulay, expressed in 1844, "his real sway in the church was far greater than that of any Primate" (i.e. senior Archbishop) (quoted by G. O. Trevelyan in *The Life and Letters of Lord Macaulay*, 1980, p. 50).

Simeon was born in 1758, the same year as William Wilberforce, champion of the slaves and his lifelong friend. His parents were affluent, and he was brought up as a young English aristocrat of the eighteenth century. At the tender age of seven and a half he was sent to the Royal College of Eton, and six years later to the Foundation (as the senior school was known). He was plain in appearance and awkward in manner, but also athletic, an accomplished horseman, and a connoisseur of smart clothes, especially silk waistcoats and flashy shoe buckles. At that time, however, he showed no interest in the things of God and had an ungovernable temper. One could hardly guess that in God's providence he was to become a powerful herald of the gospel.

What were the secrets of his effectiveness as a preacher? I will elaborate what seem to me to have been the five most important ones.

First, Simeon had a steadfast personal faith in Christ crucified.

When he went up from Eton to King's College Cambridge in 1779, he was still a godless, worldly, and carefree youth. So he was shocked to be informed by the Provost within three days of his arrival that by an ancient college rule he was "absolutely required" to attend a terminal service of Holy Communion. "Conscience told me," he commented later, "that Satan was as fit to go there as I; and that if I *must* go, I *must* repent and turn to God, unless I chose to eat and drink to my own damnation." He had three weeks in which to prepare, and made himself "quite ill with reading, fasting and prayer." The Holy Spirit was also convicting him of sin. "So greatly was my mind oppressed with the weight of my former numberless iniquities," he said, "that I frequently looked on the dogs with envy" (Carus, p. 6).

The communion service came and went, but still he had no peace. Then a week or two before Easter he bought a copy of Bishop Thomas Wilson's book *Instruction for the Lord's Supper*. Here is his own account of what happened as he read: "I met with an expression to this effect, 'that the Jews knew what they did when they transferred their sin to the head of their offering.' The thought rushed into my mind, 'What? May I transfer all my guilt to Another? Has God provided an offering for me that I may lay my sins on his head? Then, God willing, I will not bear them on my soul one moment longer.' Accordingly, I sought to lay my sins upon the sacred head of Jesus, and on the Wednesday began to have a hope of mercy; on the Thursday that hope increased; on the Friday and Saturday it became more strong; and on the Sunday morning (Easter Day) I woke early with those words upon my heart and lips 'Jesus Christ is risen today! Hallelujah! Hallelujah!' From that hour peace flowed in rich abundance into my soul, and at the Lord's table in our chapel I had the sweetest access to God through my blessed Savior" (Carus, p. 9).

Simeon's somewhat dramatic conversion was no flash in the pan, soon to be extinguished. It was no sudden springtime blossoming, whose flowers quickly withered and dropped and died. On the contrary, he never lost his vivid sense of personal indebtedness to the cross of Christ. In his early sixties he could write: "It is now a little over forty years since I began to seek after God, and within about three months of that time after much humiliation and prayer I found peace through that Lamb of God who taketh away the sins of the world. . . . From that time to the present hour I have never for a moment lost my hope and confidence in the adorable Savior, for though, alas, I have abundant cause for humiliation, I have never ceased to wash in that fountain that was opened for sin and uncleanness, or to cast myself upon the tender mercy of my reconciled God."

It seems to me that one might well single out this freshness of spiritual experience as the first indispensable quality of the effective preacher. No amount of homiletical technique can compensate for the absence of a close personal walk with God. Unless he puts a new song in our mouth, even the most polished sermons will lack the sparkle of authenticity.

When Simeon lay on his deathbed in 1836, he was disturbed by the doctor, the nurse, the three servants, and the two curates who were all fussing around him. "I wish to be alone, with my God," he said, "and to lie before him as a poor, wretched, hell-deserving sinner. . . . But I would also look to him as my all-forgiving God—and as my all-sufficient God—and as my all-atoning God—and as my covenant-keeping God. . . . I would lie here to the last, at the foot of the cross, looking unto Jesus; and go as such into the presence of my God" (Carus, page 810).

It was right, then, that after his death a memorial tablet should have been erected on the south wall of the chancel of Holy Trinity Church, which describes him as one who "whether as the ground of his own hopes or as the subject of all his ministrations determined to know nothing but Jesus Christ and him crucified."

Second, Simeon was willing to suffer for what he believed and preached.

In 1782, only three years after his conversion, he was elected a Fellow of King's College, was ordained into the pastorate of the Church of England, and began his ministry at St. Edward's Church, "in good old Latimer's pulpit" as he put it (Carus, p. 21).

It is hard for us to comprehend his sense of isolation and loneliness as an evangelical believer at that time. He wondered if anybody existed who shared his experience and convictions. "I longed exceedingly to know some spiritual person," he wrote, "who had the same views and feelings with myself; and I had serious thoughts of putting into the papers . . . an advertisement to the following effect: 'that a young clergyman who felt himself an undone sinner, and looked to the Lord Jesus Christ alone for salvation, and desired to live only to make known that Savior unto others, was persuaded that there must be some persons in the world whose views and feelings on this subject accorded with his own, though he had now lived three years without finding so much as one; and that if there were any minister of that description, he would gladly become his curate and serve him gratis'" (Carus, p. 22).

Even during those early days of intense loneliness God richly blessed his ministry at St. Edward's. Within a month or two the building was full, "and a considerable stir was made among the dry bones" (Carus, p. 24). "He preaches at a church in the town," wrote John Berridge to John Newton, "which is crowded like a theater on the first night of a new play" (Marcus Loane, p. 179).

But Simeon was to remain at St. Edward's less than a year. He had often walked past Holy Trinity Church, which had been the pulpit of those two great Puritans, Richard Sibbes and Thomas Goodwin, and which was in the heart of the university campus. As he went by, he would say to himself, "How should I rejoice if God were to give me that church that I might preach his gospel there, and be a herald for him in the midst of the University."

God answered his prayer, and he was appointed to Holy Trinity later that same year. Little did he anticipate the violent opposition which awaited him, however, because of his known evangelical views. In spite of (or perhaps because of) the Evangelical Revival associated with the names of Wesley and Whitefield, which had been spreading throughout Britain for over forty years, Evangelicals were suspected and feared as dangerous "enthusiasts." I have read (though I have been unable to confirm) that there is a church bell in Cambridge which still bears the inscription "Glory to God and damnation to enthusiasts."

At all events, when Simeon began his ministry at Holy Trinity, the seatholders (who paid to reserve places for themselves and their family) not only boycotted the services themselves, but locked the doors of their high, old-fashioned pews, so that nobody else could occupy them. Then, when Simeon had benches put in the aisles, the church wardens dragged them out into the street and churchyard. For more than ten years the congregation had to stand. The same wardens even tried several times to lock Simeon out of his own church, while rowdy students did their best to break up the services. Sometimes both the church and the adjoining streets were scenes of "the most disgraceful tumults." Filth and stones were flung, and on at least one occasion Simeon's face was seen streaming with rotten eggs as he left the church. And if the students showed their disapproval by means of such violence, the faculty treated him with a more refined contempt, and both slandered and ostracized him.

It was not easy to bear a decade of such sustained opposition. But Simeon determined to win his way by "faith and patience" (Carus, p. 44). A text which at that time was never far from his thoughts was 2 Timothy 2:24: "The servant of the Lord must not strive, but be gentle unto all men, apt to teach, patient." On one occasion, when he was in great distress on account of the opposition, he went for a walk with his Greek Testament in his hand, and prayed that God would comfort him from his Word. Opening his Testament he read, "And as they came out, they found a man of Cyrene, Simon (Simeon) by name; him they compelled to bear his cross." "When I read that," he wrote, "I said, 'Lord, lay it on me, lay it on me. I will gladly bear the cross for thy sake'" (Carus, p. 676).

Gradually the tide turned. Growing numbers of students came to Holy Trinity to listen to him, impressed by his learning, courage, and sincerity. Seatholders began to relent and to open their locked pews. As the years passed, his reputation grew throughout the University. He became Dean and Vice-Provost of his College, and on numerous occasions Select Preacher before the University.

For fifty-four years he remained Vicar of Holy Trinity Church. He had become so widely honored that when he died, all the shops closed (although it was market day), University lectures were suspended, and mourners lined up four deep all round the great court of King's College, waiting to pay their final tribute to his memory.

The story of Simeon is a signal example both of the inevitability of opposition whenever the gospel is faithfully preached, and of the fulfillment of the promise of Proverbs 16:7 that "when a man's ways please the LORD, he makes even his enemies to be at peace with him."

Third, Simeon was wholly and thoughtfully faithful to Scripture.

Without doubt this was his most distinctive characteristic both as a disciple and as a preacher. His faithfulness took several forms.

To begin with, he sought to be personally submissive to whatever God had said in his Word. In consequence, anticipating the modern hermeneutical debate about the blindspots which our cultural inheritance and ecclesiastical traditions create within us, he tried to divest himself of all preconceptions and to listen to God's Word with an open, unprejudiced, and impartial mind. "I have long pursued the study of Scripture with a desire to be impartial," he once said to his friend J. J. Gurney. ". . . In the beginning of my inquiries I said to myself, 'I am a fool; of that I am quite certain.' One thing I know assuredly, that in religion of myself I know nothing. I do not therefore sit down to the perusal of Scripture in order to impose a sense on the inspired writers, but to receive one, as they give it me. I pretend (sc. claim) not to teach them, I wish like a child to be taught by them" (Carus, p. 674). Again, in his autobiographical memoirs he wrote: "I love the simplicity of the Scriptures; and I wish to receive and inculcate every truth precisely in the way, and to the extent, that it is set forth in the inspired volume. . . . I soon learn that I must take the Scriptures with the simplicity of a little child, and be content to receive on God's testimony what he has revealed, whether I can unravel all the difficulties that may attend it or not" (Carus, pp. 16, 25).

If Simeon had lived in our generation, I think he would have acknowledged the need for biblical "criticism"; that is, for a rigorous investigation of the cultural milieu, historical background, and the literary origins of every text. At the same time, I am sure he would have rejected the proud, selective, judgmental attitude which many adopt toward Scripture and would have reiterated with even stronger emphasis the necessity of cultivating the humble, openhearted simplicity of a child, and of sitting like Mary of Bethany at Jesus' feet, listening to his word.

His personal attitude to Scripture was naturally reflected in his handling of it in the pulpit. His overriding concern was so to expound Scripture that his congregation would receive it undiluted and uncontaminated by worldly wisdom. To him "biblical exposition" meant opening up some part of Scripture so that the people could feed upon it. "My endeavor," he wrote to his publisher, "is to bring out of Scripture what is there, and not to thrust in what I think might be there. I have a great jealousy on this head: never to speak more or less than I believe to be the mind of the Spirit in the passage I am expounding" (Quoted by H. E. Hopkins, p. 57). Those words seem to me to be the clearest statement ever made of the expositor's goal. Would that more preachers could wholeheartedly echo and endorse it today!

The second way in which Simeon's faithfulness to Scripture manifested itself was in his wary attitude to theological systems. He lived in a period when the controversy between "Calvinists" and "Arminians" was heated, even bitter. Yet in his preface to the *Horae Homileticae* he wrote: "The author is . . . no friend to systematizers in theology. He has endeavored to derive from the Scriptures alone his views of religion; and to them it is his wish to adhere, with scrupulous fidelity; never wresting any portion of the Word of God to favor a particular opinion, but giving to every part of it that sense, which it seems to him to have been designed by its great Author to convey" (Preface, pp. 4-5).

As Simeon went on to write, he had "no doubt that there is a system in the Holy Scriptures (for truth cannot be inconsistent with itself)" (Preface, p. 5). Nor was he opposed to every attempt to synthesize or systematize the teaching of Scripture, for he himself did it in every sermon he preached, setting his exposition down in an orderly and systematic way. What he feared was the development of a complete and rigid system; for then, when new light breaks forth from the Word, the systematizer is faced with the painful dilemma of either adapting his system to absorb the freshly perceived truth or of trimming the truth to fit his system. The latter is the temptation of tidy minds.

Indeed, Simeon suspected that every systematizer is guilty of a little bit of editing and manipulating. "Of this he is sure, that there is not a decided Calvinist or Arminian in the world, who equally approves of the whole of Scripture. He apprehends that there is not a determined votary of either system who, if he had been in the company of St. Paul, whilst he was writing his different epistles, would not have recommended him to alter one or other of his expressions. But the author would not wish one of them altered: he finds as much satisfaction in one class of passages as in another; and employs the one, he believes, as often and as freely as the other. . . . He is content to sit as a learner at the feet of the holy apostles, and has no ambition to teach them how they ought to have spoken. . . . He bitterly regrets that men will range themselves under human banners and leaders, and employ themselves in converting the inspired writers into friends and partisans of their peculiar principles" (Preface to *Horae Homileticae*, pp. 5-6).

There is a valuable warning here for us to heed in our own day. Works of systematic theology we shall gratefully and profitably read. But all the time we shall be wise to hear Simeon whispering in our ear what he said to students in one of his conversation parties, "Be Bible Christians, and not system Christians" (Pollard, p. 15).

This leads me to mention another way in which Simeon's faithfulness to Scripture was expressed. It concerns the biblical paradoxes (containing a contradiction which is apparent, not real), and even more the biblical antinomies (in which the contradiction seems real enough and cannot be logically resolved). His favorite example was again the Calvinist-Arminian controversy between divine sovereignty and human responsibility. Simeon (like Calvin himself) was convinced that we do not have to choose between these, since Scripture teaches both. For example, he was fond of quoting two texts from John's Gospel. According to one, Jesus said "you will not come to me, that you may have life" (John 5:40); according to the other, "no man can come to me unless the Father who sent me draws him" (John 6:44). The "will not" and the "cannot" are both plain; the problem is how to reconcile them.

Simeon summed up his position in relation to the biblical antinomies in these words: "The truth is not in the middle, and not in one extreme; but in both extremes," even if you cannot reconcile them. He was aware how his critics would respond. "Go to Aristotle," they would say, "and learn the golden mean." "But, my brother," Simeon would reply, "I am unfortunate: I formally studied Aristotle, and liked him much. I have since read Paul, and caught something of his strange notions, oscillating (not vacillating) from pole to pole. Sometimes I am a high Calvinist, at other times a low Arminian, so that if extremes will please you, I am your man. Only remember, it is not one extreme that we are to go to, but both extremes" (Carus, p. 600).

Is it not illogical, however, to embrace two opposite positions which appear to exclude each other? Yes, it may be illogical to the human mind, but who requires us to resolve all antinomies logically? "When I come to a text which speaks of election," he said to J. J. Gurney in 1831, "I delight myself in the doctrine of election. When the apostles exhort me to repentance and obedience, and indicate my freedom of choice and action, I give myself up to that side of the question" (Carus, pp. 674-5). In defense of his commitment to both extremes, Simeon would sometimes borrow an illustration from the Industrial Revolution. "As wheels in a complicated machine may move in opposite directions and yet subserve a common end, so may truths apparently opposite be perfectly reconcilable with each other, and equally subserve the purposes of God in the accomplishment of man's salvation" (Preface, p. 5).

Fourth, Simeon dedicated himself to the ministry of preaching.

He was quite clear that, according to the New Testament, the ordained ministry is pastoral in nature, not priestly. That is, its direction is primarily manward, not Godward. The pastor is a shepherd, called to tend the sheep of God's flock by feeding them. God's ministers are first and foremost ministers of his word, stewards of his revelation, charged to teach people out of it. "Ministers are appointed of God," he said, when expounding 2 Timothy 2:25,26 (sermon 2250) "to instruct the world in the things which belong to their everlasting peace." Again, on 2 Timothy 4:1,2 (Sermon 2258) in which Paul urged Timothy to "preach the Word," the minister "is not at liberty to amuse the people with the fancies and conceits of men, but must declare simply the mind and will of God. He is sent of God for that very end. He is an ambassador from God to man, authorized to declare on what terms God will be reconciled to his rebellious subjects." Moreover, he must do so "with assiduity," "with fidelity, and "with perseverance."

Next, Simeon took trouble to prepare his expository sermons. He was a lifelong student of Scripture. So deeply had he absorbed its message that his sermons are saturated with biblical quotations and allusions. Yet he did not come by this thorough knowledge easily. It was the fruit of the most diligent labor. "There is nothing in the whole universe to be compared with the Scriptures of truth," he said in Sermon 2187, "nothing that will so enrich the mind, nothing that will so benefit the soul. To treasure them up in our minds should be our daily and most delightful employment. Not a day should pass without adding to their blessed store, and not only in memory and mind, but in heart and soul." Not that he relied for growing understanding on his studies alone; he knew that the illumination of the spirit was also indispensable. To enforce this, he used the illustration of the sundial. On a dull and cloudy day it does not tell us the time; but when the sun breaks through, and shines upon the dial, immediately the finger points. So "for the attainment of divine knowledge we are directed to combine a dependence on God's Spirit with our own researches. Let us, then, not presume to separate what God has thus united."

In order to give himself to Bible study and prayer, Simeon exercised stern self-discipline and rose at four o'clock every morning. Early rising did not appeal to his natural tendency to self-indulgence, however, especially on dark winter mornings in East Anglia where the bitterly cold north-easterly wind seems to blow straight from the snows of Siberia. On several occasions he overslept, to his considerable chagrin. So he determined that if ever he did it again, he would pay a fine of half a crown to his "bedmaker" (college servant). A few days later, as he lay comfortably in his warm bed, he found himself reflecting that the good woman was poor and could probably do with half a crown. So, to overcome such rationalizations, he vowed that next time he would throw a guinea into the river. This (the story goes) he duly did, but only once, for guineas were scarce; he could not afford to use them to pave the riverbed with gold (Moule, p. 66).

Apart from his daily, prayerful Bible study, Simeon never

spared himself in the actual preparing of his Sunday sermons. "Few cost him less than twelve hours of study," wrote Carus, "many twice that time, and some several days" (p. 84), and then, when he had written his sermon out, he would read it over "half a dozen times at the least" (Carus, p. 63), in order to familiarize himself with his message and avoid the necessity to read it word for word.

Such a rigorous daily and weekly regimen of study meant that he had little time left for other things. To be sure, he visited and counseled, maintained a wide correspondence, and arranged his "conversation parties" for groups of students. He was also conscientious in the wider life of the church, especially in the leadership he gave to the Eclectic Society, in his promotion of Christian missions to both "the heathen" and the Jews, in encouraging ministerial candidates and young clergy, and in securing the "ad vowsons" (i.e., the right of appointment) to many churches, in order to ensure a continuity of evangelical ministry in them. Nevertheless, in spite of all this varied service, he steadfastly refused to become an activist, lest he should exhaust his limited physical resources and so damage or detract from his primary ministry of God's Word. "My own health, through mercy," he wrote some thirty-five years after his ordination, "is as good as at any period of my life; and by means of constant and extraordinary caution, my voice in public is as strong almost as ever. But I am silent all the week besides. . . . I compare myself to bottled small beer: being corked up, and opened only twice a week, I make a good report; but if I were opened every day, I should soon be as ditch-water" (Carus, p. 445).

Next, Simeon cultivated a direct and simple style. The preachers of his day were mostly dry and academic, and the Victorians who followed him tended toward flowery verbosity. Simeon resisted both temptations. He started a new tradition of biblical exposition. He aimed, he said, at "unity in his subject, perspicuity in his arrangement, and simplicity in his diction" (Carus, p. 719). Again, "I think that every sermon should have, like a telescope, but one object in the field" (p. 717). In consequence, there is in his sermon outlines, Arthur Pollard has written, "a clarity, orderliness and directness that is all too rare in the writings of our own time," let alone of his (Pollard, p. 7). Reading his outlines today, one is amazed at the entire absence of padding. The prose is straightforward and fluent. The sentences are short, and for the most part lack subordinate clauses. He practices a great economy of words, and eschews the habit of adding adjective to adjective like the carriages of a train. He uses antithesis with effect, sprinkling his text liberally with "not—but" sentences. He asks himself questions, and immediately answers them with a resounding "yes" or "no." One is never in doubt about his meaning.

Every sermon is carefully structured, beginning with an introduction which opens up the topic, continuing with two or three main points which are sometimes subdivided, and concluding with an "Address," "Application," or "Entreaty," which drives the message home by calling on the congregation to make precise and practical responses (usually two at a time).

The fifth and last characteristic of Simeon for which I thank God is that he was a man of unalloyed personal authenticity.

There was no dichotomy between the man and his message, between the person and the preacher. There was nothing devious about him. He was a transparent Christian, who hated humbug.

One indication of this was the earnestness of his bearing and manner while preaching. He knew how much his academic colleagues despised religious "enthusiasm." It was not done in those days for preachers to betray their emotions in the pulpit. Deep thinking and deep feeling were supposed to exclude one another. But Simeon did not care what people thought of him. He feared God, not man. He was not like the Pharisees who "loved praise from men more than praise from God" (John 12:43).

Besides, he had a clear objective in every sermon. He wrote in his preface to *Helps to Composition* that he wanted his work to be judged by this test, whether it tended uniformly "to humble the sinner, to exalt the Savior, and to promote holiness" (Carus, p. 188). These goals were far too serious to play with or joke about. So he was determined to be himself. "His whole soul was in his subject," wrote William Carus his biographer, "and he spoke and acted exactly as he felt. Occasionally indeed his gestures and looks were almost grotesque . . . but his action was altogether unstudied . . . and always sincere and serious" (Carus, p. 63). "Whoever heard a dry sermon from Simeon's lips?" asked Canon Abner Brown, and to answer his own question told of the little girl who heard him preach for the first time and turned to her mother saying: "O Mama! What is the gentleman in a passion about?" (Quoted by H. E. Hopkins, p. 65).

Simeon's personal authenticity was mostly clearly revealed, however, not on public occasions (whether in the pulpit or elsewhere) but in private when he was alone with God. He knew his imperfections of character, and needed to humble himself before God in repentance. The hot temper of his unregenerate youth was never wholly subdued by the Holy Spirit. He could be awkward, even brusque. After he had visited his friend Henry Venn, the latter's three daughters could not help laughing at his clumsy mannerisms. So their father asked them to go outside and pick him a peach. Not knowing what was in his mind, they did so. But being early summer, it was green, unripe, inedible. "Well, my dears," commented their father, "it is green now, and we must wait; but a little more sun and a few more showers, and the peach will be ripe and sweet. So it is with Mr. Simeon" (Moule, p. 44). He was right. Simeon mellowed with age, and the fruit of the Spirit grew ever riper within him.

Yet he never lost his sense of indebtedness to Christ crucified for the forgiveness of his sins, and he knew what it was to walk humbly with his God. After describing his conversion he wrote: "with this sweet hope of ultimate acceptance with God, I have always enjoyed much cheerfulness before men; but I have at the same time labored incessantly to cultivate the deepest humiliation before God. I have never thought that the circumstance of God's having forgiven me was any reason why I should forgive myself . . . there are but two objects that I have ever desired for these 40 years to behold; the one is my own vileness; and the other is the glory of God in the face of Jesus Christ; and I have always thought that they should be viewed together. . . . By this I seek to be not only humbled and thankful, but humbled in thankfulness before my God and Savior continually" (Carus, pp. 518-520).

At one of his weekly tea-parties somebody asked Simeon: "What, Sir, do you consider the principal mark of regeneration?" It was a probing question. With the current popularity of the "born-again movement," one wonders how the average evangelical believer would reply today. This was Simeon's answer: "the very first and indispensable sign is self-loathing and abhorrence. Nothing short of this can be admitted as an evidence of a real change. . . . I want to see more of this humble, contrite, broken spirit amongst us. It is the very spirit that belongs to self-condemned sinners. . . . This sitting in the dust is most pleasing to God . . . give me to be with a broken-hearted Christian, and I prefer his society to that of all the rest. . . . Were I now addressing to you my dying words, I should say nothing else but what I have just said. Try to live in this spirit of self-abhorrence, and let it habitually mark your life and conduct" (Carus, pp. 651-652).

"Self-loathing," "self-condemnation," "self-abhorrence." The words grate on modern ears. The contemporary craze is for a bigger and better self-image. We are exhorted on all sides to love ourselves, forgive ourselves, respect ourselves, assert ourselves. And to be sure, as in all heresies, there are a few grains of truth in this one. For we should gratefully affirm ourselves as creatures made in the image of God, and as children of God redeemed by Christ and indwelt by his Spirit. In this mercy of God our Creator and Savior we are to rejoice greatly, and there is much exhortation to such joy in Simeon's sermons.

But to rejoice in God is one thing; to rejoice in ourselves is another. Self-congratulation and the worship of God are mutually incompatible. Those who have a high view of themselves always have a correspondingly low view of God. It is those who have seen God high and lifted up, exalted in indescribable glory above the universe, who become overwhelmed with a sense of their own sinfulness and unworthiness. It was so with every biblical character who glimpsed the holiness of God. Moses was afraid to look, Isaiah cried out in dismay, Ezekiel fell down prostrate before God's throne, while Job actually said, "Now my eyes have seen you; therefore I despise myself and repent in dust and ashes" (42:5,6). Would it be too much to say that personal authenticity begins here, when we are on our faces before God? This is "the broken and contrite heart" which is a sacrifice pleasing to God (Psalm 51:17). Modern men and women may value "self-esteem," but God thinks differently. "This is the one I esteem," he says: "he who is humble and contrite in spirit, and trembles at my word" (Isaiah 66:2).

Of this truth Simeon remains a conspicuous example; I will therefore let him have the last word. In May 1832 he wrote to his friend Daniel Wilson, Bishop of Calcutta: "Repentance is in every view so desirable, so necessary, so suited to honor God, that I seek that above all. The tender heart, the broken and contrite spirit, are to me far above all the joys that I could ever hope for in this vale of tears. I long to be in my proper place, my hand on my mouth, and my mouth in the dust. . . . I feel this to be safe ground. Here I cannot err. . . . I am sure that whatever God may despise (and I fear that there is much which passes under the notion of religious experience that will not stand very high in his estimation), he will not despise the broken and contrite heart. I love the picture of the heavenly hosts, both saints and angels: all of them are upon their faces before the throne. I love the Cherubim with their wings before their faces and their feet. . . . For me, I feel that this is the proper posture now, and will be to all eternity. . . . " (Carus, pp. 695-6).

Then, on recovering from an illness three years before he died, Simeon returned to the same theme: "Standing as I do on the very brink and precipice of the eternal world, I desire nothing so much a broken and contrite spirit. . . . I hang upon the Savior, as actually perishing without his unbounded mercy and unintermitted care. I look to him as the very chief of sinners; and in this frame of mind I find perfect peace" (Carus, p. 716).

A year later he referred to this as "the religion of a sinner at the foot of the Cross" (Carus, p. 731).

Our proud, self-confident, self-congratulatory generation urgently needs to recover this biblical perspective. I do myself. It is the acme of health and holiness.

John R. W. Stott

Bibliography

Balleine, G. R. A *History of the Evangelical Party in the Church of England*. First published Longmans Green, 1908; Church Bookroom Press, 1951.

Carus, William, ed. *Memoirs of the Life of the Rev. Charles Simeon*. Hatchard 1848.

Hopkins, Hugh Evan. *Charles Simeon of Cambridge*. Hodder & Stoughton, 1977.

_____. *Charles Simeon Preacher Extraordinary*. Grove Books, 1979.

Loane, Marcus L. *Cambridge and the Evangelical Succession*. Butterworth, 1952.

Moule, Handley C. G. *Charles Simeon*. First published 1982, IVP 1948.

Pollard, Arthur, ed. *Let Wisdom Judge*. IVP, 1959.

Simeon, Charles. *Horae Homileticae* in 17 volumes. 1819.

_____. *An appendix to the Horae Homileticae in 6 volumes*. 1828.

_____. *Horae Homileticae in 21 volumes*. 1832.

Smyth, Charles. *Simeon and Church Order*. CUP, 1940.

Part I
GOD AND MAN

JEHOVAH: A JEALOUS GOD

*"The LORD, whose name is Jealous, is a
jealous God" (Exodus 34:14).*

Practical religion is entirely based upon the character of
God. If he were, as many foolishly regard him to be, "a Being
like ourselves," very little duty or service would be all he could
reasonably require. But being a God of infinite majesty and unbounded mercy, it is not possible to serve him with too much fear
and love. Nor can he be too strict in exacting from us the utmost
that we are able to pay. In view of this, the feeling of jealousy
which may seem at first sight incompatible with our notions of the
Supreme Being may very appropriately be ascribed to him. We
may justly say, as in our text, "the Lord, whose name is Jealous, is
a jealous God."

Let us first contemplate:

I. THE CHARACTER OF GOD, AS HERE DESCRIBED

Jealousy *does* exist in Jehovah. In man jealousy is a painful
experience that arises from suspecting that the due regard owed to
us is given to someone else who has no right to it. This can inflict
such a deep wound, especially in a husband who conceives himself
to have been dishonored by his wife, that nothing can ever heal
it. "Jealousy," says Solomon, "is the rage of a man; therefore he
will not spare in the day of vengeance; he will not regard any at

ransom; neither will he rest content, although you give him many gifts" (Proverbs 6:34,35). In God also, it burns with a most fierce flame. "They have moved me to jealousy" says God; "and a fire is kindled in my anger, and it shall burn to the lowest hell, and shall consume the earth with her increase, and set on fire the foundations of the mountains. I will heap mischief upon them, and will send my arrows upon them" (Deuteronomy 32:21-23). In the same way the prophet Nahum says, "God is jealous; and the LORD revenges; the LORD revenges, and is furious; the LORD will take vengeance on his adversaries; he reserves wrath for his enemies" (Nahum 1:2).

Nor is this unworthy of his character. For because of his inconceivable glory, he deserves to stand without any rival in our affections. Because of what he has done for us in creation, in providence, and in grace, especially in the gift of his dear Son to die for us, this is so. I may add that it is also because of the relationship in which he stands as "the husband of his church" (Isaiah 54:5) that he has further claims for our supreme concern. If he sees that we permit in any way some competition to be against him, he will be jealous. Indeed, he could not consistently with his own perfections dispose of these obligations, even for a moment. "He cannot give his glory to another" (Isaiah 42:8). He would cease to be God if he would suffer his own inalienable right to be withdrawn from him, and not express his indignation against the idolatrous offender. It is his very "Name" and nature to be jealous. To those who love him, he is a God of love and mercy; so when he is alienated from their affections, he is indeed "a jealous God, and a consuming fire" (Deuteronomy 4:23,24).

From this awareness of his character, let us now proceed to note:

II. OUR DUTY AS A RESULT OF THIS

We must not act inconsistently in any way within the relationship we have with him. We must not suffer therefore,

1. *Any alienation of our affections from him.* We are bound to love him with all our heart, and all our mind, and all our soul, and all our strength. Nothing is to be loved by us other than what is secondary to him and for his sake. If we allow anything under

heaven to rival our concern for him, then we are guilty of idolatry (Colossians 3:5). Nothing is excepted, when the apostle says, "Set your affections on things above, and not on things on the earth" (Colossians 3:2). Therefore we must take care not only to eschew loving anything above him, but to "hate even father and mother, and our own lives also" in comparison with him.

2. *Any lessening of our concerns for him.* God speaks of our espousals to him as a time of peculiar love (Jeremiah 2:2). That season we are mostly delighted with everything that brings us in closer communion with him, and so express the feelings of our heart towards him. It is at such times that the reading of his word, and secret prayer, and attendance on the public services of worship are to us sources of the greatest joy. But if we become cold in these matters and the ardor of our love abates, can we suppose that he will be pleased with us? Rather will he not say to us as he did to the church at Ephesus, "I have somewhat against you, because you have left your first love"? (Revelation 2:4). Surely if a human husband will not tolerate the decline of his wife's interest, how much less will the God of heaven and earth endure such a decline on our part?

3. *Any unnecessary relationship with things which have a tendency to draw us away from him.* This is very important because of the preceding context. God requires his people not to ally themselves with their heathen neighbors, nor to accept invitations to their idolatrous feasts. He commands them to "destroy their altars, break down their images, and cut down their groves," and never to mention the gods which they worshiped. For he knew how soon "evil communications would corrupt good manners." Therefore he forbade any unnecessary intercourse with the heathen.

And has he not given a similar injunction to us? Has he not declared that as soon may "light and darkness have communion with each other, or Christ with Belial, or a believer with an unbeliever"? Therefore we must separate from the ungodly world and not be touched with the unclean thing, if he is to be "a Father unto us, and to act as becomes his sons and daughters" (2 Corinthians 6:14-18). This is a gracious, merciful warning, just as an affectionate husband would give his wife in relation to time spent with one seeking to seduce her. We must carefully attend to it and be no more "of the world than Christ himself was of the world." We must endeavor to "keep our garments clean" amid the pollutions that are around us (Revelation 3:4), and "hate even the garment spotted by the flesh" (Jude 23). We must not only be content with avoiding evil but must "abstain even from the appearance of it" (1 Thessalonians 5:22).

Address—

1. *Those who think it is an easy matter to serve God* . Although a woman may have no difficulty in performing her duties to an affectionate husband, even where the bias of her natural affections is on the side of duty, it is not so easy to undertake all that our God requires. For there our natural disposition is against it. So when the whole people of Israel were so willing to bind themselves to serve their God, Joshua warned them that they could not do it without divine help (Joshua 24:19-23). So let me tell you that if you give yourselves to the Lord and take him to be your portion, you must not use your own strength. You must look unto your "God, who alone can work in you either to will or to do."

2. *Those who are unconscious of giving God any occasion to be jealous with them.* Do not only look at your own acts, but also at the attitudes of your mind; and then judge. He says, "give me your heart." So see whether your affections have not wandered so that you are like the wild ass in the wilderness whom no one could overtake or keep from her mate until the time of mating was over. This is a humiliating but a fair description of our conduct. So if we do not acknowledge it, and humble ourselves under awareness of it, "God will surely plead with us" to our confusion (Jeremiah 2:35).

3. *Those who are ashamed of their past behavior*. Among men, the unfaithfulness of a wife may make it impossible for her to be restored to her former position. But no departures, however grievous, prevent our restoration to God's favor if we humble ourselves before him (Jeremiah 3:1) in all sincerity of heart. So in the name of God himself, I am commanded to proclaim this, and to invite the most dissolute among you to turn to him (Jeremiah 3:12-14). "Return then, unto him, and so your iniquity shall not be your ruin" (Ezekiel 18:30).

SERMON 223
SECRET THINGS BELONG TO GOD

*"The secret things belong unto the LORD our
God; but those things which are revealed
belong unto us and to our children forever,
that we may do all the words of this Law"
(Deuteronomy 29:29).*

Never were such rich mercies granted to any people than those
that were given to Israel. Nor were there ever judgments
that were so distinctly inflicted through successive ages on any
other nation than those on them. All this was in accordance with
prophecy, even with the prophecy which Moses himself delivered
to them prior to their entrance into Canaan. For all was foreseen
by God. It was also foretold with sufficient clarity, what would
happen if they did not learn to act in obedience to the divine
warnings. To find out why God dealt with them, and especially to
question his judgments (as if he had dealt unfairly with them),
would be to no purpose. For the reasons of his determinations were
hid in himself. They were only made known for their benefit. And
God expected that they would suitably develop from the information which he gave them. This seems to be the general thrust of
our text. So from this I will endeavor to show:

I. THE PROPER LIMITS OF OUR INQUIRIES INTO THE THINGS OF GOD

God has been pleased to reveal much to us concerning his nature, his dispensations, his purposes. But there is infinitely more
which he has not seen fit to communicate. For if it were, we would

7

be as capable of understanding as a child could understand the deepest discoveries of philosophy. Even what we do know we only know partially. In fact, our knowledge of everything is so superficial that it scarcely deserves to be called *knowledge*. For after all, what do we know:

1. *Of God's nature?* We are told that "he is a Spirit." From all eternity, he is a self-existent Being. "The heaven of heavens cannot contain him." What idea do we have of a Spirit? What notion can we really form of eternity and omnipresence? The greatest philosopher in the universe has no more adequate conception of these things than the small babe. Nor indeed can we in reality know anything more of the moral perfections of the deity than we do of those that we call natural. We speak of his holiness, justice, mercy, and truth. But our knowledge of these things is altogether negative. We merely know that he is not unholy, nor unjust, nor unmerciful, nor untrue; that is all.

What shall I say about his existence in Three Persons, each possessing all the attributes of deity, while there is only one God? We know that the Father is spoken of as the fountain from which all proceeds; but the Son is also spoken of as executing all that the Father has ordained for the redemption of the world; and the Holy Ghost is spoken of as applying to the sons of men all that the Son has purchased, or the Father ordained. But of these things we know nothing beyond what God has told us in his Word. If we attempt to examine them, "we only darken counsel by words without knowledge." In the contemplation of such mysteries, it becomes us to bear in mind the pointed questions of Zophar: "Can you by searching find out God? Can you find out the Almighty to perfection? He is high as heaven; what can you do? Deeper than hell; what can you know?" (Job 11:7,8).

2. *Of his dispensations?* We know that God orders everything both in heaven and in earth; and that without him "not a sparrow falls to the ground" nor "a hair from the head of one of his servants." But will anyone inform us how God overrules the minds of voluntary agents, so as infallibly to accomplish his own will and not participate in the evils which they commit? Our blessed Lord was put to death "by the determinate counsel and foreknowledge

of God." Yet throughout the whole of that scene, the agents followed entirely the dictates of their own hearts, and "with wicked hands crucified and slew him." And will anyone inform us how this was done?

If we know so little of God's providence, who shall declare to us the wonders of his grace? Will anyone tell us why the world was left four thousand years before the Savior was sent to redeem it? Or why Abraham was chosen in preference to all other persons upon earth, that the Savior should descend from him? And that it was in the line of Isaac and Jacob, rather than through the line of Ishmael and Esau, that Christ came? Will anyone tell us how the Spirit of God acts upon the souls of some to quicken, sanctify, and save them; while others never experience these operations? Can they tell why some experience his influence only so as ultimately to aggravate their eternal condemnation? Can anyone only tell us how mind operates upon matter in any one motion of his own body? If he cannot tell this, how shall he presume to judge God, "whose ways are in the great deep, and his paths past finding out"?

3. *Of his purposes?* We are assured that "God does everything according to the counsel of his own will." None can stay his hand or say to him, "What are you doing?" Who has searched the records of heaven so as to tell us what shall come to pass, either with reference to the nations or to individuals? Our blessed Lord repeatedly checked all presumptuous inquiries in these matters. When his disciples asked him, "Lord, will you at this time restore again the kingdom to Israel?" he answered, "It is not for you to know the times and the seasons, which the Father has put in his own power" (Acts 1:6,7). When Peter inquired of him about John, "Lord, what shall this man do?" our Lord replied, "If it is my will that he tarry until I come, what is that to you?"

Indeed, we know nothing of God. We know nothing of what he is, or does, or will do, any more than he has been pleased to reveal himself to us. All our inquiries respecting him should result in that profound, adoring exclamation: "O the depths!" (Romans 11:33). Instead of complaining that our knowledge is so limited, we should be thankful that it extends so far. For if little is communicated to gratify foolish curiosity, there is everything made known to us that is conducive to our present and eternal welfare.

This idea points out to us,

II. THE PROPER USE WE SHOULD MAKE OF ALL KNOWLEDGE

Everything that God has revealed is intended to have a practical effect. Everything contained in Holy Scripture has a direct bearing on some spiritual benefit to our souls. Let us briefly trace what is revealed concerning;

1. *God and his perfections*. All that is spoken about in Scripture on this sublime subject tends to fill us with holy fear, love, and confidence. It tends to bring us to God as his obedient subjects and servants.

2. *Christ and his offices*. There is no way to the Father but through the Son. When, therefore, we read of him as the Prophet, Priest, and King of his church, we are taught of necessity to look to him for the illumination of our minds, the pardon of our sins, the subjection of our spiritual enemies. We are taught to "live altogether by faith in him, who has loved us, and given himself for us."

3. *The Holy Spirit and his operations*. If we only come to God through the Son, then we only have access to him by the Spirit (Ephesians 2:18). So in desiring his gracious influences, we should seek to have the whole work of grace wrought within us, and to be "transformed into the divine image," and be "made meet for our eternal inheritance."

4. *The gospel, with all its promises and precepts*. Nothing of this is to be contemplated as a mere matter of speculation. But the whole gospel is to be embraced as a remedy, a remedy suited to our wants and sufficient for our necessities. Any promise of it is to be embraced as a basis of hope; and every precept in it is to be obeyed as an evidence of our faith and love.

5. *The realities of the eternal world*. No one ever came from heaven or from hell to inform us the condition of these places or what was the full import of those terms under which those states are displayed. Nor is it of importance for us to know more of them

in this world. We already know enough to activate our hopes and our fears. Our wisdom is to so develop our knowledge of them as to "flee from the wrath to come," and to "lay hold on eternal life." In summary "whatsoever is revealed belongs to us and to our children forever, that in all succeeding ages we should do all the words of God's Law," and to prove ourselves to him as a faithful and obedient people.

As a result we may see:

1. *The answer we should give to the proud objector.* People who sit in judgment upon God and his revealed will—as if they were capable of determining by their own wisdom what was fitting for him to reveal or do, or decide confidently on all that they see or hear—show impertinence in assuming they are competent to weigh in the balance all the mysteries of divine wisdom. With what irreverence do they revile the mystery of the Trinity of Persons in the Godhead! What do they know of the incarnation of Christ, and his atoning sacrifice, and the influences of the Holy Spirit? To all such proud objectors I say with the apostle Paul, "Nay, O Man! Who are you that flies against God?" (Romans 9:20). You completely mistake the role of reason if you think that you can sit in judgment upon such mysteries as these. Who is to judge whether the book which we call the Bible is divinely inspired? Once it is admitted to be so, then reason gives way to faith, whose role is to embrace all that God has revealed and to make use of it for the ends and purposes for which he has revealed it. And if you presume to "reprove God, you shall surely answer for it" (Job 40:2). For "He gives no account to man of any of his matters" (Job 33:13).

2. *What guidance should we give the humble inquirer?* There are many things you hear which are vastly beyond your comprehension and which you find difficult to accept. But there is a standard by which every experience may be judged and a touchstone by which every doctrine may be tried. Our blessed Lord said to those who doubted the propriety of his instructions, "Search the Scriptures: for in them you think you have eternal life; and they are they which testify of me" (John 5:39). The prophet Isaiah told his hearers to bring everything to this test: "To the Law, and to the testimony: When they speak not according to this word, it is because there is no truth in them" (Isaiah 8:20). All that is necessary

for you to know is contained in God's Word. Whatever agrees with that is true. Whatever is contrary to it is false. Whatever cannot be determined by it may well be left among those "secret things which belong to God alone."

3. *The encouragement that we are able to give to the true believer.* "The secret of the LORD," we are told, "is with them that fear him; and he shall show them his covenant" (Psalm 25:14). Yes indeed, that is most encouraging. Not that we are to suppose that God will give any new revelation to his people—we have no reason to expect that. But he will shine upon his revealed truth so that they will have a perception which others do not have. I do not have to tell you how much clearer anything is discerned when the sun shines upon it. Or how much more accurately it is seen when the eye is focused clearly upon it. Or how things that are most minute or distant are rendered clearly visible by glasses that amplify our sight. Now in all these ways God will reveal his secrets to the believing soul. By his Spirit, he will cast a flood of light upon the Word. He will make the soul more eager to apprehend his truth. By the agent of faith, truth is brought directly to the mind and thus fulfills the promise, "All your people shall be taught of God" (John 6:45). Yes, "the meek he will guide in judgment; the meek he will teach his way" (Psalm 25:9).

SERMON 1
THE CREATION OF MAN

"And God said, 'Let us make man in our image,
after our likeness'" (Genesis 1:26).

Although men constantly trace their origin to their immediate parents and frequently to their remoter ancestors, yet they rarely consider when or how they first came into existence. Nor do they ask whether any change has taken place in their nature since they came from their Creator's hands. Reason itself would teach us that there was a period when no such creature as man existed, for every effect must proceed from some cause.

It is necessary, therefore, for us to inquire into:

I. THE NATURE OF MAN, AS HERE DESCRIBED

The formation of man, however remotely we may trace his origin back, must in the first instance have been the product of some intelligent Being who was eternally self-existent. But we are not left to uncertain rational deductions. For God has been pleased to reveal to us (what could not otherwise have been known, Hebrews 11:3) the time and manner of our creation, together with the condition in which we were created. These, then, are the subjects which we now propose for your consideration.

We must note particularly,

1. *The time of man's creation.* Five days have been occupied in reducing to order the confused chaos, and in furnishing the world

13

with whatever would enrich or adorn it. Then on the sixth day, God formed man—having reserved him to the last, as being the most excellent of his works. He delayed his formation until everything in this habitable globe was suited for his purposes. It was not for us to inquire why God chose this space of time for the completion of his work, when he could as easily have formed it all in an instant. But there is one instructive lesson, at least, that we may learn from the survey which he took of every day's work. It teaches his creatures, in turn, to review their works from day to day in order that if they find them to have been good, they may be stimulated to gratitude. Or if they perceive them to have been evil, they may be led to repentance. At the close of every day, God pronounced his work to be "good."

But when man was formed, and the harmony of all the parts, all subservient to the good of the whole, was fully shown, then he pronounced the whole to be "*very* good." From this also we learn that it is not one work or two (however good they may be in themselves) that should fully satisfy our minds, but a comprehensive view of all our works as they harmonize with each other and correspond with all the ends of our creation.

2. *The manner of our creation.* In the formation of all other things, God merely exercised his own sovereign will, saying, "Let there be light," "Let such and such things take place." But in the creation of man we behold the language of consultation. "Let us make man." There is no reason to think that this was merely a form of speech such as was common among the monarchs of that day. For that is quite a modern refinement. Nor can it be an address to angels; for they had nothing to do in the formation of man. It is an address to the Son and to the Holy Ghost, both of whom cooperated in the formation of man, who was to be the masterpiece of divine wisdom and power (indeed, the work of creation is ascribed to Jesus Christ, John 1:1-3, and to the Holy Ghost, Genesis 1:2; Job 26:13; 33:4). This appears from a still more striking expression which occurs afterwards, where God says, "Now man is become like one of us, to know good and evil" (Genesis 3:22). It is also confirmed in a variety of other passages, where God, under the charter of our "Creator," or "Maker," is spoken of in the plural (see Job 35:10; Isaiah 54:5; Ecclesiastes 12:1).

However, we must not suppose that there are three gods. There is but one God. His unity is as clear as his existence. So this is intentionally marked in the very verse following our text where the expressions "us" and "our" are turned into "he" and "his." "God created man in his own image; in the image of God created he him."

Here we see an early intimation of the *Trinity in Unity*. This doctrine pervades the whole Bible and is the very cornerstone of our holy religion. It is deserving of particular notice that in our dedication to our Creator at our baptism, we are expressly required to acknowledge this mysterious doctrine, being "baptized in the name of the Father, and of the Son, and of the Holy Ghost" (Matthew 28:19).

3. *The state in which we were created.* There is some "likeness" to God even in the nature of man. "God is a spirit" who thinks and wills and acts. Man also has a spirit, distinct from his body or from the mere animal life. He has a thinking, willing substance, which acts upon matter by the mere exercise of its own volitions, except when the material substance on which it operates is bereft of its proper faculties or impeded in their use. But the image of God in which man was formed is properly two-fold:

First, it is *intellectual*. "God is a God of knowledge." He has perfect discernment of everything in the whole creation. Such, too, was Adam in his first formation. Before he had had any opportunity to make observations on the beasts of the field and the birds of the air, he gave names to every one of them, suited to their distinct natures, and which characterized them properly. But it was not merely in things natural that Adam was so well instructed. He doubtless had just views of God, his nature and perfections. He had also a thorough knowledge of himself, of his duties, his interests, his happiness. There is no such thing which could conduce either to his happiness or usefulness, which was not made known to him as far as he needed to be instructed in it. As God is light without any admixture or shade of darkness, so was Adam, in reference to all those things at least which he was at all concerned to know (1 John 1:5).

Second, *moral wholeness* is no less characteristic of the deity than wisdom. He loves everything that is good, and infinitely abhors everything that is evil. For every one of his perfections is holy. In this respect also did man bear a resemblance to his Maker.

"God made him upright" (Ecclesiastes 7:29). As he had a view of the commandment in all its breadth, so had he a conformity to it in all his dispositions and actions. He felt no reluctance in obeying it, for his will was in perfect unison with the will of his Maker. All inferior appetites were habitually subject to his reason, which in turn was subject to the commands of God. We are told respecting the Lord Jesus Christ that he was "the image of God" (2 Corinthians 4:4); "the image of the invisible God" (Colossians 1:15); "the express image of his person" (Hebrews 1:3). What the Lord Jesus Christ was upon earth, that was man in Paradise: "holy, harmless, undefiled" (Hebrews 7:26).

That man's resemblance to his Maker did indeed consist of these two things is obvious, because our renewal after the divine image is said expressly to be in knowledge (Colossians 3:10) and in true holiness (Ephesians 4:24). Well indeed does the apostle say of man that "he is the image and glory of God" (1 Corinthians 11:7).

These things being true, let us now inquire:

II. How Our Present State Differs from This

Consider again the character of man as we have seen him described, and then compare him with his present state. It becomes apparent that,

1. *Mankind is in a state of sin.* "How is the gold become dim, and the fine gold changed!" Men are now swamped in darkness and immersed in sin. They "know nothing as they ought to know," and do nothing as they ought to do it. No words can adequately express the blindness of their minds or the depravity of their hearts.

Yet all this has resulted from that one sin which Adam committed in Paradise. He lost the divine image from his own soul. He gave birth "to a son in his own fallen likeness." The streams that have been flowing for nearly six thousand years from that polluted fountain are still as corrupt as ever. O that we would consider sin habitually in this light and regard it as the one source of all our miseries!

2. *The Holy Spirit will effect a glorious change in the hearts of all who seek him!* In innumerable passages, as well as those we have

already cited (Colossians 3:10, Ephesians 4:24), the Holy Spirit is spoken of as "renewing" our souls and making us "new creatures" (2 Corinthians 5:17). What Adam was in Paradise, that shall we be "according to the measure of the gift of Christ." "Instead of the thorn shall come up the fir-tree, and instead of the briar shall come up the myrtle tree" (Isaiah 55:13). He will "open the eyes of our understanding" and cause us "to know all things" that are needful for our salvation (1 John 2:20,27). At the same time he will "turn us from darkness into light, and turn us also from the power of Satan unto God," "he will put his laws in our minds, and write them in our hearts" (Hebrews 8:10). Let us not imagine that their cause is desperate. For he who created all things out of nothing can easily create us anew in Christ Jesus. He will do it if we only direct our eyes to Christ, "we all beholding as in a glass the glory of the Lord, are changed into the same image from glory to glory, even as by the Spirit of the Lord" (2 Corinthians 3:18).

From this awareness of our predicament, let us now proceed to note:

III. What Obligations We Owe to the Ever-Blessed Trinity!

If we look no further than our first creation, we are infinitely indebted to the sacred Three for making us the subject of their consultation and for cooperating to form us in the most perfect manner. But what shall we say to that other consultation, respecting the restoration of our souls? Hear and be astonished at that gracious proposal: "Let us restore man to our image." "I," says the Father, "will pardon and accept him, if an adequate atonement can be found to satisfy the demands of justice." "Then on me be their guilt," responds his only dear Son: "I will offer myself a sacrifice for them, if anyone can be found to apply the virtue of it effectively to their souls, and to secure to me the purchase of my blood." "That shall be my charge," says the blessed Spirit; "I gladly undertake the office of enlightening, renewing, and sanctifying their souls; and I will preserve every one of them blameless unto Thy heavenly kingdom." Thus by their united efforts is the work accomplished. A way of access is opened for every one of us through Christ, by that One Spirit, unto the Father (Ephesians

2:18). So let everyone rejoice in this Triune God! And may the Father's love, the grace of Christ, and the fellowship of the Holy Ghost be with us all evermore! Amen.

SERMON 587
ORIGINAL SIN

*"Behold, I was shapen in iniquity, and in sin
did my mother conceive me" (Psalm 51:5).*

O ne of the most fundamental marks of true repentance is a disposition to see our sins as God sees them. We will not extenuate them by vain and frivolous excuses, but mark every circumstance that tends to aggravate their enormity. During their
unrepentant condition, our first parents cast the blame of their
transgression upon others . . . the man on his wife, the woman on
the serpent that had tempted her. But when true repentance was
given them, they no doubt saw their conduct in a very different
way, and took all the blame which they justly merited.

The sin of David in the tragic story of Uriah was great, beyond
all the powers of language to express. Yet there were views of it in
which none but a real penitent would notice and in which its
enormity was aggravated a hundredfold. This is the way in which
the royal penitent speaks of it in the psalm before us. Having spoken of it as an offense, not merely against man but primarily (and
almost solely so) against Jehovah himself, he proceeds to notice it
not as an isolated act or course of action, but as the inevitable fruit
of his inherent, natural corruption. We are not to suppose that he
intended by this to cast any reflection on his mother, of whom he
elsewhere speaks in the most respectful terms. Nor are we to imagine that he assumes the nature which he had derived from her as
an excuse for his wickedness.

Rather, his intention is to humble himself before God and man as a creature that is altogether corrupt. He represents his wickedness as simply that of a sample of the iniquity of which his heart was full, like a stream that issues from an overflowing fountain. This we cannot doubt is the genuine reason for the words which we have proposed to consider: "Behold, I was shapen in iniquity, and in sin has my mother conceived me."

In pursuing this vital subject, we shall endeavor to establish:

I. THE TRUTH ASSERTED

The doctrine of original sin is here distinctly taught. It is indeed denied by many, with the idea that it would be inconsistent to the goodness and mercy of God to send into the world immortal beings in any other state than one of perfect purity. But it is in vain for us to teach God what he ought to do. The question rather for us to consider is *what has God done?* What account has he himself given us of our own condition? So if the Scriptures be true, here there is no room for doubt. Here we are taught that we are the corrupt offspring of degenerate parents, from whom we derive our polluted nature, which alone since their fall have they transmitted. We shall proceed to demonstrate the reality of this:

1. *From witnesses in agreement.* Moses, in his account of the first man born into the world, expressly notices that Adam begat him not in the likeness of God (in which he himself had been originally created), but "in his own likeness" (Genesis 5:3). How different the one was from the other may be conjectured from the conduct of this firstborn, who stained his hands with his brother's blood. In his account, as well as that of after the flood, he tells us that "every imagination of the thoughts of man's heart was only evil continually" (Genesis 6:5; 8:21).

Job not only affirms the same awful truth, but shows us that it is impossible in the nature of things to be otherwise. Since a thing is radically and essentially unclean, nothing but what is unclean comes from it (Job 14:4; 15:14-16; 25:4). Likewise we have the testimony of Isaiah and Jeremiah as witnessing to the same thing (Isaiah 6:5; Jeremiah 17:9). Again we find the same teaching in the book of Ecclesiastes (9:3).

And in the New Testament, our Lord himself teaches us to regard the heart as the proper womb from which every species of iniquity is generated and from which it proceeds (Mark 7:21). The apostle Paul declares of himself, as well as all the rest of the human race, that they "are by nature children of wrath" (Ephesians 2:3). But how can we be in such a state by nature, if we are not corrupt? Can God regard as objects of his wrath creatures that possess his perfect image? No: it is as fallen in Adam that he views us, and as inheriting a depraved nature that he abhors us.

2. *From collateral evidence.* Why did God appoint the painful and bloody rite of circumcision to be administered to infants only eight days old if it was not to show that they were brought into the world with a corrupt nature? It was the strict duty of all who were in covenant with him to mortify and subdue. On the other hand, it sealed to them the blessings of the covenant, yet it also intimated that they needed to have "their hearts circumcised, to love the LORD their God."

Again, how comes it that every child, from the first moment that he begins to be active, reveals corrupt temper and attitude? If this was only true of some—that the children of wicked people alone showed such depravity—we might be led to account for it in some other way. But when, with the exception of one or two who were sanctified from the womb, this has been the state of every child that has been born into the world, then we are constrained to acknowledge that our very nature is corrupt. That is what David tells us: "we are estranged from the womb, and go astray as soon as we are born" (Psalm 58:3).

Moreover, how can we account for the sufferings and death of infants, but on the assumption that they too are partakers of Adam's guilt and corruption? Sufferings and death are the penalty of sin. We cannot conceive that God would inflict that penalty on millions of infants if they were not in some way or other under his wrath. The apostle Paul notices this as an irrefutable proof that all Adam's posterity after him and through him are partakers of guilt and misery (Romans 5:12,14).

Once again, why is it that all need a Savior? If children are not in God's eyes transgressors of his law, they cannot need to be redeemed from its curse. But Christ is as much the Savior of infants as of adults. We find no intimation in the Scriptures that any are saved without him. On the contrary, it says that "as in Adam all died, so in Christ shall all be made alive." In the temple vision showed to Ezekiel, there was one door for the prince. It was the door by which the Lord God had entered, and was forever to be closed to all except the prince (Ezekiel 44:2,3). So Christ alone enters into heaven by his own merits. To all except him that door is closed. And Christ alone is the door by which we must enter in. He is the only way to the Father. As long as the world shall stand, no child of man can come unto the Father but by Christ (John 10:9; 14:6).

So these things especially are to be taken in connection with the many specific declarations quoted already as decisive proofs that David's account of himself is true, and that it is equally true of all the human race.

Having established this truth, we now proceed to mark:

II. THE IMPORTANCE OF TAKING NOTICE OF THIS IN RECOGNIZING OUR CONDITION BEFORE GOD

Unless we bear in mind the total corruption of our nature, we can never judge aright,

1. *Our individual actions*. Even in the common courts of justice, the great object of inquiry is not so much the act that has been done as the mind of the agent. And so according to what appears to have been depraved or blameless, the sentence of condemnation or acquittal is passed upon him. Precisely so must we judge ourselves in our conduct before God.

To explain this part of our subject, let us suppose that there are two people who have been guilty of the same act of treason toward an earthly sovereign. But they have differed widely from each other in respect of the attitude with which they acted. One entered upon it unwittingly and without consciously knowing he was doing wrong. The other did so knowingly, and aware that he was rebelling against his lawful sovereign. One did it reluctantly, through the influence of someone whom he could not easily withstand. The other did so willingly, as a volunteer in the service, and as following the impulse of his own mind. One went without premeditation, being taken off his guard in a sudden moment. The other, with a fixed purpose, did so after much deliberate plotting.

In one it was a solitary act, quite contrary to the whole of his former manner of life. In the other it was frequent, as often as the temptation arose or as the occasion offered. The one proceeded with moderation, not having his heart at all on it. But the other with a fiery zeal abhorred all the authority that he was opposing. The one had his mind open to conviction, and might easily have been persuaded to renounce his error. The other was filled with self-approbation and self-congratulation, thinking nothing of his risks and dangers if it might help to bring about the utter subversion of the government.

Take these two persons and decide whether, in spite of the appearance of their acts as being the same, there was not an immense difference between the measure of their criminality in the judgment of a righteous judge? There can be no doubt about this. But then take any other sin whatever (for all sin is treason against the King of kings) and examine how far it has been voluntary, deliberate, habitual. How far has it been against light and knowledge? How far has it proceeded from a heart radically averse to God and holiness? Let sins of omission be examined in this way, as well as sins of commission. Then the things which are now accounted light and venial will appear hateful in the extreme, not merely as blighted "grapes of a degenerate vine," but as "grapes of Sodom, and clusters of Gomorrha." Then their enormity will be felt as intensely as we regard the evils normally labeled utterly hateful.

2. *Our general character*. If our actions have not been openly sinful, we are ready to congratulate ourselves as having little basis for shame and remorse. But if we consider "the enmity of the fleshly mind against God," and view our utter want of all holy affections and our exceeding proneness to some besetting sins, we shall see how little reason we have for failing to see ourselves in the vilest of mankind. We shall see how much cause, indeed, there is in gratitude to God for his preventing grace that has restrained us from many evils into which others have run. But we can take no credit for ourselves as being better than others. If we see bitter fruit produced by others, we shall remember there is a root of it all in ourselves. If we see in others the streams of wickedness, we shall bear in mind that the fountain of it all is in ourselves also. Thus, however free we may be from any flagrant enormity, we shall be

ready to acknowledge with Paul, that "in us, that is, in our flesh, dwells no good thing." We shall say with Job, "Behold, I am vile! I repent, and abhor myself in dust and ashes." So far from indulging in self-preference and self-esteem, we shall find there are no other names more suited to describe us than those by which Paul designates his own character, "Less than the least of all saints," and "The very chief of sinners."

From this understanding of our natural corruption we may learn:

1. *How greatly we need the renewing influence of God's Spirit.* Outward reform may suffice for outward sins. But where the heart itself is so corrupt, we must have "a new heart given to us," and "be renewed in the spirit of our minds." With such hearts as ours, it would be impossible for us to enter into the kingdom of heaven or to enjoy it even if we were there. We could not bear the sight of so holy a God. Nor could we endure to spend our lives in such holy employments. So know that "all things must pass away; and all things must become new." "That which is born of the flesh is flesh." The stream cannot rise higher than the spring's source. If you are to enjoy the things of the Spirit, you must be "born of the Spirit," who alone can impart the faculties necessary for that objective. Let your prayer then be like that of David, "Create in me a clean heart, O God, and renew a right spirit within me!" (Psalm 51:10).

2. *How carefully we should watch against temptation.* If we carried about with us a load of gunpowder which would explode with a single spark, we should be extremely careful to avoid whatever might subject us to danger. If our hearts, then, are so corrupt, should we not in the light of temptations that are so thick around us look well to our ways, and pray to our God to keep us from the evils of an ensnaring world? Well did our blessed Lord say, "Watch and pray, that you enter not into temptation . . . the spirit may be willing, but the flesh is weak." Whoever reflects on David's state prior to his fall will not fear for himself, but cry out to God, "Hold thou me up, and I shall be safe!" "Uphold me with Thy free Spirit, and take not thy Spirit from me!" To all, then, we say, "Be not high-minded, but fear." And "Let him that thinketh he stands, take heed lest he fall."

SERMON 1074
THE NEW COVENANT

*"And they shall teach no more every man
his neighbor, and every man his brother,
saying, 'Know the LORD:' for they shall all
know me, from the least of them unto the
greatest of them, saith the LORD: for I will
forgive their iniquity, and I will remember
their sin no more" (Jeremiah 31:34).*

In order to give a clear view of this subject, we shall state:

I. THE BLESSINGS OF THE NEW COVENANT

These are specified by the prophet and copied exactly by the apostle, so that we should strictly adhere to them without attempting to reduce them to any other order than that which is here observed. In the new covenant then, God undertakes,

1. **To write his law in our hearts.** This is a work which none but God can effect. The kings were commanded to write a copy of their law, each one for himself. But although they might write it on parchment, they could not inscribe it on their own hearts. However, God engages to do this for all who embrace the new covenant. He will make all the laws which he has revealed agreeable to us. He will reveal to us their excellence. He "will cause us to delight in them after our inward man." He will make us see that the moral "law is holy, and just, and good" even while it condemns us for our disobedience to its commands. "The law of faith" (that is to say, the gospel) is also a marvelous exhibition of God's mercy and grace that exactly suits the needs of our souls. He will engage our wills to submit to his. He will dispose our souls to be energized

in obedience to his commands. This he has repeatedly promised (Ezekiel 36:26,27). This he will fulfill to all who trust in him.

2. *To establish a relation between himself and us.* By nature we are enemies to him, and he to us. But when we embrace his covenant, he will "give himself to us as our God, and take us for his people." In being our God, he will exercise all his perfections for our good. He will give us his wisdom to guide us, his power to protect us, his love and mercy to make us happy, his truth and faithfulness to preserve us to the end. In taking us for his people, he will incline us to employ all our faculties in his service. Our time, our wealth, our influence—yes, even all the members of our bodies and all the powers of our souls— will be used as his, for the accomplishment of his will and the promotion of his glory. We can see this illustrated in the life of the apostle Paul. God took as much care of him as if there had been no other creature in the universe. In turn, he devoted himself to God as much as if his faculties had not been capable of any other use or application. The effects of this relationship are indeed clearly seen in all the Lord's people. But the difference is in degree only, not in the reality and substance.

3. *To give us the knowledge of himself.* There is a knowledge of God which cannot be attained by human teaching. It is a spiritual, experimental knowledge which is accompanied by suitable attitudes and affections. God will give this to those who lay hold on his covenant. "He will reveal himself to them, as he does not unto the world." He will "put them into the cleft of the rock, and make all his glory to pass before their eyes." He will proclaim to them his name, the LORD, the LORD God, merciful and gracious (Exodus 33:18-23; 34:5-7). He has promised that "all his people shall be taught of him" (Isaiah 54:13; John 6:45), "the least as well as the greatest," yes, the least often *in preference* to the greatest (Matthew 11:25; 1 Corinthians 1:26-29). In proof that this promise is really fulfilled to all who receive the gospel, the apostle John declares it to be an acknowledged fact: "We know that the Son of God is come, and has given us an understanding to know him that is true" (1 John 5:20).

4. *To pardon all our iniquities.* Under this new covenant we have access to "the fountain opened for sin and for uncleanness." By

washing in it, "we are cleansed from all sin" (1 John 1:7). Whatever transgressions we may have committed in our unregenerate state, they are all put away. "Although they may have been as scarlet, they will become white as snow; although they have been red like crimson, they are as wool."

Until now we have spoken only generally of the blessings of the new covenant. Let us now consider then more particularly, while we state:

II. THE DIFFERENCE BETWEEN THE OLD AND NEW COVENANTS

We have already seen that by "the old covenant" is meant the Mosaic covenant, made with the Jews on Mount Sinai. There is a wide difference between this and the gospel. They differ:

1. *In the freeness of their grants*. The Mosaic covenant imposed certain conditions that had to be fulfilled on the part of the Jews. All the blessings of that covenant depended on their fidelity of their commitment to it (Exodus 24:6-8). But we find no condition specified in the new covenant. Must we attain the knowledge of God and become his people and have his law written in our hearts? Yes, indeed, but these are not acts of ours which God requires in order to bestow other blessings upon us. Rather, they are blessings which he himself undertakes to give. If any argue that repentance and faith are conditions which we are to achieve, we will not dispute about a term. You may call them conditions if you please, but what we wish to affirm is that they constitute a part of God's free grant to the gospel covenant. So they are not new conditions in the same sense that the obedience of the Jews was the condition upon which they held the promised land. They are, as we have just said, *blessings freely given to us by God*. They are not acts of our own on which we can found our claim to other blessings.

It is worth observing that the apostle, mentioning this grant of the new covenant, particularly specifies that God, "finding fault with" the Jews for their violations of the old covenant, says, "I will make a new covenant" (Hebrews 8:8). Had he said, "Commending them for their observation of the inferior covenant, God says, I will give you a better covenant," then we might have supposed that it was given as a reward for services rendered. But when it was given because of the hopeless state to which their violations of the former covenant had reduced them, the freeness of this covenant appears in the strongest light.

2. *In the extent of their provisions.* We shall note again the different blessings as they occur in our text. God wrote his law upon tables of stone and put it into the hands of those with whom his old covenant was made. But according to his new covenant, he undertakes to put it into our inward parts and to write it on our hearts. What a glorious difference this is! And how beautifully and exultingly does the apostle point it out to his Corinthian converts (2 Corinthians 3:3).

God indeed established a relationship between himself and his people of old. But although this relationship was nominally the same as ours, it was by no means realized to the same extent. To true believers among them he was the same as he is now. But what was he to the people at large, with whom the covenant was made? He no doubt interposed for them on many occasions in an external way. Outwardly they acknowledged him. But his communications to us are internal, and our devotion to him is real and spiritual.

Under the old covenant, God revealed himself to his people in types and shadows. The ceremonies which he appointed were so obscure and varied that they could not be known to the populace unless the people carefully instructed each other. Because of this it was commanded that children should inquire into the reason of various institutions (as that of the Passover and the Feast of Unleavened Bread and the Redemption of the Firstborn). Their parents were to explain these things to them (Exodus 12:26, 27; 13:8, 14, 15). But with us there are only two institutions, and these are the plainest that can be imagined. The great truths of our religion are so interwoven with our feelings that a person whose desires are after God needs no other teacher than that of God's Word and Spirit. And although the instructions of ministers or of theologians and of parents are still extremely helpful, yet many a person obtains the knowledge of God and of salvation without being indebted to any one of them. It is indeed a fact that many people remote from church life and from instruction of every kind—except the blessed book of God—are so often richly taught by the

Spirit of God as to shame those who enjoy the greatest external advantages (see 1 John 2:27).

The forgiveness of sins which was guaranteed under the old covenant was not such as to bring peace into the conscience of the offender: "the sacrifices which he offered could not make him perfect in regard to conscience"; nor indeed were any means appointed to obtain pardon for some particular offenses. But under the new covenant, "all who believe are justified from all things, from which they could not be justified by the law of Moses" (Acts 13:39). "Being justified by faith, they have peace with God" (Romans 5:1). "A peace that passes understanding," "a joy unspeakable and glorified" is granted now.

How glorious does this new covenant then appear in this contrast, and what reason have we to adore our God for the rich provisions contained in it!

3. *In the duration of their benefits.* The annual repetition of the same sacrifices under the old covenant was intended to intimate to the people that their pardon was not final. Had their guilt been completely removed, the apostle rightly observes that "they would then have ceased to be offered, because the worshipers would have had no more conscience of sins." But since the sacrifices were annually renewed, they were in fact no more than "a remembrance of sins made every year" (Hebrews 10:1-3). But under the new covenant, God engages to "remember our sins and iniquities no more." They are not only forgiven by him, but forgotten; not only canceled, but "blotted out as a morning cloud" (Isaiah 44:22). Not only are they removed from his face, but they are cast behind his back "into the depths of the sea" (Micah 7:19).

He put away his former people "although he was a husband unto them." But to us his "gifts and callings are without repentance" (Romans 11:29). This is particularly noted by the prophet in the verses following our text (35-37). They are also worth considering in the comment of the inspired apostle. It shows the superiority of Christ's priesthood to that appointed under the law. He confirms his position from this circumstance, that the sacrifices offered by the Levitical priests could never take away sin, and therefore were continually repeated; whereas Christ's sacrifice, once offered, would forever take away sin and "perfect forever all them that are sanctified."

He then adduces the very words of our text, saying in these words, "the Holy Ghost is a witness to us." In promising first that "the law should be written in our hearts" and then that "our sins and iniquities should be remembered no more," he had attested fully the sufficiency of Christ's sacrifice. He gave ample assurance that those who relied upon it should never have their sins imputed to them (Hebrews 10:11-18).

It is unnecessary to multiply any further words upon this subject. For the old covenant, with all its benefits, was to continue only for a limited period. But the new covenant is to continue to the end of the world, and its benefits to the remotest ages of eternity.

We infer from this two things:

1. *The folly of making self-righteous covenants of our own.* Why did God give us another covenant if the first was adequate for our necessities? Shall we then revert to the old covenant or form new ones of our own upon the same principle? Take your own covenants and examine them, and see what grounds of hope they really afford you. We give you permission to dictate your own terms. Say, for example, "You are to repent and amend your lives; and on those conditions God shall give you eternal life." Can you repent, can you amend your lives, by any power of your own? Have you agreed with God what shall be the precise measure of your repentance and amendment? Have you attained the measure which you yourselves think to be necessary, so that you can say "My conscience witnesses for me that I am fully prepared to meet my God?" If not, see what a state you have brought yourself to. You need no one else to condemn you. For God may say, "Out of your own mouth will I judge you." Do not be so mad as to cast away the Lord's covenant for such delusive projects of your own. Instead of depending on your own weak efforts, go and lay hold on that better covenant, which provides everything for you as the gift of God in Christ Jesus.

2. *The blessing of those who obey the gospel.* You have "a covenant which is ordered in all things, and sure" (2 Samuel 23:5). You have a Mediator who, having purchased for you all the blessings of this covenant, will infallibly secure them to you by his efficacious grace and all-prevailing intercession. So put your con-

fidence in him. Use him daily, if I may say so, to maintain your interest in it. Give him the glory of every blessing you receive. Your enjoyment of such benefits will be progressive, as long as you continue in the world. Let your desires for them be more and more enlarged. In due time you shall enjoy them in all their fullness. For it is in heaven alone that you will fully possess them. There you shall be perfectly able to understand the meaning of that promise, "You shall be my people, and I will be your God" (Revelation 21:3).

SERMON 1594
THE DIVINITY OF CHRIST

"In the beginning was the Word,
and the Word was with God,
and the Word was God" (John 1:1).

What amazing dignity and majesty are displayed in these brief but comprehensive words! The other evangelists begin their histories at the period of our Savior's incarnation. But the apostle John carries us back to eternity itself. He informs us not only of what Christ did and suffered, but of who he was. He calls him by a very distinctive name: *The Word;* and in other places, "The Word of Life" (1 John 1:1,2). He also speaks of "The Word of God" (Revelation 19:13). This name, applied to the Messiah, was not completely unknown to the Jews. It seems peculiarly proper to the Son, because it is by the Son that God has in all ages revealed his mind to man. Perhaps this very explanation of the term was intended by the apostle John when he says, within a few verses after my text, "No man has seen God at any time: the only-begotten Son, who is in the bosom of his Father, he has declared him" (vs. 18).

But without dwelling upon that conjecture, let us consider:

I. THE TESTIMONY GIVEN HERE TO THE LORD JESUS CHRIST

The beloved apostle, speaking of the Lord Jesus, declares here:

1. *His eternal existence.* "In the beginning was the Word," even before the creation existed, either in heaven or in earth. From him

every created being derived its existence (v. 3). So the apostle Paul informs us also that "by him were all things created that are in heaven and that are in earth, visible and invisible, whether they be thrones or dominions or principalities or powers. All things were created by him and for him. And he is before all things, and by him all things consist" (Colossians 1:16, 17). Although he was born into the world in time, yet in his divine nature he existed from eternity. "He is the same yesterday, today, and forever" (Hebrews 13:8). "He is the Alpha and Omega, the beginning and the end, the first and the last" (Revelation 1:8,11).

2. **His distinct personality.** "From all eternity he was with God," "having a glory with him before the worlds were made" (John 17:5). Having perfect participation in all that the Father possessed, whether of wisdom and knowledge (Matthew 11:27) or of authority and power (John 5:17). This appears from the counsel that was held, as it were, between the Father and the Son, respecting the formation of man (Genesis 1:26); and man's consequent expulsion from Paradise (Genesis 3:22); and the confounding of the projects of man's apostate race by changing their language at Babel (Genesis 11:7). So the Lord Jesus is said to have "come forth from God" (John 16:27, 28), even "from his bosom," where he had his everlasting abode. The importance of this truth is marked by the repetition given by the apostle John in the words that follow my text: "the same was in the beginning with God."

3. **His proper deity.** "The Word was God," even "the mighty God" (Isaiah 9:6), "the great God" (Titus 2:13), "God over all, blessed forever" (Romans 9:5). "He was in the form of God; and thought it not robbery to be equal with God" (Philippians 2:6); and was therefore rightly "named Immanuel, God with us" (Matthew 1:23); and is with truth declared to be "God manifest in the flesh" (1 Timothy 3:16).

Now that this is not a mere speculative subject, I will proceed to show:

II. The Deep Interest We Have in It

The very question "whether our Savior be God, or only a created being?" indicates what an extremely important subject this is. So realize that Christ is truly God as well as man. On this truth depend the following:

1. *The efficacy of all that he did and suffered for us on earth.* Had he only been a creature, he could only have done what was his duty to do. Therefore he could have merited nothing at the hands of God, or at all events could have merited only for himself. But being God, his whole undertaking was gratuitous. There was no obligation whatever for him to do anything or to suffer anything for our sake. What he did and suffered therefore may well be put to our account, all the more so because it was concerted between him and his Father when he undertook to redeem our ruined race. His sufferings, although only for a season, may well be regarded the same as the eternal suffering of man. His obedience to the law may justly be considered as if all mankind had obeyed it. In both one and the other, his deity stamps an infinite value so that "he having been made sin for us, we may well be made the righteousness of God in him" (2 Corinthians 5:21).

2. *The efficacy of all that he is still doing for us in heaven.* Our adorable Savior is seated there at the right hand of God. All judgment is committed to him, that he may complete for his people the work which he began on earth. He is appointed "head over all things to the church" (Ephesians 1:22). If we suppose him to be merely a creature, how could he attend to all at once and supply the necessities of all in every part of the universe at the same moment? But there is no room for such speculation, seeing he is the omnipresent, omniscient, almighty God. "Our help is, indeed, laid upon one that is mighty" (Psalm 89:19), "in whom dwells all the fullness of the Godhead bodily" (Colossians 2:9). So we do not fear, however great our necessities may be, but are fully assured that "he is able to save to the uttermost all that come unto God by him" (Hebrews 7:25).

See then, brethren:

1. *How inconceivably great is the condescension of our God!* I do not wonder at the unbelief of those who call in question the divinity of Christ. For if it were not so fully revealed—as it is impossible for a truly enlightened man to doubt it—I should be ready to doubt it myself. So inconceivable does it appear that God should become a man and make himself the surety and substitute

of his own rebellious creatures. But he *is* God and therefore can do it. He is, and therefore cannot be judged by the finite capacity of man. In doing what he has done, he has acted like himself. He is God, and therefore I believe all that he has done for sinful man. Although himself eternal, he has been born in time. Although eternally with God, he has come down and tabernacled with man. Although himself the true and living God, he has become a man, yea, and died for man upon the cross. I believe it, because he has revealed it. I believe it, because nothing less than this would have been adequate for my needs.

2. *What unbounded consolation he has provided for sinful man.* This doctrine meets my every need. I have guilt, which nothing less than "the blood of God" can wash away (Acts 20:28). I have corruptions, which none but the Spirit of God can subdue and mortify. I have wants, which none but the all-sufficient God can supply. And having Jehovah for my friend, my surety, my righteousness, my all, I fear nothing. I hope in him, believe in him, glory in him, and make him "all my salvation and all my desire." Trusting in him, I will defy all my enemies (Romans 8:31); and "believing in him," I will anticipate in my soul all the glory and blessing of heaven (1 Peter 1:8).

SERMON 1748
SALVATION BY CHRIST ALONE

*"Neither is there salvation in any other: For
there is none other name under heaven
given among men, whereby we must be
saved" (Acts 4:12).*

F rom the account given to us of the miracles performed by our
blessed Lord, we should also be led to acknowledge him not
only as the true Messiah, but consider what we ourselves may expect from his hands. His apostles Peter and John have healed a
man who had been lame from his birth. The spectators were
amazed and were ready to acknowledge the honor of this miracle
to them. But they told them by whom it had been done, even by
Jesus, whom the Jews had rejected. Yet despite their contempt of
him, it was by this miracle that he had proved himself to be "the
head-stone of the corner" (v. 11). The apostles then had directed
the attention of their hearers to their own eternal interests and
assured them that as Jesus alone restored the cripple to the use of
his limbs, so Jesus alone could save them from everlasting perdition. It is evident that the text refers not to bodily healing, but to
salvation, which the apostles themselves and all their hearers
stood in need of.

In discussing the words before us, it will be proper to note:

I. WHAT IS IMPLIED

Nothing can be more clearly implied than that there is salvation for us in Christ. It may be thought unnecessary to insist so

plainly and obviously on this truth, especially among those who call themselves Christians. But this truth is far from being universally known. The basis for it is very little considered. If it were as well understood as we are apt to imagine, there would still be the necessity of dwelling often upon it because of its great importance, and of determining with the apostle Paul "to know nothing among us but Jesus Christ, and him crucified".

To confirm this, we shall appeal to:

1. *The typical representations of Christ.* There were a great variety of sacrifices under the Law which typified the Lord Jesus Christ. The lamb that was offered every morning and evening foreshadowed "the Lamb of God that should take away the sin of the world." The scapegoat, which bore the iniquities of all Israel into the uninhabited wilderness, expressed in a vivid way the removal of our guilt by its transfer upon the head of Jesus. To dwell upon all the ceremonies that were appointed on different occasions for the expiation of sin is needless. Suffice it to observe that "the blood of bulls and of goats could not take away sin." If those offerings had not respect to Christ, they were altogether unworthy, even to be prescribed to man or to be accepted for him. But the efficacy of those sacrifices for the end for which they were instituted proves without a doubt the infinitely greater efficacy of the sacrifice which Christ in due time offered on the cross (Hebrews 9:13, 14).

2. *The positive declarations concerning him.* Nothing can be conceived more clearly or strongly than the declarations of Scripture concerning Christ's sufficiency to save. How forcibly has the prophet marked the extent (Isaiah 45:22), the fullness (Isaiah 1:18), and the freeness (Isaiah 55:1, 2) of his salvation! He invites "all the ends of the earth," even persons defiled "with crimson sins," to accept all the benefits of the gospel "without money and without price." In the New Testament the same things are spoken with all the energy that language can muster. All without exception are exhorted to come to Christ (Matthew 11:28; John 6:37) with the full assurance that he will cleanse them from all sin (1 John 1:7; Acts 13:39) and bestow upon them freely all the blessings of grace and glory (John 4:10; 7:37, 38). Is all this a mere

delusion? It surely is if Christ is not "able to save to the uttermost all that come unto God by him" (Hebrews 7:25).

3. *Matter of fact.* We can draw aside the veil of heaven and point to some before the throne of God who are such monuments of grace as to leave no doubt respecting the sufficiency of Christ to save any others, whoever they may be. See that man, a murderer; he was not satisfied with shedding the blood of some of his fellow men or of those who deserved to die. He "made the very streets of Jerusalem run with blood, and that with the blood of innocents." Yet this was only a small part of the guilt that he contracted, so various and enormous were his crimes. Yet is he, even Manasseh, a chosen vessel in whom God is, and forever will be, glorified.

You see that woman also? We do not know the details of her life, but she was so vile and notorious a sinner that it was a disgrace to notice her. Yet our Lord's condescension to notice her was made a ground of doubting his divine mission. Yet she also, although once possessed by seven devils, is now in glory. While still on earth she received the assured witness from our Lord himself that her sins, numerous as they were, were all forgiven (Luke 7:47, 48). Now she is singing the triumphs of redeeming love as loudly as any in heaven.

We could easily refer to a host of others whose enormities were very great, yet who were "washed, justified, and sanctified, in the name of the Lord Jesus, and by the Spirit of our God" (1 Corinthians 6:9-11). But enough has been said to put out of all question the blessed truth that we are insisting on—that Jesus is a Savior, one who is great and able to deliver all who trust in him (Isaiah 19:20).

Let us now turn our attention to:

II. WHAT IS EXPRESSED

What solemn assurances are in this text! One would have supposed that the first would have been quite sufficient. But the apostle thought that no repetitions were superfluous, nor any accumulation of words too strong on such a subject as this. Indeed, it is of infinite importance to every one of us to know that as there is salvation for us in Christ, so "there is no other salvation in any other."

1. *There is not*. In whom else can we find the requisites of a Savior? In whom can we find such sufficiency, either of merit to justify or of power to renew a sinner? If we were to ask the highest angel in heaven to give us of his merit, he would tell us that "he himself is only an unprofitable servant; for he does no more than is his duty to do" (Luke 17:10). If we were to entreat him to change our hearts, he would have to confess his utter inability to do such a great thing. Shall we then look to ourselves? We are full of sin. Our merit is found . . . where? Not in heaven truly, but in the lake that burns with fire and brimstone (Romans 3:9). "Nor have we in ourselves a sufficiency even to think a good thought" (2 Corinthians 3:5), much less to renew ourselves after the divine image. None but Jesus could atone for sin. None but Jesus could yield such an obedience to the Law as should be capable of being imputed to others. None but Jesus can send down the Holy Spirit into the souls of men or say to them, "My grace is sufficient for you" (2 Corinthians 12:9). Therefore "there is no other name under heaven given among men whereby we can be saved."

If there were any other Savior, the most eminent of God's servants would have had some intimation of it. Abraham, the friend of God and the father of the faithful, would probably have heard of him. But he knew of none other. He sought acceptance through Christ alone and was justified solely through faith in him (Romans 4:3-5). David too, the man after God's own heart who was inspired to write so much respecting Christ, would probably have been acquainted with such an important fact in order to enjoy his own salvation. But he sought refuge in none but Christ: "Purge me with hyssop, and I shall be clean; wash me, and I shall be whiter than snow" (Psalm 51:7). At least we might hope to have some information of this kind given by the apostle Paul, who was more fully instructed in the mind and will of God than any other person. Yet he knew of no other name but that of Jesus. He renounced all hope "in his own righteousness, that he might be found in Christ" (Philippians 3:9). "He determined to know nothing, in all his service, but Jesus Christ and him crucified" (1 Corinthians 2:2).

So whether we dwell upon the insufficiency of all creatures to take the place of a Savior, or the utter ignorance of all the prophets and apostles concerning the appointment of any creature to hold that office, we may be sure that there is none other than the person mentioned in the text—who is a man indeed, but is at the same time "God over all, blessed for evermore."

2. *There cannot be.* We do not presume to be wise beyond what is written or to say what God might have done if it had pleased him. We are fully warranted by the Scriptures to say that consistent with God's honor as the moral governor of the universe, man could not have been saved without a mediator. Nor could any mediator except Jesus have been found to execute all that was necessary for our salvation. It was necessary that the justice of God should be satisfied for the violations of his law. His holiness needed to be displayed in its marked abhorrence of sin. His truth had to be kept inviolate by the execution of his threats. His law had to be honored, as well as its precepts obeyed, by the carrying out of its penalties. Now none but Jesus, who is God as well as man, could effect all these things; and therefore none but he could save us.

But there is also another basis on which we may deny that any other could save us. If we were indebted to any other, either for righteousness or strength, we could not join in the songs of the redeemed in heaven, but must separate from the heavenly choir (Revelation 7:9, 10). We must then ascribe to ourselves or to some other the honor of our salvation. But how could this be consistent with the dignity of Jehovah, who has determined "that no flesh should glory in his presence"? It is in vain to say that the glory would ultimately be given to him. For if we are saved *by* or *for* anything of our own, we may, and must, take the glory to ourselves (Romans 4:2). That would create discord in heaven and be irreconcilable with the honor of the divine majesty.

Address—

1. *To the careless.* Why are men so indifferent about their spiritual welfare? Is it because they are not in danger of perishing? If that were so, why is so much said regarding salvation? Why are we warned so strongly against relying on any but Jesus Christ? Surely the very circumstance of Christ being sent down from heaven to die for us is enough to alarm all our fears and to convince us that if the salvation offered us could be procured by none but him, the danger of those who are not interested in him must

be inexpressibly great. So let the careless ponder this and flee for refuge to the hope that is set before them.

2. *To the self-righteous*. It is difficult to convince those who are looking *partially* to Christ that they are really renouncing him altogether. The Scriptures are so plain about this that there cannot be the smallest doubt about it. Salvation is "of faith, on purpose that it may be by grace" (Romans 4:16). If it is partially or wholly by our own works, it ceases to be of grace. It must be wholly of grace or wholly of works (Romans 11:6). It must completely exclude boasting, or else admit it. But boasting must be excluded wholly (Romans 3:27). Therefore all dependence whatever on our own works must be completely and forever renounced (Romans 3:20). If we will not accept salvation on these terms, "Christ shall profit us nothing" (Galatians 5:2, 4).

3. *To the despondent*. The person healed by Peter and John was a very apt symbol of our state by nature and practice. "We are transgressors from the womb." But however desperate our condition may be, there is in Jesus sufficiency of power and grace to make us whole. "His name, through faith in his name, shall give us a perfect soundness in the presence of God and man" (Acts 3:16; 4:10). So let none complain as if they were beyond the reach of mercy. For there is nothing impossible with Jesus. "With him there is mercy; with him is plenteous redemption; and he shall redeem Israel from all his sins" (Psalm 130:7, 8).

Part II
THE NATURE OF THE GOSPEL

SERMON 1933
EVANGELICAL RELIGION

"I am determined not to know anything among you, save Jesus Christ, and him crucified" (1 Corinthians 2:2).

At different times it has pleased God to reveal himself to men in different ways. Sometimes he has done so by visions, sometimes by voices, sometimes by suggestions of his Spirit to their minds. But since the completion of the sacred canon, he has principally made use of his written Word, which has been explained and enforced by men whom he has called and qualified to preach his gospel. Although he has not precluded himself from conveying again the knowledge of his will in any of the former ways, it is through the written Word only that we are now authorized to expect his gracious instructions. This, whether read by ourselves or published by his servants, he applies to the heart, and makes effectual for the illumination and salvation of men. God is not confined to means; but he condescends to employ the stated ministry of his Word for the diffusion of divine knowledge.

But this circumstance, so favorable to all classes of the community, imposes on them a duty of utmost importance. For if there is a well from which we are to receive our water supplies, it is necessary for us to make sure that its waters are healthy. Likewise, if we are to receive instruction from men who are weak and fallible as ourselves, it becomes us to try their doctrine by the touchstone of the written Word. "Prove all things, and hold fast that which is good." Preachers then have this awesome responsibility—they set before their people "the sincere milk of the Word." In no way can

47

they "corrupt the word of God" or "handle it deceitfully; [but] by manifestation of the truth commend themselves to every man's conscience in the sight of God" (2 Corinthians 2:15-17; 4:2).

It thus appears that we are deeply interested in this one essential question: What is truth? What then is the truth which ministers of the gospel are bound to teach and which their people should be anxious to hear? We shall have no difficulty in answering this question if we only consult the passage that we have before us. For in it the apostle Paul explicitly declares what was the great scope of his ministry and the one subject which he labored to unfold. He was not preoccupied with the subtleties that might draw the attention of philosophers. Nor was he influenced with the kind of knowledge that might have a high reputation among men. On the contrary, he studiously avoided all that gratified the pride of human wisdom, and was determined to adhere simply to one subject—the crucifixion of Christ for the sins of men. "I came not unto you," he says, "with excellency of speech or of wisdom, declaring unto you the testimony of God: for I am determined not to know anything among you, except Jesus Christ and him crucified."

It is the intent of this discourse to explain and vindicate this determination of the apostle.

I. Its Explanation

By preaching Christ crucified, we are not to understand that he dwelt continually on the fact or history of the crucifixion. He does speak of having "set forth Christ as it were crucified before the eyes" of the Galatians and therefore may have enlarged upon the sufferings of Christ as the means of stimulating gratitude toward him in their hearts. Yet there is no reason to suppose that he wanted simply to dwell on that tragic scene, as though he hoped by that to convert their souls. Rather it was the doctrine of the crucifixion that he insisted upon.

This he calls "the preaching of the cross." This consisted of representing "Christ crucified, to the Jews a stumblingblock, and to the Greeks foolishness; but to the true believer, the power of God and the wisdom of God" (1 Corinthians 1:23, 24). Invariably, the apostle spoke of the death of Christ from two perspectives: as the ground of our hope, and as the motive for our obedience.

With the former, the apostle not only asserts that the death of Christ was the appointed means of effecting our reconciliation with God, but that it was the *only* means by which it could be. He represents all, whether Jews or Gentiles, as under sin and in a state of guilt and condemnation. He insists that as we are all condemned by the law, we can never be justified by the law. This can only occur in the way that God has provided for us in the gospel (Galatians 3:22, 23). He asserts that "God has set forth his Son to be a propitiation through faith in his blood, to declare his righteousness in the remission of sin, that he may be just, and the justifier of them that believe in Jesus" (Romans 3:25,26).

So he requires all, Jews as well as Gentiles, to believe in Jesus in order to be justified by faith in him (Galatians 2:15, 16). So jealous is he of everything that may interfere with this doctrine or be supposed to serve as another basis of our acceptance with God, that he shows that if anything else will do, it will render his death of no avail (Galatians 5:2-4). Indeed more—if he himself, or even an angel from heaven, should ever propose any other basis of hope to sinful man, he will denounce him with a curse. Lest this denunciation be overlooked, he repeats it with increased emphasis: "As we have said before, so say I now again, if any man preach any other gospel unto you than that you have received, let him be accursed" (Galatians 1:8, 9).

He ascribes every blessing we possess to the death of Christ. We are "reconciled to God by the blood of his cross." We are "brought nigh to him," "having boldness and access with confidence" even to his throne. We "are cleansed by it from all sin." Yes, "by his one offering of himself he has perfected forever them that are sanctified."

But there is one passage in particular where a multitude of spiritual blessings are all referred to him as the true source from whom they flow. This is the first chapter to the Ephesians, where within the space of eleven verses the same truth is repeated eight or nine times. To enter into the full force of the passage, we can think of the apostle Paul as maintaining the truth in opposition to all its most determined adversaries. He later labors to the uttermost to exalt Christ in the eyes of those who trusted in him. So we can imagine him saying: "Have we been chosen before the foundation of the world? It is in Christ. Have we been predestined to the adoption of children? It is in and by him. Are we accepted? It is in the Beloved. Have we redemption, even the forgiveness of sin? It is in him, through his blood. Are all, both in heaven and earth, gathered together under one Head? It is in Christ, even in him. Have we obtained an inheritance? It is in him. Are we sealed with the Holy Spirit of promise? It is in him. Are we blessed with all spiritual blessings? It is in Christ Jesus."

When the apostle has labored thus to impress our minds with the idea that our whole salvation is in and by the Lord Jesus Christ, is it not surprising that anyone can be ignorant of it? Yet we know that many people, even those who have studied the Scriptures and have read this passage many times, have never yet seen its force. They have not been led to see that Christ is the fountain "in whom all fullness dwells" and "from whose fullness we must all receive grace for grace."

But we have also seen that there is another aspect in which the apostle speaks of the death of Christ, mainly as a motive for our obedience. While he was emphatic on the necessity of relying upon Christ and of basing our hope of salvation solely on his obedience unto death, the apostle is no less earnest in promoting the interests of holiness. While he showed believers as "dead to the law" and "without law," he also insisted that they were "under the law to Christ." They were as much bound to obey every detail of it as ever (1 Corinthians 9:21; Galatians 2:19). He emphasized the necessity of obedience to it in all its aspects. Also, when the doctrines which he had emphasized were in danger of being abused for unholy purposes, he expressed his own utter abhorrence of such practice (Romans 6:1, 15). He declared that "the grace of God, which brought salvation, taught them that denying ungodliness and worldly lust, they should live righteously, soberly, and godly in this present world" (Titus 2:11, 12).

He shows us that a life of holy obedience is the great purpose that Christ has for all his people. Indeed, the very name *Jesus* proclaimed that the object of his coming was "to save his people from their sins." This was the scope and purpose of his death, even to "redeem them from all iniquity, and to purify unto himself a peculiar people zealous of good works." This was also the purpose of the resurrection and ascension to heaven. "Therefore he both died, and rose, and revived, that he might be the Lord both of the dead and the living."

With the importance of these things before him, the apostle

Paul labored more abundantly than any of the apostles in his holy vocation. He proceeded with a zeal which could not be quenched, and with an ardor which nothing could dampen. He had privations, labors, imprisonments, deaths; but these were of no account in his eyes. "None of these things moved him, neither counted he his life dear unto him, so that he might finish his course with joy, and fulfill the ministry that was committed to him."

What was the principle by which he was so motivated? He tells us himself that he was impelled by a sense of obligation to Christ for all that he had done and suffered for him. "The love of Christ constrains us," he says, "because we must judge that if one died for all, then we are all dead; and that he died for all, that they who live should not henceforth live unto themselves, but unto him who died for them and rose again" (2 Corinthians 5:14, 15). This is the principle which he desired to be universally accepted and which he longed to impress on the minds of everyone. "We beseech you, brethren," he says, "by the mercies of God, that you present your bodies a living sacrifice, holy, acceptable to God, which is your reasonable service" (Romans 12:1). We do not need to inquire what the mercies are that he refers to. For they are the great mercies guaranteed to us in the work of redemption. So he says elsewhere, "You are bought with a price; therefore glorify God in your body and in your spirit, which are his" (1 Corinthians 6:19, 20).

This is what the apostle means then by the phrase "Christ crucified." This consists of two aspects: of being in Christ for salvation, and of obedience to the law for his sake. Neither can be separated and taken alone, else ministry would be unbalanced and unsuccessful. If he had neglected to set forth Christ as the only Savior of the world, he would have betrayed his trust and led his hearers to build their hopes on a foundation of sand. On the other hand, if he had neglected to inculcate holiness and to set forth redeeming love as the great incentive to obedience, he would have been justly charged with what has often been falsely imputed to him, namely an antinomian spirit. His doctrines would have deserved the odium which has most unjustly been cast upon them.

But he did not err in either direction. He never forgot the foundation nor the superstructure. He distinguished properly between them, keeping each in its place. Thus we see the great symmetry of truth in our text.

II. THE VINDICATION OF THE TEXT

It was not merely from enthusiastic fondness for one aspect, but from the fullest conviction of his mind that the apostle adopted this resolution. So literally he says, "I determined, as a result of my deliberate judgment, to know nothing among you save Jesus Christ and him crucified. I have made it, and will ever make it, my theme, my boast, and my song." We shall now look to see the reasons he insisted on this matter so exclusively and with such evident delight.

III. BECAUSE IT CONTAINED ALL THAT HE WAS COMMISSIONED TO DECLARE

"It pleased God to reveal his Son in the apostle, that he might preach him among the heathen." So the apostle Paul tells us, that "this grace was given to me to preach the unsearchable riches of Christ." This, I say, was his office. This too is the ministry of reconciliation which is committed to ministers in every age. It is that "God was in Christ reconciling the world unto himself, not imputing their trespasses unto them" (2 Corinthians 5:18, 19). Indeed, to the apostles the commission was to "go forth into all the world, and to preach the gospel to every creature." To us it has been assigned as a more limited sphere. But the subject of our ministry is the same as theirs. We have the same dispensation committed to us. "Woe unto us if we preach not the gospel!"

Yet today the term *evangelical* is used as a term of reproach, as though men no longer needed to be evangelized. It is not that we want to justify the use of unnecessary language. But the distinctions which are made in Scripture still must be made by us. Otherwise why should God himself make them? Now it cannot be denied that the apostle characterizes the great subject of his ministry as the gospel. Neither can it be denied that he complains of some teachers in the Galatian church who introduced another gospel, which was not the true gospel, but a perversion of it (Galatians 1:6, 7). Here he lays down the distinction between doctrines which are truly evangelical and others which have no just title to that name. Of course, wherever the same differences lie between the doctrines maintained, the same terms must be proper to distinguish them. So a just view of these distinctions is necessary in order to guard us against error and to be established in the truth.

I am anxious that we should be clearly understood about this matter. For it is not our design to enter into any dispute about the use of a term, or to vindicate any particular party. We want with all clarity to insist simply that we have the most accurate and precise ideas of what we are talking about.

We have seen that it was the great subject of the apostle's preaching, which he emphatically and exclusively called the gospel. So if we attend to what he is telling us in the text, we shall see what really constitutes evangelical preaching. The subject of it must be "Christ crucified." That is to say, Christ must be set forth as the only foundation for a sinner's hope. Likewise holiness in all its aspects must be insisted upon. A sense of Christ's love in dying for us must be inculcated as the mainspring and motive for all our obedience.

The manner of expressing this doctrine must also accord with the apostle's text. The importance of the doctrine must be so firm as to make us determined never to know anything else, either for the salvation of our own souls or for the subject of our public preaching. Seen in its transcendent excellence, we must rejoice and glory in it ourselves. We need to show its fruitfulness in a life of entire devotedness to God. We must call upon our hearers also to rejoice and glory in it, and to display its sanctifying effects in the whole of their lives and conversation.

Thus an evangelical is one who preaches and lives, personally and in his ministry, in the light of the apostle's message. To be indifferent to this doctrine or to corrupt it by a self-righteous or antinomian mixture is only a denial of what we mean by evangelical. Yet we are not talking here about this term as referring to some subculture. We are referring to the spirit and preaching of those who base their faith upon this text.

Now we may ask, is there anything here which a minister ought not to preach or which every Christian should not feel? Is there anything that is merely enthusiastic, sectarian, uncharitable, or worthy of reproach? Is the apostle absurd in what he is saying, or contemptible? Or if a scoffing and ungodly world were to make glorying in the cross of Christ a matter of reproach, should those who are so reproached abandon the gospel for fear of being called evangelical? Or should they not rather, like the apostles, "rejoice that they are counted worthy to suffer shame, if shame it be, for Christ's sake"?

The fact is indisputable that the apostle's commission was to preach Christ crucified. He was to do this chiefly, constantly, and exclusively. That was why he was justified in his determination "to know nothing else." The same resolution is also our wisdom, whether with reference to our own salvation or to our ministry to the church of God.

Let us now proceed to the second reason for the apostle's determination. He determined to know nothing but Christ and him crucified because it contained all that is conducive to the blessing of man. Many things may amuse man, but there is nothing else that can contribute to man's true blessing. Put him in a position of deep distress. Let him be weighed down by a sense of sin. Let him be oppressed with great calamity. Let him become so ill that he borders on death. In all of these circumstances, nothing will satisfy his mind but a view of this glorious subject.

Let him hear of his good works, and he will doubt in a way that cannot be resolved. Tell him of repentance and of Christ supplying his deficiencies; he will still be at a loss to find out whether he has attained the right measure of penitence or of goodness that is necessary to meet the demands of God. But speak to him of Christ and his dying for the sins of men, then he will be assured "that none that come unto him shall be cast out." Then he will be assured that he has purged us "by his blood from all sin." Then he will be assured that Jesus clothes us with his own undefiled righteousness. Then he learns that "where sin abounded, grace has much more abounded" (Romans 5:20, 21). Set forth to him the freeness and sufficiency of the gospel of salvation, and he will lack for nothing. Then he will realize that Christ is "a rock, a sure foundation." Thus assured, he will build without fear that "whosoever believes in Christ shall not be confounded." Then he will hear the Savior say, "This is life eternal, to know you the only true God, and Jesus Christ whom you have sent." Having this knowledge, he trusts that the word of Christ will be fulfilled to him. "Who is he that condemns? It is Christ that died, yes rather, but is risen again, who is even at the right hand of God, who also makes intercession for us" (Romans 8:34).

If a sense of guilt afflicts some, others are distressed by lack of victory over their inner lives. To them the doctrine of Christ crucified is the only effective remedy. To consider eternal rewards and punishment may be a powerful incentive; but efforts based on these motives alone will always savor of constraint. They will never be spontaneous, hearty, affectionate, and unreserved. But let a sense of redeeming love preoccupy the soul, and the heart becomes enlarged, and "the feet are set at liberty to run the way of God's commandments." We are not saying that everyone who professes to have experienced the love of Christ will always walk consistently with that profession. For there may be falls and offenses even among the apostles themselves. But we insist that there is no other principle in the whole universe that is so powerful as the love of Christ. When this principle is seen in action, no command is ever considered grievous. The yoke of Christ is easy in every sense, and his burden is light. Indeed, the service of God will be perfect freedom, and the labor of our souls will be to "stand perfect and complete in all the will of God." This was the apostle's own experience, and this was the effect of his own ministry on the hearts of thousands. What else then would he want or could he proclaim in comparison with this reality?

Moreover, he determined to know nothing but this subject, because nothing could be added to it without weakening or destroying its efficacy. As we have noted, the subject of Christ crucified consists of both a foundation and a superstructure. Now, the apostle Paul declares that if anything whatever is added to that foundation, it will make void the whole gospel. An honorable mention of something that could have been added was the rite of circumcision, because it was God's special appointment, which in the Old Testament had been emphasized by God himself. But the apostle says in reference to that rite, that if anyone submitted to it with a view to confirming his interest in the gospel, "Christ should profit him nothing." Such a person would have "fallen from grace," since he had in fact denied the gospel completely. So unless one built rightly on this foundation, "his work would be burnt up as wood or stubble." So with such a view of the subject, what could have induced the apostle to add anything to it?

But the apostle speaks even more emphatically about it. For he tells us that not only adulterating the subject would destroy its efficacy, but even a superficial statement of the truth would make it of none effect. For God is exceedingly jealous of the honor of his gospel. When it is proclaimed plainly and simply, it is effectual for the salvation of men. But when it is made ornate with human eloquence and expressed in "words which man's wisdom teaches," it will not work. God would have "our faith to stand, not in the wisdom of men, but in the power of God." So the apostle Paul, although eminently qualified to express it with all the charms of oratory, deliberately laid aside "all excellency of speech, or of wisdom in declaring the testimony of God." Instead, he "used all plainness of speech" so that it should not be "in the enticing words of man's wisdom" and thus make "the cross of Christ of none effect" (1 Corinthians 1:17; 2:1, 4, 5).

Further vindication is unnecessary. For if this subject contained all that he was commissioned to declare, it comprised all that was necessary for the blessing of man. If nothing could be added to it without weakening or destroying its efficacy, he would have defeated the purpose of his own ministry if he had done otherwise.

If these things are so, then we may venture to give the following advice.

First, *let us take care that we know Christ crucified* . Because many are born and educated in a Christian country, they are ready to take for granted that they are instructed in this wonderful subject. But there is almost as much ignorance of it prevailing among Christians as among the heathen themselves. The name of Christ indeed is known, and we compliment him with the name of Savior. But the nature of his office, the extent of his work, and the excellency of his salvation are known to few.

Do not think this is an exaggeration. Let us appeal to everyone's conscience. Do we find that the apostle's views of Christ are common? Do we find many so filled with admiring and adoring thoughts of this ministry, as to count all things but loss for the excellency of the knowledge of it? Do such say, "God forbid that I should glory, save in the cross of our Lord Jesus Christ"? On the contrary, do not we find that there is an almost universal jealousy on the subject of the gospel so that those who follow most closely to the apostle's steps are despised? Of course, we should be glad to be found false witnesses in relation to these attitudes. Yet we also hope that there will be an increasing love for the gospel pervading the whole land. I pray God that it may prevail more and more and be embraced by every one of us; not superficially, partially, theoretically, but clearly, fully, and practically.

Second, *let us adopt the apostle's determination for ourselves.*

Doubtless, as members of society, there are many other things which we are concerned to know about. Whatever may be our profession in life, we ought to be well acquainted with affairs in order to perform our duties to the best advantage that we can for others. Above all we need to employ our knowledge diligently and conscientiously. But as Christians, we have one object of pursuit which deserves all our care and our efforts. Yes, it is simply to know nothing but Christ and him crucified. This is the subject which even "the angels in heaven are ever desiring to look into." It is this that we can investigate for our whole lives, and yet leave depths and heights unfathomed and unknown.

The apostle Paul, after preaching Christ for twenty years, did not conceive of himself as having yet attained all that he might, and therefore he still desired to know Christ more and more, "in the power of his resurrection and in the fellowship of his suffering." This we may well desire also, and count all things but loss in comparison to it.

Finally, *let us show the wisdom of our intent by the holiness of our lives.* The doctrine of Christ crucified has and always will appear "foolishness" in the sight of the ungodly. When it was preached by an apostle himself, he seemed to men to be a babbler and deceiver. There is only one way that we can display its excellence in such a manner that we effectively "put to silence the ignorance of foolish men." This is "by well- doing." That is to say, that we show the sanctifying and transforming efficacy of this doctrine. The apostle Paul tells us that "by the cross of Christ the world was crucified unto him, and he unto the world" (Galatians 6:14). Such is the effect that it should produce in us. We should show that we are men of another world, and men too of "a more excellent spirit." We should show the fruits of our faith in every relationship of life. In doing so, we may hope "to win by our good conversation" many who never have submitted to the word preached.

But we must never forget where our strength lies, or on whose aid we must entirely depend. The prophet Isaiah reminds us of this: "Surely shall one say, in the LORD have I righteousness and strength." Our Lord himself plainly tells us that "without him we can do nothing." Since "we have no sufficiency in ourselves to help ourselves," and God has "laid help for us upon One that is mighty," let us "live by faith in the Son of God." Let us receive "daily out of his fullness that grace" that shall be "sufficient for us."

Let us bear in mind that this is the central part of the knowledge of Christ crucified. As "all our fresh springs are in Christ," so we must continually look to him for "the supplies of his Spirit." Let us have him for our wisdom, our righteousness, our sanctification and redemption.

(Preached before the University of Cambridge, in March 1811, to express Simeon's view of evangelical Christianity.)

SERMON 2009
THE GLORY OF THE GOSPEL
ABOVE THAT OF THE LAW

"If that which was done away was glorious,
much more that which remains is glorious"
(2 Corinthians 3:7-11).

In vindicating his claim to apostolic authority, the apostle appeals to the Corinthians against the false teachers with proofs and evidences of his divine mission, since the work of God upon their hearts clearly showed that his ministrations among them had been attended with a power that was more than human (vv. 2, 3, 5, with 1 Corinthians 9:2). By thus substantiating his title to apostolic authority, he is led almost incidentally to mention the excellency of the gospel which he was sent to preach. Then he goes on to show that the deference due to him was all the more, in proportion to the excellency of the gospel which he ministered to them. Dignified as the status of Levitical priesthood was, it was not to be compared with that of those who preached the gospel. The law, as ministered in the "letter" of it, proved fatal to all who trusted in it; but the gospel was a source of "life" to all who warmly embraced it. The one, as a mere "letter, killed." The other, as a quickening "spirit, gave life" (v. 6).

Having touched upon this point, the apostle now proceeds to expand it more fully with the words of this text. For a fuller understanding of this we shall consider:

I. THE DIFFERENT TERMS BY WHICH THE LAW AND THE GOSPEL ARE DESCRIBED HERE

The law is called "the ministration of death and of condemnation." As given to Adam in paradise, the law "was ordained to life," and would have entitled him to life if he had continued to obey it (Romans 7:10). But as it was republished by Moses, it was never intended to give man any title to life. Nor could it possibly give life, because every human being is corrupt and is incapable of giving to it perfect obedience (Galatians 3:21; Romans 8:3). The law is a perfect transcript of God's mind and will. It makes known to man the whole extent of his duty. It requires a perfect obedience to every one of its commands. If transgressed in any one particular, it denounces death. It says to every soul of man, "The soul that sins, it shall die."

At the very time that it so rigorously demands perfect obedience, it neither imparts to man any strength for obedience, nor does it provide any remedy for a single act of disobedience. So it is called in our text "a ministration of death and of condemnation." Its voice to everyone is, "Do this and live; transgress and perish." But as every man has transgressed it, and so can never do all that it commands, it condemns to death every child of man. As the apostle Paul has said: "As many as are of the works of the law are under the curse. For it is written, 'Cursed is every one that continues not in all things that are written in the book of the law to do them'" (Galatians 3:10). It is not enough to *desire* to do them, but to *do* them. And not only do some, but *all*. Nor is it temporarily, but in *continuance*—from the first to the last moment of our lives. Nor can there be any exception in favor of someone, for *every one* must stand or fall, be saved or "cursed" according to this law. Consequently, since every one is born under this law, "every mouth must be stopped, and all the world become guilty before God" (Romans 3:19).

The gospel is called "a ministration of righteousness and of the Spirit." Since the law condemns all, the gospel applies a remedy. It reveals a Savior who by his own obedience unto death has "made reconciliation for iniquity, and brought in an everlasting righteousness" (Daniel 9:24). This righteousness is revealed to us in the gospel to be apprehended by faith (Romans 3:22). It is actually given "to," and put "upon," "all who believe" in Jesus (Romans 3:21, 22). This righteousness is totally independent of any obedience to the law on our part. It exists in Christ alone, and it is imputed to us by faith (Romans 4:5, 6). So far from being augmented by any works of our own, it is made void by the smallest dependence that we have on our own works (Galatians 2:21; 5:4). We must renounce all hope in ourselves before we can have any part in the righteousness of Christ (Philippians 3:9). So the gospel is called "a ministration of righteousness" because it reveals a righteousness commensurate with all the demands of the law, and offers that righteousness to every man who will believe in Christ. It declares that "Christ himself is the end of the law for righteousness to every one that believes" (Romans 10:4). The law was given as a ministration of death specifically to shut men up to this righteousness and to constrain them to seek salvation in the way provided for them (Galatians 3:22, 23).

The gospel is also "the ministration of the Spirit." In the first stages, the spirit was given in his miraculous powers to attest the truth and divine authority of the gospel. That purpose having been fully answered, his miraculous powers are no longer exercised. But his gracious influences still continue, and will continue to the end of time. He is still sent "to convince the world of sin, and of righteousness, and of judgment." It is still his office "to glorify Christ," and to "take of the things that are Christ's, and to show them unto us." He still enlightens the mind and sanctifies the souls of them that believe. He is still, as the Comforter promised to the Church, operating in the saints as "a Spirit of adoption," "witnessing with their spirits that they are the children of God," and "sealing them unto the day of redemption." To no one is he imparted for these purposes except through the gospel of Christ. But wherever the gospel is faithfully ministered, he accompanies it with these blessed influences, producing holiness and comfort in all who truly receive it.

Thus the gospel supplies what the law knew nothing about. As we have said before, the law spoke nothing of pardon to the guilty or of strength to the weak. But the gospel administers both. And that in such an abundant measure as is adequate for all the needs of the whole world. It ministers righteousness sufficient to justify the most guilty sinner upon earth. It imparts the Spirit so that the weakest may be more than conqueror over all the enemies of his soul.

Corresponding with this description of the law and of the gospel were the following:

II. THE DIFFERENT DEGREES OF GLORY BELONGING TO EACH

1. *The Law was truly glorious*. It was proclaimed by God himself with an audible voice in the midst of such displays of glory as had never before been seen upon earth. So that it might never be forgotten, it was written also by the finger of God in tables of stone. Moreover, the person through whom it was given to Israel had such glory imparted to him that the people of Israel were no more able to look steadfastly upon his face than upon the face of the meridian sun. While this reflected a very high degree of glory upon the law itself, it was intended specifically to intimate to all Israel that they were unable to apprehend the full scope and the meaning of the law (v. 13)! They thought it was a covenant by means of which they could obtain acceptance with God. Instead, it had an infinitely higher office, that "of a schoolmaster to bring them to Christ, that they might be justified by faith" (Galatians 3:24). But this, which was its chief glory, they were not able to discern. In consequence of their ignorance of its true meaning, they supposed it to be of everlasting obligation. Instead, with all its attendant rites and ceremonies, it was only to continue until Christ should come, and then to give way to a more perfect dispensation. Still, when all the circumstances associated with its declaration are considered, it was yet exceeding glorious.

2. *But the gospel was far more glorious*. As imparting life, it must necessarily be far more glorious than that which only brought death. For the law really did bring death inasmuch as if there had been no law, there would have been no transgression; consequently there would have been neither sin nor death (Romans 4:15; 1 John 3:4). In revealing such a way of salvation too, it is inconceivably glorious. How mysterious is the record, "that God has given unto us eternal life; and this life is in his Son; that whoso has the Son has life; and he that has not the Son of God, has not life" (1 John 5:11, 12). Finally, "He was made sin for us, who knew no sin, that we who had no righteousness might be made the

righteousness of God in him!" (2 Corinthians 5:21). Well is this called "the glorious gospel of the blessed God"! For in it are "riches" of love that are altogether "unsearchable," and heights and depths that can never be explored.

Another ground of excellence is that the gospel also transforms the soul into the divine image. This exalts it infinitely above the Law. Instead, the Law irritates and inflames the corrupt principle within us, rather than tending to put all in subjugation to it (Romans 7:5, 8). But the gospel both frees us from the dominion of sin and liberates us from all its penal consequences: "The law of the Spirit of life in Christ Jesus makes us free from the law of sin and death" (Romans 8:2).

The gospel also, as being God's last dispensation, will endure forever. The Law, which was only introductory to it, is completely abolished. In this respect also its superiority to the Law is therefore great and indisputable.

Comparing the two, we see the difference between them. The luster imparted by one was external, on the face of Moses. The change that is wrought by the other is internal, in the heart and in the soul. In the one, the radiance shone from only one person. In the other, it is conferred on all who believe. In the one, it passed quickly away. In the other, it is abiding, even to the end of life, and throughout eternal ages. In the one, it is veiled from the sight of all. In the other, it is to be displayed for the instruction of all, that all may see in it the hand of God (vv. 2, 3) and learn to glorify its divine author (Matthew 5:16). It may be said that "that which was made glorious had no glory in this respect, by reason of the glory that excels." For in truth, although the Law shone like the starry heavens on the brightest night, the gospel, like the meridian sun, has eclipsed its splendor and cast a veil over all its glory.

Nor let this be a matter of speculation only. For let us consider:

III. THE CONDUCT WHICH THIS SUPERIOR DISPENSATION DEMANDS

1. **Of Ministers**. The result of these considerations upon the apostle was to make him "use great plainness of speech." Unlike Moses, he would not "put a veil upon his face" to hide any part of the splendor of this gospel (vv. 12, 13). Instead, he would preach

it with all fidelity, and by the fullest possible "manifestation of it, commend himself to every man's conscience in the sight of God" (2 Corinthians 4:2).

This is what *we* must do, and it is indeed through grace our delight to do it. Yes, brethren, we declare to you freely that the law, as a covenant of works, is abolished. A new covenant with a better Mediator and with better promises is proposed to you in the gospel. This new covenant provides, as you have heard, *righteousness* for the guilty and *strength* for the weak. It authorizes every believer to say, "In the LORD I have righteousness and strength" (Isaiah 45:24). O that we might be instrumental to bring you into a near and full acquaintance of this better dispensation! Never should we forget that our one great office is to make it known to you, and to bring you to the enjoyment of all its blessings. We would go up to the holy mount ourselves to receive it from God, and we would come down with it in our hands and in our hearts to proclaim it to you (1 Corinthians 15:3; 1 John 1:1-3).

We do proclaim it to you at this moment. We do declare it to you, that the most guilty sinner in the universe may now find acceptance with God through the blood and righteousness of the Lord Jesus Christ. We also declare that a new heart shall be given you, and a new spirit shall be put within you, and the whole law of God be written in your hearts, if only you will believe in him. For he will send down his Holy Spirit upon you, as he has promised, and by his gracious influences upon your soul will "cause you to keep his statutes and his judgments" (Ezekiel 36:25-27). All this shall be "ministered unto you abundantly through the knowledge of our Lord and Savior Jesus Christ," if only you will come to him. Then it shall be given to you "freely, without money and without price."

Your minds should be intent upon this great subject. You should seek to grow daily in its knowledge. You should come up to the house of God with the same preparation of heart to receive the Word of God from your ministers as the Israelites did to receive the law from the hands of Moses. Your state of mind should be like that of Cornelius and his company when Peter came to preach the tidings of salvation to them: "Now are we all here present before God, to hear all things that are commanded you of God" (Acts 10:33). As there is no veil put over our face, so you should beg of God that no veil will remain on your hearts. The law was hid from

Israel without involving them in any guilt or danger, if only they complied with it as far as it was revealed to them. But "if the gospel be hid from you, you must eternally perish" (2 Corinthians 4:3). It is the only possible way of salvation, and it can only save by operating effectually both on the understanding and the heart (1 Thessalonians 2:13). So beg God to upset the devices of Satan, who continually strives to hide this gospel from you. Entreat him "to shine into your hearts to give the light of the knowledge of the glory of God in the face of Jesus Christ" (2 Corinthians 4:4, 6).

At the same time, you must remember that in this respect the obedience that you pay must correspond with the privileges that you enjoy. Being liberated from the Law, you are freed also from all servile hopes and fears. So your service must be no longer that of a slave, but of a child. You must serve God, not in oldness of the letter, but in the newness of the Spirit (Romans 7:6). In this way you will obtain all the blessings which the gospel is intended to impart. For the intent of this gospel is to assimilate you to that Savior who proclaims it to you. While you receive it from him, a portion of his splendor must cling to you so that all who behold you may see truly that you have been with Jesus. You must be "his epistle" to an ungodly world. So plainly must the characters be written on your heart and life, that they may be "known and read of all men." This writing must daily be more visible. Daily shall the radiance around you increase, if you live near to the Lord and contemplate continually the wonders of his love. For "if with un-veiled face you behold as in a mirror the glory of the Lord, you shall be changed into the same image from glory to glory by the Spirit of the Lord" (v. 18).

Sermon 2091
The Cross of Christ

*"God forbid that I should glory, save in the
cross of our Lord Jesus Christ, by whom the
world is crucified unto me, and I unto the
world" (Galatians 6:14).*

Whatever he does, the Christian is characterized by a
singleness of eye and by simplicity of mind. All others,
even when they appear to be more zealous for God, have mixed
and selfish ends in view. We see this in the Judaizing teachers,
who insisted on the observance of circumcision and Jewish ritual.
They wanted it to be thought that they were motivated only by a
dutiful sense to Moses and to God. But they were impelled by
other secret motives. They were preachers of the gospel, but
knowing how offensive the simple preaching of the cross was to
both Jews and Gentiles, they sought to make it palatable by blend-
ing it with certain observances. They did this to avoid the persecution which a simple exhibition of Christ crucified would have
brought upon them. They had an eye also to their own glory. For
they pretended to be leaders of a party in the church, and they
labored to exalt themselves by increasing the number of their own
followers. They were not motivated by a real desire to approve
themselves to God. While endeavoring to enforce the observance
of the Law upon others, they did not keep the Law themselves.

All such corrupt practices the apostle Paul abhorred. While he
disdained to seek his own glory, he was proof against the fear of
man, laboring only to advance the glory of his divine Master and
for the salvation of those to whom he ministered. "They," he says,
"who constrain you to be circumcised, desire to make a fair show

in the flesh." "But God forbid that I should glory, save in the cross of our Lord Jesus Christ, by whom the world is crucified unto me, and I unto the world."

In this commendation of the cross of Christ, we see first of all:

I. His Views of Its Excellency

By "the cross of Christ" he means the doctrine of salvation through a crucified Redeemer. This he preached, and it was the great subject of all his ministry. Although it was "to the Jews a stumblingblock and to the Greeks foolishness," yet he would "know nothing else" (1 Corinthians 2:2) and "glory in nothing else."

1. *He gloried in it as displaying such wonders as love and mercy to the whole world.* For here the plan of salvation was suited to and sufficient for the needs of the whole world. All were involved in one common ruin. All needed atonement to be offered for their sins. The whole universe could not present one capable of expiating their guilt. The highest archangel was as incompetent to it as was the blood of bulls and goats. But God in his infinite mercy had devised a way. He had entered into covenant with his only begotten Son. He agreed that he should assume our nature and "make his soul an offering for sin." His sacrifice was accepted on our behalf.

This stupendous plan has been executed. The Lord Jesus Christ has "been made in the likeness of men, and has become obedient unto death, even the death of the cross." And having "borne our own sins in his own body on the tree," he has been exalted to the right hand of God and is the Head and Forerunner of his people. He now offers salvation unto all freely, "without money and without price." The persons sent out and commissioned by him to preach his gospel are empowered to declare that "God was in Christ reconciling the world unto himself, not imputing their trespasses unto them" (2 Corinthians 5:19). To every living person is this message sent, with full assurance that "they who believe in Christ should never perish, but shall have eternal life" (John 3:16).

In this wonderful mystery the apostle Paul saw such honor reflected in all the divine perfections, and such blessedness secured to man that he could not but glory in it, and determined never to glory in anything else.

2. *He commends the cross of Christ as ample provision for his own soul.* The apostle Paul felt himself to be the very "chief of sinners," deserving of God's worst punishment. But this Savior had revealed himself to him even in the midst of all his wickedness, and by a signal act of grace had not only pardoned his sins, but had appointed him to preach to others that salvation of which he was so remarkable a monument. By the manifestation of Christ to his soul, he was assured of mercy and acceptance with God. At that moment he no more doubted his own salvation than he did his existence. The blessing which was thus imparted to him, he had been the means of imparting to others, even to hundreds and thousands of the Gentile world. Could he then be insensitive to the value of what had filled his soul with such peace and joy, and which through his ministry had been spread with such unspeakable blessings all around him? No, he could not but commend to others what had been so effective for his own benefit, and glory in the cross as "all his salvation and all his desire."

There is a special reason for glorying in the cross, he mentions:

II. HIS EXPERIENCE OF ITS POWER

The words "by whom" should be translated rather "by which." For it is to the doctrine of the cross as received into his soul, and not to Christ's personal agency upon his soul, that he traced the effects produced.

The world was in the apostle's eyes an object that was crucified. He himself was crucified in respect to it. This is a remarkable image, and deserves particular attention: "The world was crucified to him." For a person dying upon a cross, however dear he may have been to us, is no longer an object of desire. As soon as his life is given up, his body will be given to us to bury out of sight. We can no longer look to him for any of those comforts which are derived from social intercourse. All relation to him, all dependence upon him, all satisfaction in him, are now dissolved. Every tie that once bound us together is broken, and "we know him no more."

The apostle further adds that "he also was crucified to the world." This does not mean that the world despised him and wished him buried out of its sight. That was certainly true, but it is not this that is being intimated here. The expression suggests that while the world was as a crucified object in his eyes, he beheld everything in it as a man would who was himself dying on a cross. He may have loved the world intensely; but now he loves it no more. He may have sought its pleasures, its riches, and its honors with the most insatiable ardor; now he has no desire for anything in it. He feels himself dying, and he has no wish to improve his few remaining moments for his own benefit and the benefit of those around him. It is like the penitent thief. If crowns and kingdoms could have been given him for the few remaining hours that he had to live, they would have been of no value whatever to him.

Thus the apostle looked upon the world and everything in it. There was nothing in it that he desired: "the lust of the flesh, the lust of the eye, and the pride of life," they are all lighter than vanity in his estimation. He had now no longer any taste for them. He felt that whether his life would continue a longer or shorter time, he had nothing to do but to honor God and benefit his fellow creatures as far as he had opportunity, and to seek the salvation of his own soul. All that the world could either give or take away was "counted by him as dung, that he might win Christ, and be found in him."

How did he attain to such an extraordinary degree of deadness to the world?

This holy feeling was wrought in him entirely by the cross of Christ. It was this that filled his soul with such joy as to render all earthly satisfactions as worthless and distasteful as the husks of swine. It was this which raised him above those vain hopes which the Judaizing teachers stimulated and above those unworthy fears with which their fidelity to God was assailed. The sense of love to his Redeemer constrained him. When menaced with all that the world could inflict, he could say, "None of these things move me, neither count I my life dear unto me, so that I may but finish my course with joy, and fulfill the ministry committed to me." Nor was this a vain hope. For his whole life testified that this was his actual experience. The doctrine which formed the only basis of his hopes had a transforming effect, such as no other principles under heaven could have produced.

But you must not suppose that this state of mind was peculiar to the apostle. For the cross of Christ also produces the same effect in others. From this we see therefore,

1. **How sublime are the Christians' views!** The cross of Christ is that, and that alone, on which every Christian under heaven will glory. The very words of our text afford the best comment on that description which the apostle gives to the cross of Christ, when he calls it "the wisdom of God and the power of God." So unfathomable are the counsels of divine wisdom contained in it, that all the angels of heaven are searching into it with a thirst that is insatiable. Such is its efficacy, that nothing can withstand its influence. By this then, my brethren, you may judge whether you are Christians in deed and in truth, or whether you are only such in name only. For a nominal Christian is content with proving the way of salvation by a crucified Redeemer. But the true Christian loves it, delights in it, glories in it, and shudders at the very thought of glorying in anything else. So what then are your views and your feelings? Do you see how base and unworthy it would be to glory in anything else? Are you not indignant at the very thought of so treating your adorable Redeemer? Be assured that it will be thus with you, if your heart is fully enlightened and if you have "learned of the Father as the truth is in Jesus."

2. **How heavenly is the Christian's life.** He is in the world. But he is "not of it: he has overcome the world; and this is the victory by which he has overcome it, even his faith." "His treasure is in heaven, and his conversation is also there." See him, and you will behold "a man of God"; a man "born from above," and a man "filled with the Holy Ghost." Such is a man "walking as Christ himself walked." In Christ we see the figure used in our text completely illustrated. "He had not even where to lay his head." Yet, "when the people would have taken him to make him a king, he withdrew and hid himself from them." Among the early Christians too, you see the same spirit. For "they were not of the world, even as Christ was not of the world." Seek then, beloved, after this high and holy attainment. Walk with a holy indifference to the world. Show yourselves above all the things of time and sense. "Set your affections on things above, and not on things of the earth." Let all your joys flow from the contemplation of his cross. Then you shall "dwell in God, and God in you." You shall be "one

with God, and God with you." The very moment that the ties between the world and you shall be finally dissolved by death, you shall soar as on eagle's wings to take possession of the crowns and kingdoms that await you in a better world.

Part III

WARNINGS

Sermon 41
The Christian's Birthright

"And Esau said, 'Behold, I am at the point to die: and what profit shall this birthright do to me?'" (Genesis 25:32).

W e may consider it a general rule that no one abstains from anything which he has determined to do because of some excuse of expediency or a necessity to justify it. Yet we have a tragic example of expediency which is not abnormal but a common and almost universal attitude amongst us today. For Esau, having come home from hunting with an unusual appetite and exhaustion, set his heart upon his brother's meal. He was not only willing to sell his birthright for it, but he confirmed with an oath the alienation of that inheritance to which by primogeniture he was entitled. He sought to justify his conduct with this foolish and false apology: "Behold, I am at the point to die; and what profit shall this birthright be to me?" The fact is, as the historian informs us, he "despised his birthright."

I. Esau's Contempt of His Birthright

Among the Jews there were many important privileges attached to primogeniture. For the firstborn was by God's appointment to have dominion over his brothers (Genesis 27:29, 37; 49:3). He was to enjoy a double portion of his father's inheritance (Deuteronomy 21:15, 17). Besides these civil privileges, he also had some some sacred ones. For the Messiah, of whom he was to be a type, and who in reference to the ordinances of birthright is called "the first-born among many brethren" (Romans 8:29), was to be descended from him. Yes, in some sense the firstborn had a better prospect even of heaven itself than the rest of his brethren, because the expectation of the Messiah, who was descended from him, would naturally cause him to look forward to that great event and inquire into the office and character which the promised seed should sustain.

But Esau despised these privileges.

He accounted them of no more value than a mess of pottage. Nor did he immediately repent of his folly and wickedness. For if he had seen the evil of his conduct, he would surely have tried to get the agreement annulled. If his brother Jacob had refused to reverse it, he should have entreated the mediation of his father so that he might be reinstated in his natural rights. But we read of no such effort. On the contrary, we are told, "He did eat and drink, and rose up and went his way." So little was the value that he attached to it; indeed, he utterly "despised his birthright." It is for this reason that he is condemned by the apostle as a profane person (Hebrews 12:16). Had he disregarded only temporal benefits, he would have been guilty of folly. But because his contempt was of spiritual blessings, it was indeed profanity.

Of course, Jacob's conduct in this whole affair was despicable. But Esau's was inexpressibly vile. Yet he is found to have many followers if we look around us.

II. THE ANALOGY BETWEEN HIS CONDUCT AND OUR OWN

The Christian too has a birthright. While the true Christian does not have any temporal advantages similar to those enjoyed by the right of primogeniture, yet he is made an heir of God and a joint-heir with Christ. He has a distinguished interest in the Savior and has an indisputable title to the inheritance of heaven. Thus those who have attained the full possession of their inheritance are called "the general assembly and church of the firstborn" (Hebrews 12:23). Yet the majority are like Esau.

In one instance this privilege was separated from what we have said. Both were alienated from the firstborn; the former being given to Joseph, and the latter to Judah, as a punishment of Reuben's iniquity in lying with his father's concubine (1 Chronicles 5:1, 2).

1. *They have the same indifference about spiritual blessings.*
Some make the same excuse given by Esau, that he did not know
a Savior nor the inheritance that he despised. But we have had
the Savior fully revealed to us. We know what a glorious place the
heavenly Canaan is. Yet too many of us think as lightly of Christ
and of heaven as if he or it were of no interest to us. So we are
ready at any time to barter them away for the most trifling gratification. What then is this, but to imitate the profanity of Esau?

2. *Some have the same insatiable thirst for earth and sensual indulgence.* Although Esau pretended that he was almost dying, it
was only an excuse for his profane conduct. For it cannot be conceived how in the house of such a wealthy man as Isaac, there was
not, or might not easily be procured, something to satisfy the
natural hunger. But he was bent upon having his brother's pottage, whatever it cost.

And is it not so with those who yield to uncleanness, indulgence, or any base passion? Do they not sacrifice their health,
their reputation, yes, even their very souls for a momentary indulgence? Do they not say in fact, "Give me the indulgence of my
lust; I must and will have it, whatever the consequence. If I cannot have it without the loss of my birthright, be it so. Let my hope
in Christ be destroyed; let my prospects of heaven be forever
dimmed. Let my soul perish. Welcome hell; welcome damnation!
But give me the indulgence for which my soul longs." This sounds
very crude. But is this not realized in the lives and actions of the
majority of mankind? Indeed it is so. Like a wild ass, when seeking
her mate, will defy all endeavors to catch and detain her, so are
those who persist in spite of all that is set before them. There are
no persuasions, no promises, no threats, no consequences, either
temporal or eternal, that can divert them from their purpose
(Jeremiah 2:23, 24).

3. *They have the same lack of remorse for selling their birthright
for something of no value.* Esau never had any remorse for what he
had done. For when the birthright was actually given to Jacob, he
"cried with an exceeding bitter cry, 'Bless me, even me also, O my
father'" (Genesis 27:34). Yet he never humbled himself for his

---

*His extreme eagerness may be seen in his own words, "Give me that *"red, red."* En-
chanted with the color, he was determined to get it, whatever it might be, and whatever it
might cost. It is from this that the name *Edom*, which signifies red, was given to him (v.
30).

iniquity, nor did he pray to God for mercy, nor did he endure patiently the consequences of his profanity. On the contrary, he comforted himself with the thought that he would murder his brother as soon as his father was dead (Genesis 27:41, 42). And is this not also true of most people? They go on, but none say, "What have I done?" Instead of confessing and bewailing their guilt and folly, they continue to the utmost, or even indeed presume to justify their impieties. Instead of crying day and night to God for mercy, they never bow their knee before him; or if they do so it is only in a cold and formal manner. Instead of submitting to the rebukes of Providence and kissing the rod, they are rather like a wild bull in a net, determined to add sin to sin. Even Judas himself had greater penitence than they. Alas! Alas! What a resemblance does almost everyone around us bear to this worthless wretch, this monster of profanity!

May I address those who are still despising their birthright? Reflect for a moment on your folly and your danger. Place yourself for a moment on a deathbed situation and say, "I am about to die. What shall it profit me now for having all my past lusts and pleasures?" Will you continue to justify yourselves as you now do, and congratulate yourselves on having been so gratified with your vices and inclinations? Suppose on the other hand that you were dying like Isaac, in the faith of Christ. Would you then say, "What shall it profit my birthright to me now?" Would it then appear a trifling matter to have an interest in the Savior, and to have a title to heaven? Consider further, how likely it is that you may one day, like Esau, seek earnestly the inheritance that you sold and yet find no place of repentance in your Father's bosom!

We do not mean to say that a true penitent will be rejected. But the apostle indicates—as daily experience demonstrates—that as Esau could not secure the revocation of his father's word, although he sought it desperately with tears, so we may cry with great bitterness and anguish on account of the loss that we have sustained. Yet we may never so repent as to regain our forfeited inheritance (Hebrews 12:17). In any case, if we do not obtain a title to heaven while we are here, we may come to the door and knock, like the foolish virgins, and be dismissed with scorn and contempt. Having "sown the wind, we shall reap the whirlwind." So let us then "seek the Lord while he may be found, and call upon him while he is near."

Reflect also on those who value their birthright above everything else. Among the crowd who pour contempt on spiritual blessings, there are some who know their value and have tasted their sweetness. Yet how often temptations arise that will divert our attention from these great concerns and impel us with almost irresistible energy to commit sin! How can we do in one moment what we shall have occasion to regret for all eternity! Let us then watch and pray that we enter not into temptation. For however firm we may imagine our title is to heaven, let us beware lest our subtle adversary deprive us of it. Let us fear, lest a promise being left us of entering into the heavenly rest, any of us should seem to come short of it (Hebrews 4:1).

SERMON 195
THE DANGER OF PROSPERITY

"It shall be, when the LORD your God shall
have brought you into the land which he
sware to your fathers, to Abraham, to Isaac,
and to Jacob, to give you goodly cities which
you built not, and houses full of good things
which you did not fill, and wells dug which
you did not dig, vineyards and olive trees
which you did not plant; when you have
eaten and are full, then beware lest you forget
the LORD, which brought you forth out of the
land of Egypt, from the house of bondage"
(Deuteronomy 6:10-12).

We cannot help noticing in this passage the confidence with which Moses assured the Israelites with regard to their ultimate success in occupying the land of Canaan. They had not yet passed over Jordan, yet he speaks to them as if they were already in full possession of the land. It was so certain that God would fulfill all his promises which he had made to their fathers. At the same time, we cannot but be struck with the warning which is given here of man's tendency toward ingratitude, of the tendency of prosperity to deaden all the finer feelings of the soul. So the caution which he gives them leads me to set before you:

I. THE NATURAL INGRATITUDE OF MAN

This is found to occur generally:

1. *In relation to man's earthly concerns.* We are impressed with the distinct goodness of God to Israel in giving them so many blessings for which they had never labored. Indeed, this is only one example of what he has done for man since the beginning of the world. For Adam, when he was formed in Paradise, found

every comfort prepared for him. It is thus with every child that is born into the world. Everything according to his situation in life is provided for his needs. He has the full benefit of the labors of others for which he never contributed the smallest item. Throughout all our lives we enjoy the same advantages. For God has so ordained that every man, in seeking his own welfare, also contributes to the well-being of those around him. One man "builds houses." Another "fills them with good things." Another "digs wells." Another "plants trees of different species." All according to their own occupations provide well- being for others which would have been impossible for them to have otherwise enjoyed, but for this provision of God. He has made private interest the means of advancing the public welfare. The only difference between the Israelites and ourselves is that what they gained by the bloody extermination of the original inhabitants, we enjoy in a sweet and peaceful participation with the lawful owners.

Now it might well be expected that we should trace back all these blessings and be filled with thanks to God as the Author and Giver of them all. But the evil about which the Israelites were warned is also realized in us to a great measure. We too rest in the gift and forget the Giver. When we seek to provide things for ourselves, we run into the same error against which they were warned. We ascribe our achievements to our own skill or ability, instead of recognizing that they are entirely the gift of God (Deuteronomy 8:17, 18). So in this respect we are not only like the animals, but we actually degrade ourselves below them. For "the ox knows his owner, and the ass his master's crib, while we neither know, nor consider." We do not regard our adorable Benefactor (Isaiah 1:2, 3; Jeremiah 2:32).

2. *In relation to even the welfare of his soul*. The deliverance of Israel from Egypt was typical of our deliverance from far worse bondage. Is it possible that we should ever forget this? Suppose it is possible for man's ingratitude to extend to all that Israel experienced in Egypt, in the wilderness, and in Canaan. Is it possible that man's depravity should be so great as to make him completely forget all the blessings of redemption? Can it be that man should forget what his incarnate God has done for him in laying aside all the glory of heaven, and taking upon him our fallen nature, and bearing our sins in his own body on the tree that he might deliver

us from the bondage of corruption and bring us to the everlasting possession of a heavenly inheritance?

Yes, it is not only possible, but *certain* that men are as forgetful of this as they are of their obligations for temporal blessings. Indeed, it is a fact that many are far more thankful for their temporal mercies than they are for this which infinitely exceeds all others. How shall we then consider their guilt? We have seen that their ingratitude for temporal blessings makes them less than the animals. And I am not certain that their ingratitude for spiritual benefits does not reduce them below the fallen angels themselves. For whatever guilt these miserable creatures may have, at least we know this—that they never poured contempt on the One who took their nature and bore their iniquities to deliver them. This is a depravity that is distinctive to man. This is the depravity that dominates every child of man. Of how awful it has prevailed in all of us our consciences bear witness. For our character is all too clearly described in these words: "When they knew God, they glorified him not as God, neither were thankful" (Romans 1:21).

This increases rather than diminishes because of the abundance of his mercies. As we shall see, we ought to point out:

II. THE GENERAL EFFECT OF PROSPERITY UPON HIM

The real purpose of God's mercies is to fill us with humility and gratitude before him. But because of the corruption of our nature, success:

1. *Inflates those with pride who should be humbled.* This was its sad effect on Israel. Or as the prophet complains, they "sacrificed to their own net, and burned incense to their own drag" (Habakkuk 1:16). If we look at the general effect of prosperity among us, we will find that success in business, or social climbing in society, are generally the fruitful parents of pride and arrogance and self-conceit. See how the money-minded businessman expands his wealth and is proud as if he had been the cause of his own success. Note how all his former meekness is turned into conceit about his own standing, and his overbearing manner to those below him (compare Deuteronomy 8:17, 18 with 1 Timothy 6:17). Indeed, the saying is all too often realized in every level of society, "Jeshurun waxed fat, and kicked" (Deuteronomy 32:15).

But can ever this be a way for spiritual advance? It certainly cannot be with real piety. But it may assume the appearance of real piety. Devotees of religion, when they have acquired more knowledge of theology, are very liable to be conceited with it and to "become in their own conceit wiser than their teachers." So there are many who set up as "teachers, while they yet do not understand what they say, nor what they affirm." Many, because they have some vague idea of what is spiritual, pour contempt on others as being too worldly.

To all such conceited professors I would say, "Be not high-minded, but fear." "Let him that thinks he stands, take heed lest he fall."

2. *Lulls into security those whom it should challenge.* The effect of affluence, especially when it is self-achieved by hard work, is to be less industrious and to make its possessor like the rich fool in the Gospel. "So, you have much goods laid up for many years; eat, drink, and be merry" (Luke 12:16-21). Indeed, leisure is looked upon as the reward of hard effort. Its prospect is man's greatest incentive to diligence. But success, instead of weakening, should rather *increase* our efforts for further success; not from a covetous desire to advance further, but with the desire to enlarge the means that we have of doing good. For wealth and all its associated influence should be considered as a talent that is not hidden in a napkin, but to be improved for God.

What should be the result of increased awareness of divine truth and of a deepened confidence in God? Should not these things stimulate us to more action in the service of the Lord in the light of his grace to our souls? So I say then, let not any of you because of your prosperity be "settled on your lees." Rather let every blessing, whether temporal or spiritual, be used as a motive to further exertion as a means of honoring your heavenly Benefactor.

Let us now address:

1. *Those who have succeeded in the world.* The example of David is what you should follow. When he was assured by God that his kingdom would be established in his family, he "went in, and sat before the LORD, and said 'Who am I, O LORD God, and what is my house, that you have brought me here?'" (2 Samuel 7:18). So let your success affect you in this way, and see the hand of God in it all. Acknowledge your own unworthiness and adore the grace

that has made you have so many prospects. Never forget that prosperity can be a snare which ruins thousands (Proverbs 13:22). If it makes your situation more comfortable in this world, it also hinders your progress even like clods of "clay upon your feet" with respect to the world above (Compare Habakkuk 2:6 with Hebrews 12:1 and Matthew 19:23, 24).

2. *Those who have been reduced by adverse circumstances*. How often it has happened that what prosperity could not give, adversity did. For generally in success, we forget God. But "in the time of adversity we consider." "In their affliction," says God of his people of old, "they will seek me early"; "they will pour out a prayer when my chastening is upon them." Is not this what you have found? When however painful your sufferings may have been, they call for congratulations rather than for condolence? For the prosperity of the soul is what really matters. See to it then that in whatever you decay, you grow in grace. Realize that if only you keep your eyes fixed, not on things visible and temporal, but on those things which are invisible and eternal, "your light afflictions, which are but for a moment, shall work for you a far more exceeding and eternal weight of glory" (2 Corinthians 4:17).

SERMON 490
THE SIN OF REPROVING GOD

"He that reproves God, let him answer for it"
(Job 40:2).

Job's friends had failed to convince him. And no wonder! For they had adopted the wrong kind of argument for their purpose. Job was faulty, exceedingly faulty, before God; but not in the way that his friends imagined. He had complained of God in very irreverent and unholy terms. He had complained of God as "multiplying his wounds without cause" (Job 9:17). He had even condemned God as an oppressor: "I will say to God, 'Do not condemn me: Show me wherefore you contend with me. Is it good for thee that thou should oppress, that thou should despise the work of thine hands, and shine upon the counsel of the wicked? Thou inquirest about my iniquity, and searchest after my sin. Thou knowest I am not wicked'" (Job 10:2, 3, 6, 7).

He then even challenges God to a debate concerning the righteousness of his own proceedings, not doubting that if God will only give him a chance to plead his own cause, without oppressing him by his power, he will prove God to be in error about him. "Withdraw thine hand far from me; and let not thy dread make me afraid: Then call, and I will answer; or let me speak and answer thou me" (Job 13:21, 22). In reply to all this, God takes up the cause. And with an immediate reference to such expressions as I have already cited, he says, "He that reproves God, let him answer for it."

Now, in case there are those who think there are none so presumptuous today as to "reprove God," I will inquire:

I. WHO ARE THEY THAT MAKE SUCH AN OFFENSIVE CHARGE?

Irreverent as such conduct is, there are multitudes who are guilty of it.

1. *Those who dispute his Word.* Only the truly humble will receive the word of God without argument. To some it is too sublime, containing doctrines which human reason cannot comprehend. To others it is too simple, offering salvation by faith alone without any deeds of the Law. To others again, its precepts are too strict, requiring more than man can perform. While, on the other hand, its promises are too free, seeing that a man has nothing to do but to rest upon them, and they shall all be fulfilled to him.

Some deny its efficiency for the instruction of men in the way of life, and put on a footing of equality with it their own unwritten traditions. They even deny also its suitability. They affirm that if read indiscriminately by the laity, "it will do more harm than good." If it be in any translation into common tongues, they denounce it as "a deadly pasture" that will destroy the flock.

What is all this, but to "reprove God," and to say to him, "You have revealed your Word in a way that is unsuitable to the needs of your people and unfit for their perusal." Some declare this even with regard to their own translations of the Bible. So accordingly they take the Bible out of the hands of the laity and allow none to read it without their special permission. I marvel that there can be found upon the face of the whole earth people that will submit to such impious and such deadly tyranny as this. But this whole church shall answer for it before long.

2. *Those who criticize his providence.* Here again everyone will be found guilty before God. For it is no uncommon thing to hear people who even bear the Christian name speaking of luck, fortune, and chance, as if there were no God in heaven, or as if there were things beyond his reach and control. And when afflictions are multiplied upon us, how commonly do we criticize and mur-

mur against God, instead of saying as we ought, "The cup which my Father has given me, shall I not drink it?"

Perhaps it may be argued that our complaints are not so much made against God as against those who are the immediate instruments of our affliction. But whatever the creature may be, it is only a "rod," a "staff," a "sword" in Jehovah's hands. Although God leaves men to the unrestrained outworking of their own corrupt hearts, he overrules everything they do for the accomplishment of his own will. Even the crucifixion of our blessed Lord was "in accordance with God's determinate counsel and will" (Acts 2:23; 4:28). "Nor is there evil in the city, but it must be traced to God as the doer of it" (Amos 3:6) so far at least as the sufferer is concerned. And as Moses, when the people murmured against him and Aaron, told them that their murmurings were in reality against God himself (Exodus 16:7, 8), so I must say that murmurings of every kind, against whoever or whatever it is directed, is in fact a reproof of God himself, without whom not a sparrow falls to the ground, nor does so much as a hair fall from our heads.

3. *Those who condemn his grace.* The sovereignty of God and the disposal of his blessings are most offensive to the proud heart of man. We arrogate to ourselves a right to dispense our favors on whomever we will. Yet we deny that right to God. The apostle Paul places this in a very striking point of view. God has said by the prophet, "Jacob have I loved, but Esau have I hated." The apostle then, arguing with a proud objector, replies: "What shall we say then? Is there unrighteousness with God? God forbid. For he says to Moses, 'I will have mercy on whom I will have mercy, and I will have compassion on whom I will have compassion.' So then, it is not of him that wills, nor of him that runs, but of God that shows mercy. For the Scripture says unto Pharaoh, 'Even for this purpose have I raised you up, that I might show my power in you, and that my name might be declared throughout all the earth.' Therefore has he mercy on whom he will have mercy; and whom he will, he hardens. Will you say then unto me, why then does he still find fault? For who has resisted his will? Nay but, O man, who are you that replies against God? Shall the thing formed say to him that formed it, 'Why have you made me thus?' Has not the potter power over the clay, and the same lump to make one vessel to honor and another to dishonor?" (Romans 9:13-21).

Here is the very point both stated and answered. Man's proneness to call in question the grace of God is here affirmed, and is plainly declared to be a reproving of God himself.

Seeing that so many are obnoxious to the charge here exhibited, I will show,

II. What Is Meant by the Warning That Is Here Given to Them

I have already noticed Job's challenge to Jehovah to answer him. Now God, in reply, challenges the offender if he can answer *him*. But there are only two ways in which any answer can be given. It must be either in the way of self-approving vindication, or in the way of self-abasing humiliation. Let both be heard.

1. *In a way of self-approving vindication.* To apply like this, a man must maintain three points: God is bound to consult me in what he does; I am competent to sit in judgment on his proceedings; I know better than God himself does what it becomes him to do. But who can maintain these points and make them good against God? Read the two preceding chapters and it will soon appear what claim man has upon God. It is from him that he derives his very existence and who keeps him in existence every breath he draws. As to judging God's ways, as well might a peasant sit in judgment on the works of the greatest statesman or philosopher. Who among us would submit to have all his views and pursuits criticized by a child that has only just learned to speak? Yet that is the way in which we are presuming to sit in judgment upon God. When a candle can add to the light of the meridian sun, then we may hope to counsel God how best to rule the world and how most effectively to advance his own glory. If, then, we cannot make good our own cause against God, then we must answer him in a different way.

2. *In a way of self-abasing humiliation.* It was in this way that Job replied. "Then Job answered the LORD, and said, 'Behold I am vile; what shall I answer thee? I will lay my hand upon my mouth. Once have I spoken; but I will not answer; yea, twice; but I will proceed no further'" (vv. 3, 4). Later Job says: "I have uttered what I did not understand; things too wonderful for me, which I

knew not. Wherefore I abhor myself, and repent in dust and ashes" (Job 42:3, 6). O brethren! *This* is the answer for every one of us to give! For "God will assuredly be justified in all that he has done, and will be clear when he has judged" (Psalm 51:4). He will vindicate his own honor and put to silence every proud objector.

So instead of reproving God, let us have this habit of our minds in future. And under all circumstances, let us maintain a humble dependence upon his goodness, and have a meek submission to his will. This is our duty, our interest, our happiness. We expect this from our own children. Shall we show less regard for God than we poor fallible creatures expect from our children? Let us lie as clay in the hands of our all-wise, all-gracious God, and leave him to perfect his work in his own way. Let us have no anxiety in our minds, but seek only to fulfill his will and glorify his name. It was by a very circuitous route that he brought the Israelites to Canaan. But we are told, "He led them by the right way." And so we, whatever trials we may meet with in this wilderness, shall in the end have the same reason to glorify our God as Job himself had (James 5:11), and as all the saints have had from the beginning of the world.

SERMON 669
THE NEED FOR INTEGRITY

"The deeds of faithless men I hate;
they will not cling to me" (Psalm 101:3).

In whatever position God has placed us, it is our duty to improve our influence for God. So especially those who are in positions of leadership in a community (like magistrates) may be most influential by exerting all their power in the promotion of what is good. David felt this was his responsibility. So in beginning his reign in Hebron after the death of Saul, as well as later coming into full possession of the kingdom, he wrote this psalm as a declaration of his determination to repress evil and to encourage good to the best of his abilities. This he did both among his court and among his more immediate servants in his own household.

Let us consider therefore,

I. THE WORK HE COMPLETELY REJECTS

There are two points to which he seems to refer:

1. **A lack of integrity in morals.** Carelessness about principle has often been excused because of expediency. The most subtle forms of argument can be used to vindicate it. But integrity, undeviating integrity, is what should dominate the Christian's mind. There are many things which constitute what is called a sense of honor that can never be admitted in the character of a real saint. The laws of honor have their origin from man. And as they derive their

95

authority from man, so they refer only to the judgment of man in their keeping. These therefore may bend to the times and circumstances.

But the Law of God is inflexible. Our submission to it must be constant under all circumstances. It must regulate the ends which we propose, the means that we use in pursuit of them, and the way in which we proceed throughout the whole of our deportment. In everything we must try to approve ourselves to God and to act as if we were in his immediate presence. So any departure from the strict line of duty, in whatever circumstances we are placed, must be avoided. Our whole conduct toward mankind, in whatever relation they stand to us, must be such that with changing circumstances we should still think it right to keep them. God requires that "truth should be in our inward parts" (Psalm 51:6). Every act, every word, every purpose and desire of our hearts ought to be in strict accordance with it.

2. **A lack of constancy in religion.** There are many who having begun well no longer behave wisely and "turn aside from the holy commandment delivered to them" (2 Peter 2:21). There are many causes for this declension. It begins sometimes with a neglect of religious duties or in the mere formal performance of them. Sometimes it begins in the secret indulgence of some hidden lust. Sometimes "the care of this world, the deceitfulness of riches," and the desire for other things which have no direct reference to religion choke the seed that has been sown in our hearts and prevent it from bringing forth any fruit to perfection (Matthew 13:22). But whatever it is that turns us from God, it should be disapproved in others and avoided by ourselves. For it can be subtle and give us the excuse to extenuate, if not to altogether justify, our practice of it. By its operation it turns us aside from God and from the pursuit of heavenly things. So it becomes an evil work which should be renounced by us.

But we must be careful not to impute to any line of duty the evils which arise from our own lack of care in their pursuit. There is nothing which we may not make an occasion for sin. Someone may say, "I have scholarly pursuits which occupy my mind with such intensity that I cannot afterwards concentrate upon heavenly things." Another may say, "I have manual labor which makes it difficult for me to have heavenly contemplation." In these cases, the duty of these people is not to renounce the labors to which in the course of providence they have been called, but to implore God that they may be given some measure of spiritual strength to combine the duties which they have tended to separate. Nor can we doubt that if they are upright in heart they will be given grace sufficient for the conscientious carrying out of their duties. What is important for them to recognize is that they have to guard against every inordinate desire. For it is from their inward desires, rather than from their outward duties, that they may be in danger of being drawn away from God.

The conduct of the Psalmist, in connection with such "work," shows:

II. The Attitude Which We Should Show Toward It

1. *In principle we should abhor it*. We should be attracted toward God as the compass is to the magnetic north. A compass needle may be deflected from its proper direction, but it will never cease from a tremulous motion until it has returned to its proper rest. So it should be with us. We do not know what deviations a sudden impulse of temptation may cause for a moment. But as soon as we perceive that we have been deflected, even in thought, from the perfect line of duty, then we should neither sleep nor rest until we return with repentance to our God. The direction given to us by God is "Abhor that which is evil; cleave to that which is good" (Romans 12:9). And whether with regard to morals or religion, this must be habitual for our minds. We must be "Israelites indeed, in whom there is no guile" (John 1:47).

2. *In practice we should avoid it*. We can never be too careful about our ways. At sea the sailor is often driven from his course by currents of which he is not aware. He will only find his deviation off course by the observations that he makes. So it is possible for a Christian to be deflected by a corrupt bias, until he has carefully compared his ways with the unerring standard of the Word of God. So it is necessary to heed the divine counsel, "Prove all things: hold fast that which is good" (1 Thessalonians 5:21). We must be extremely careful that we be able to "keep a conscience void of offense toward both God and man." For we are passing

through a polluted world, and it is very difficult to "keep our garments altogether undefiled" (Revelation 3:4). But if we come in contact with evil, we must take care that it does "not cling to us." It must be the one effort of our lives to be "sincere and without offense, until the day of Christ" (Philippians 1:10).

Address—

1. Carefully note the beginnings of decline. "Examine yourselves, whether you be in the faith," says the apostle. "Prove your own selves" (2 Corinthians 13:5). Let the first symptoms of spiritual decline be carefully noted by you, and make this an occasion for increased diligence in setting your heavenly course. By such vigilance you will avoid many evils. Happy it would have been for David if he had marked the first risings of lust which the sight of Bathsheba excited in his soul. How happy it would be for us if we determined through grace to abstain not only from evil but from the first desires for it, and even "the very appearance of it," whether in the heart or in life (1 Thessalonians 5:22).

2. Avoid the occasions and ways of it. Our Lord teaches us to pray that we may "not be led into temptation." Indeed, if we willingly subject ourselves to temptation, we cannot expect to be kept. We must "take heed to our ways" and avoid the scenes of vice and folly. Avoid the company, the conversation, the books, and the sights that would trap us, if we are to be preserved "holy and unblameable and unreproveable in the world." If we "come out from among the ungodly, and touch not the unclean thing, then will God be a Father unto us, and we shall be his sons and daughters, saith the Lord Almighty" (2 Corinthians 6:17, 18).

SERMON 1159

THE CAUSES AND SYMPTOMS OF SPIRITUAL DECAY

"Ephraim has mixed himself among the people: Ephraim is a cake half baked. Strangers have devoured his strength, and he does not know it; yea, gray hairs are here and there upon him, yet he knows it not"
(Hosea 7:8,9).

When the body is sick we inquire about the symptoms of the disorder and try to trace it to its cause. The same thing is true with reference to the soul, and indeed to the state of nations as well as individuals. So the prophet is representing the declension and almost desolate condition of the ten tribes. In the words before us, he describes the particular sins which had provoked God to forsake them. He describes the fearful consequences of their transgressions. The Israelites had, in direct opposition to God's command, united themselves with the heathen and incorporated many of their idolatrous rites with the worship of the true God. They were even "mad upon their idols," while they were cold and indifferent to what related to Jehovah. Because of this, God gave them into the hands of their enemies. Pul, king of Assyria, exhausted their treasures by the tribute that he imposed (2 King 15:19). The king of Assyria reduced their armies to a mere shadow, "making them even as the dust of the threshing floor" (2 Kings 13:7). The evidence and proof of decay were seen everywhere, and these indicated the approaching dissolution of the nation. Yet the people were so infatuated that they were unconcerned and felt secure as if they had been in the safest and most flourishing condition.

But it is not our intention to enter any further into the history of the ten tribes. Rather, we shall draw your attention to our own personal concerns, of which theirs was a type and shadow. So we shall proceed to point out the causes and symptoms of spiritual decay.

I. THE CAUSES

The two things mentioned in the text will be found to be among the most important sources of decline in the divine life:

1. *An undue connection with the world.* Some intercourse with mankind is necessary in order to do our civil and social duties. But if we mix with the world by choice, we shall go contrary to the commands of God and suffer loss in our souls. So we are enjoined to "come out from among them, and be separate" (Romans 12:2; Psalm 45:10, 11). God even appeals to us with regard to the impossibility of maintaining with propriety any intimate communion with them (2 Corinthians 6:14-17). Our Lord characterizes his followers as being no more of the world than he was himself (John 17:14). But some professors of religion connect themselves more closely and involve themselves more deeply with the world's business than they need to do. Others associate themselves as companions of the world. Others are so blinded by their passions as to unite themselves with them in marriage. What can we expect from such conduct? Will it not expose us to many temptations? Are we not, when so compromised, likely to drink into the spirit of the world, and to be drawn into a conformity to their ways? Surely the falls and apostasies of many must be traced to this source. It will be well that this evil does not become fatal to some of us.

2. *A partial regard for God.* A "cake" that is heated upon coals and is only "half-baked" will be burnt on one side and soft and doughy on the other. This aptly describes the state of those who are cold and indifferent to things relating to religion, while excessively enthusiastic in their pursuit of other objects. Yet what could be more common than such a condition? Some professors are so intent on their worldly business, and have their hearts so engaged in it, as scarcely to have any zeal left for better things. Some are occupied with this or that favorite study, in comparison with which the Bible, prayer, and communion with God have no charms for them. Some are inflamed by politics and are never

happy except when they are discussing political matters. Some are so intent upon the polities of religion, such as baptism or church government, that they seem to think an agreement with them in their opinions on these subjects is essential to salvation as well as piety itself. Some again are heated by controversy about certain doctrines while alas! they pay little attention to their duties, especially those of humility and love. No wonder the soul languishes when eternal interests are thus postponed to matters of inferior importance. If we were to don a holy profession, we must be penetrated through and through with a fervent regard to God; all other things must be subordinated to the one thing needful.

Having traced the causes of spiritual decay, let us notice,

II. THE SYMPTOMS

In the light of what we have observed concerning the Israelites, we shall mention three marks which, in the progressive stages of decay, will show themselves in a soul's decline:

1. **Inward weakness.** The exercise of true religion requires our utmost effort. Without fixity of purpose, intensity of thought, ardor of desire, and resoluteness of conduct, we cannot progress in our Christian course. But when we have declined from God, all these are relaxed accordingly. The bow is unstrung and cannot send the arrow to the mark (Hosea 7:16). We take up the Bible, but it is a sealed book. We address ourselves to prayer, but our mouths are shut, and we cannot utter a word before God. Duties which once were easy become arduous and irksome. Temptations which once had lost all their force now obstruct our way and entangle our feet. The Cross, which was once the object of holy glorying and served only to stimulate us to fresh exertions, now becomes an object of terror. Instead of taking it up cheerfully, we try as much to avoid it.

Let us look and see whether "strangers have not devoured our strength," and whether "the things which remain in us are not ready to die" (Revelation 3:2).

2. **Outward evidences of that weakness.** "Gray hairs" are evidence of declining strength. At first they are thinly interspersed, but afterwards they are diffused over the whole head. Thus the

symptoms of decline, which are small at first and scarcely visible except on close inspection, develop. However, they will appear when the inward weakness has begun. There will be a visible alteration in temper. A proud, imperious spirit will show itself more readily. Fretfulness and impatience arise more easily. A change will occur in our dealings with the world. We become less open, less generous, less scrupulous about adhering to truth or in practicing the tricks of the trade. There will also be deterioration of our condition seen in our families. There will be less attention paid to their spiritual interests. The Word of God will not be read to them with such practical and relevant concern. Nor will devotions be exercised. They degenerate into a mere form.

But it is in the closet that the symptoms of our decline will be seen especially. Probably prayer will become mere lip-service, and not infrequently entirely omitted. The Scriptures will be glanced over in haste, or else lie wholly neglected. In brief, there will be no delight in God, no peaceful serenity of mind, no joyful hope of life to come. These things will be exchanged for gloom and depression, for sighs and sorrows, for an accusing conscience and a dread of death.

3. *Insensibility under such weakness*. Things have now gone far when this trait appears. For it is the natural effect of sin to blind the eyes, to harden the heart, and to sear the conscience (1 John 2:11; Hebrews 3:13; 1 Timothy 4:2). It is said twice of the Israelites in the text, "they knew it not." They had contracted a stupid indifference that bordered on judicial blindness and infatuation. This is the state to which many professors of religion are reduced. Others will see their gray hairs, but they do not. They have ceased to look into the glass of God's law or to examine themselves. They have quieted their minds by some worldly expedient of business or company or by comparing themselves with others. Their condition is deplorable indeed! If they are not soon aroused from their lethargy, they will have reason to wish they had never been born or never seen the light of gospel truth (2 Peter 2:20, 21).

Address—

1. *Those who are trusting in a formal religion*. True religion is a state of holy, active exertion in the things that belong to God.

God says to us, "My son, give me your heart" (Proverbs 23:26). Without this, our services are of no value. See to it then, my brethren, that you get your hearts quickened by the Spirit of God. You must not be satisfied merely with seeking: "You must try to enter in at the strait gate" (Luke 13:24). You must "take the kingdom of heaven by violence" (Matthew 11:12). Seek then that you may be "renewed by the Spirit in your inward man," and be enabled so to fight as to conquer, so to run as to win the prize (1 Corinthians 9:24, 26).

2. *Those who profess to experience "the power of godliness"*. The deceitfulness of the human heart is amazing. We all see defects in others of which they themselves are not conscious. And can we suppose that we ourselves are not also blind to our own defects? Yes indeed, and perhaps the very locks of hair which we think to be our greatest ornament are full of gray strands. Perhaps our graces are rather the resemblance than the reality of virtue. Our humility may be affectation, our zeal pride, our confidence presumption. Let us then "be jealous over ourselves with a godly jealousy" (2 Corinthians 11:2). Let us search and try ourselves (Lamentations 3:40). Let us beg of God to search and to try us (Psalm 139:23). Let us be careful that we set out well, and then labor to "go on from strength to strength, until we appear before God in Zion" (Psalm 84:7).

SERMON 464
DEATH

"Man gives up the ghost, and where is he?"
(Job 14:10)

While afflictions wean us from the love of this present world, they also serve to make us familiar with the thoughts of death, which are repulsive to our nature. Yet they can be transformed into a source of desire and hope (See Job 7:1-10; 14:1, 2). Yet it is proper for us to contemplate this subject while we are in a state of health and prosperity. Especially it should help to make the departure of others to the eternal world an occasion of considering what our own state may shortly be.

Man consists of soul and body. In death these are separated, the body returning to its native dust and "the soul returning to God who gave it." This separation must quickly take place, whatever be our rank, our age, or our employment. The very instant that "our soul is required of us," it must be given up. Nor can the skill of all the physicians in the world assist us in warding off the stroke of death a single hour.

When the hour comes, "man gives up the ghost, then where is he?" While he is yet alive we can find him. His status in life will help us in our inquiry. The student, the mechanic, the man of pleasure, yes, even the traveler may be sought for, each in his own vocation, and may be found without great difficulty. But who shall find the man when once his spirit has taken its flight to the invisible world? For he will no more return to his former abode. He will have no more intercourse with his former friends. The house he has built or the books he has written may remain. But he himself will be far away, and the place that he has inhabited shall know him no more. Even a tree that is cut down may sprout again. But not so with the man who dies: "He shall pass away as a morning cloud and shall be seen no more" (Ecclesiastes 3:20).

Then where is he:

1. *As to any opportunity of serving God?* Once he had at least one talent entrusted to him, and he might have approved it for God. Now it is taken from him. Whatever he once possessed of bodily or mental power, of time, wealth, influence, all these are gone forever. He can do no more for God than if he had never existed in the world.

2. *As to any means of benefiting his own soul?* Time was, when he could read the blessed book of God and draw near to the throne of grace and pour out his soul in prayer and lay hold on the promises of the gospel and seek from the Savior, the Lord Jesus Christ, such communications of grace, mercy, and peace as were needful for him. Now this time has passed away. There is no access to God now. There is no help from the Savior now. There is no scope for repentance now. None of these things remain once the soul is removed to the eternal world (vv. 7-12). The work that is unfinished now will remain unfinished forever.

3. *As to any hope of carrying into effect his purposes and desires?* There are few who are so hardened that they have not given some thought or desire of turning to God before they die. For the gay, the industrious, the dissolute, the fit time for religious services has not yet come. But yet all have a secret conviction that the concerns of the soul deserve at least some attention. So they hope that in a dying hour at least, they shall in spite of all their levity realize that one thing is needful. Perhaps the youth waited until they were more settled in life. Perhaps they waited until their children should grow up and give them more leisure to follow the dictates of their better judgment. Those who were absorbed in earthly affairs only waited until they were able to retire from the world and to devote a good measure of their attention to heavenly things. But "the day is closed upon them; the night is come, in which no man can work." "Their soul being, as it were, prematurely and unexpectedly required of them," their hopes were never realized and their desires never accomplished.

4. As to any possibility of preparing for his eternal state? The fight is over, the race is closed, the crown awarded. There is no return to the field of action. There is no further scope for amended efforts. "As the tree falls, so it lies," and so it will lie to all eternity. Pardon, peace, holiness, glory, are all at an unapproachable distance to him who dies without having attained the possession of them. There is an impassable gulf between him and heaven. He must take his portion forever in that place for which he alone has prepared.

Permit me, then, now to ask:

1. If the time were come for us to "give up the ghost," where should we be? This is a thought which ought frequently and deeply to occupy all our minds. Of individual people we can know very little. Respecting characters, we may form a very correct judgment. For instance, we know where the man who dies impenitent shall be (Luke 13:3, 5). We know where the man who has not fled to Christ for refuge will be (John 3:18, 36). We know also where the hypocritical professor will be (Matthew 7:21-23). And if we candidly look into our own character, we may form a very accurate estimate about our future destination. So I beg you then to examine carefully the state of your own souls, in reference to your penitence, to your faith, to your obedience to God's commands. Then say, as before God, what expectations such an inquiry will authorize. Reflect too, I pray you, on the inconceivable difference between those two states to which you must go. Recognize the different emphasis with which the reflections in my text will be uttered by your surviving friends, according as their hopes or apprehensions about you are formed.

2. As the time for your giving up the ghost will shortly come, "where should you now be?" Are the scenes of gaiety and dissipation those which we should chiefly resort to? Or rather should it be the house of God where we delight to dwell? Should it not be your own closet that is frequently visited for the purposes of reading, meditation, and prayer? In brief, should you not live as dying men, and improve your time in preparation for eternity? Realize the thought of your feelings on that day, when in the eternal world you shall say "Where am I?" How blessed is that thought if you died in the state of acceptance with God, and how contrasted it is with the anguish if you died under his displeasure! So I urge you brethren, waste no more time in vanity and folly, but attend now to the great concerns of your souls. So if the inquiry is made here or in the invisible world, "Where is he?" the answer may be, "He is blessed forever, in the bosom of his God."

Part IV

REPENTANCE

SERMON 1533
REPENTANCE

*"Except you repent, you shall all likewise
perish" (Luke 13:5).*

These words are twice repeated by our Lord within the space
of three verses. Why are they so repeated? Our Lord intended
to check that common tendency which we all have to judge
others. Rather, he would lead us to judge ourselves and to prepare
for that awful judgment which shall before long be passed upon us.
Some of his hearers in the context of what he had spoken told him
of the Galileans who had been slain by Pilate in the very act of
offering their sacrifices, and whose blood had mingled with their
sacrifices. Seeing that they intended to insinuate that this calamity was a judgment from God on account of some terrible wickedness, our Lord rectified their error, and taught them to look at
themselves instead of judging and condemning others. Such
calamities as these, he observed, fell indiscriminately on the righteous and the wicked; but there was a day coming when a just dis-
crimination would be made. Then the impenitent would be subjected to God's heaviest judgments.

Seeing what emphasis our blessed Lord laid upon these truths,
we cannot be thought uncharitable if we expound them to you according to their true import. In order to do this we will point out,

I. THE NATURE OF REPENTANCE

All are ready to imagine that they know what repentance is, although in truth, very few have any just notions about it. It consists in:

1. *A humiliation before God on account of sin.* Although this is not denied, few are aware what kind of humiliation is required.

It must be *deep.* It is not just a slight, superficial sorrow that will suffice. For sin is a dreadful evil, and must be lamented in a way that is suited to its enormity. Hear how God himself teaches us to deplore its commission. "Be afflicted, and mourn, and weep; let your laughter be turned into mourning, and your joy into heaviness. Humble yourselves under the mighty hand of God" (James 4:8-10). Such was the compunction that was felt by the three thousand on the day of Pentecost (Acts 2:37). Such was also the overwhelming sense of guilt which David felt (Psalm 38:4; 51:3). And such was the contrition of Ezra, when he confessed before God his own and his people's iniquities (Ezra 9:5, 6). This is the humiliation which God requires; and everything that falls short of this he will despise (Psalm 51:17).

It must be *ingenuous.* There is a sorrow, like that of Felix or Judas, that arises from convictions of the natural conscience, but which ends in despair. But this is in no way acceptable to God; for it will consist with a love of sin and a hatred of God's law. The person who is impressed with it would prefer a life of sin, provided only that he might be assured of escaping the punishment attendant on it. Rather our sorrow should resemble that of the Corinthian church when they had seen their error and were humbled for it with "a sorrow which wrought in them a repentance not to be repented of." "For behold," says the apostle, "this self-same thing, that you sorrowed after a godly sort, what carefulness it wrought in you, yea, what clearing of yourselves, yea what indignation, yea what fear, yea what vehement desire, yea what zeal, yea what revenge. In all things you have approved yourselves to be clear in this matter" (2 Corinthians 7:10, 11).

In them we see what we consider as eminently characterizing true repentance. That is, an ingenuous shame on account of their past conduct, a readiness to justify God in any judgments he should inflict on them, a hatred of their sin, and a determination through grace to walk more circumspectly in the future. Wherever there is experience like this, there is the grace of God in truth (Ezekiel 20:43, 44).

It must be *abiding*. Transient emotions, of whatever kind they be, can never be regarded as constituting true repentance. The confessions of Pharaoh (Exodus 9:27; 10:16, 17), and Saul (1 Samuel 24:16-18; 26:21) appear to indicate a change of heart. But no real change was wrought in them, as was evident from their reverting almost immediately to their former ways. Most people, if they had experienced the humiliation of Ahab, would be ready to consider themselves real penitents. But his subsequent conduct showed the insincerity of all his professions (1 Kings 21:27-29; 22:27). Far different from this must our contrition be, if we would ever be accepted of our God. We must retain the impressions which have been made upon us so that we say with Hezekiah, "I will go softly all my years in the bitterness of my soul" (Isaiah 38:15). Instead of accounting our acceptance with God a reason for putting off this disposition of mind, we should regard it rather as a motive to still deeper humiliation. This is the design of God in exercising mercy toward us (Romans 2:4). This is the inseparable effect where that mercy is properly received (Ezekiel 16:63).

2. *Turning to God in newness of life*. This also must be acknowledged as essential to true repentance; but do not let this change be misunderstood.

It must be *cordial*. It is not the service of a slave under the influence of fear and dread, but it is the result of a conviction that sin is an intolerable bondage, and that the service of God is perfect freedom. Whatever change proceeds not from the heart, it is mere hypocrisy (Jeremiah 3:10). What characterizes sound conversion will engage all the faculties of the soul (Jeremiah 24:7). Thus it is represented by Solomon in his intercessory prayer (2 Chronicles 6:37, 38). It is what the prophet Joel commands: "Turn you even to me with all your heart, with fasting and with weeping and with mourning" (Joel 2:12).

It must be *progressive*. Conversion is not a work that is accomplished all at once, or is ever perfected in this life, but it is what we need in order to press forward to higher attainments. Even Paul himself, toward the close of his life, did "not consider himself as having attained perfection, or apprehended all for which he himself had been apprehended of Christ Jesus. Hence he, like a person in a race, forgot all that was behind, and reached forward for that which was before" (Philippians 3:12-14). Although the body is perfect in all its limbs, even in earliest infancy, yet it grows in every limb until it reaches manhood. So does the new man advance toward "the full measure of the stature of Christ" (Ephesians 4:13). We should "grow in grace," and so grow as to make our "profiting to appear." Indeed, we may not be able to see any actual progress at every short interval, any more than we can see the advance of the sun every minute. Yet we perceive after some time that the sun has continued on its course. Likewise our path must be like the shining light, which "shines more and more unto the perfect day." We must be "going on to perfection," and aspiring after that which is proposed to us as the proper aim of our ambition. This is "to stand perfect and complete in all the will of God" (Colossians 4:12).

It must be *uniform*. Nothing whatever is to divert us from this duty. We are not ever to be influenced by times or circumstances so that we neglect the positive duty because of fear of man or because we are tempted by some earthly advantage. The changes which we see in the conduct of the apostle Paul did not come from any deviation from principle, but from a strict adherence to principle. His one object was to save the souls of men. In those things that were non-essential, he accommodated himself to their habits and prejudices in order to promote his main design. But when he saw that any evil was likely to arise from a particular act of conformity, he was as immovable as a rock. Thus we may vary our conduct on particular occasions, provided we can appeal to God that we are motivated by a regard for the welfare of others and not by any personal considerations of our own. But in no instance whatever must this principle be stretched to violate any known duty of the dictates of our own conscience. Life itself must be of no value in our eyes in comparison of God's honor and the preservation of a conscience void of offense toward God and man.

It must be *unreserved*. Not only must we labor to undo what we have done amiss by making restitution of ill-gotten gain and warning those whom we have led into sin, but we must strive to mortify sin of every kind in every degree. Everyone has some "sin that more easily besets him," and to which he will be more strongly tempted. This sin is different in different persons. In one it may be pride, in another passion or lust or covetousness or ambition and the love of praise or sloth; but whatever it is, our victory over it is a just criterion of our condition. If it leads us captive, we are still carnal and unrenewed. Whatever repentance we may fancy ourselves to have experienced has all been ineffectual. We are yet in our sins. We are "in the gall of bitterness and the bond of iniquity." Our right eye must be plucked out if it causes us to offend; and our right hand must be amputated. There is no alternative for us but to part with that, or else to suffer the miseries of hell (Mark 9:43-48).

Such is the view which God himself gives us of repentance. To this alone does he attach any hope of salvation: "Repent and turn yourselves from all your transgressions; so iniquity shall not be your ruin" (Ezekiel 18:30).

These views of repentance will appear all the more important if we consider,

II. THE NECESSITY OF IT

The word which we translate "likewise" may possibly be intended to show the resemblance between the calamities that awaited the impenitent Jews and those which had befallen the people just spoken of. But as we are more interested in what relates to ourselves, we shall take a broader view of the subject than attempt a parallel, which would be more curious than useful. We can say then in reference to repentance that the necessity for it is:

1. *Indispensable*. Eternal happiness or misery depends upon this: "Except we repent, we must all perish." It is not for us to say what God *might* do. It is sufficient to know what he *will* do. He has appointed repentance as the means of obtaining reconciliation with him. He has given his own Son to die for us, in order that the guilt of sin having been expiated by the blood of the cross, he may be able to receive returning sinners in a perfect consistency with the demands of law and justice. This should be clearly understood. He has not appointed repentance to atone for sin. If we could shed rivers of tears, they could never wash away the smallest sin. It is only the blood of Christ that can cleanse from sin. No other fountain ever was or ever can be opened for sin and for uncleanness, but that which issued from the wounds of our adorable Redeemer.

But repentance is necessary in order to prepare our souls for a worthy reception of his divine mercies, and for a suitable improvement of them. So although it cannot atone for sin or merit anything at the hand of God, it is still indispensable. If we do not repent, we must forever remain in the snare of the devil, and the gates of heaven will assuredly be closed against us (2 Timothy 2:25, 26). The declaration of our text will certainly be fulfilled. Sooner shall heaven and earth pass away than one jot or tittle of it ever fail. So know that whatever is implied in the "perishing" of an immortal soul, this is the lot of every impenitent sinner.

2. *Universal.* There are distinguished authors who have tried to prove that there are some who do not need to repent. Our Lord *does* say, "I came not to call the righteous, but sinners to repentance"; and that "there is more joy among the angels over one sinner that repents, than over ninety and nine just persons who need no repentance." These authors imagine there is a class of people whose natures are so pure and their conduct so blameless that they are given no occasion for repentance. But the former of these passages relates to those who thought themselves righteous and who, from a conceit of their being "whole," despised the offered assistance of a physician (see Matthew 9:12, 13). The latter clearly refers to those who have already been converted to God, and are as sheep living in the fold of Christ. Such are considered secure, while those who are unconverted are in real danger. As the recovery of a lost sheep affords more real pleasure to its owner than the possession of a hundred that have not strayed, so the angels are filled with preeminent joy at the conversion of one whom they had considered as in a lost and perishing condition (Luke 15:7). So these passages cannot be understood to sanction the idea that there are any persons so good that they do not need repentance.

The apostle Paul collects a multitude of texts to prove that "there is none righteous, no, not one: that all have sinned, and come short of the glory of God: and that therefore every mouth must be stopped, and all the world become guilty before God" (Romans 3:9-10). "There is not a man that lives and sins not," says Solomon. "In many things we offend all," says the apostle James. "If we say we have no sin, we deceive ourselves," says the apostle John, and "the truth is not in us." So where shall we find those who need no repentance?

Is such a one more righteous than Job, of whom God himself testified that "there was none like him in the earth, a perfect and upright man, one that feared God and eschewed evil"? Supposing we argue that he was equal to Job. Would he not then need to repent? Hear what Job says concerning himself: "If I justify myself, my own mouth shall condemn me. If I say, I am perfect, it shall also prove me perverse. Although I were perfect, yet I would not know my soul. I would despise my life. If I washed myself with snow water, and make my hands never so clean, yet thou shalt plunge me in the ditch and my own clothes shall abhor me" (Job 9:20, 21, 30, 31). So let those who maintain such an unscriptural sentiment lay to heart the warning of the Almighty: "You say, 'Because I am innocent, surely his anger shall turn from me.' Behold, I will plead with you, because you say, 'I have not sinned'" (Jeremiah 2:35). If they do not humble themselves now, let them be ready to maintain their own cause against God in the day of judgment.

We repeat that the necessity of repentance is universal, and we entreat everyone to apply the declaration to his own soul: "Except you repent, you shall all likewise perish."

Address—

1. *To those who think themselves penitents*. What has been said on the nature of repentance may well lead us to examine ourselves and to fear lest we should deceive our own souls. So we entreat you all to bear in mind the particulars which you have heard, and apply them to yourselves. If in anything we appear to have pressed a point too far, let the confession which we always utter at the Lord's Supper be taken in connection with it. It will be found that we have not uttered a single thought which is not contained in that exercise.

So we cannot but urge all who are in the habit of frequenting the Lord's table to inquire whether their repentance is what in prayer they profess it to be. We are told by our church what is required of those that come to the Lord's Supper, namely, to examine themselves whether they truly repent of their former sins. We now most earnestly recommend this examination, lest in the midst of all "your sacrifices" the wrath of God breaks out against you and you "perish" in a far more fearful manner than ever the Galileans did (v. 1).

2. *To those who desire to repent.* Do not delay for a moment to carry out your purpose, lest death find you unprepared to meet your God. Knowing the terrors of the Lord, we would persuade you so to turn to him that you may have no reason to dread them. Remember not to address yourselves to the work of repentance in your own strength. For it is God alone who can give it to you. He has "exalted the Lord Jesus to his own right hand on purpose to give you repentance and remission of sins" (Acts 5:31). But if you are tempted to doubt whether he will bestow it upon you, know that "he is not willing that any should perish, but that all should come to repentance" (2 Peter 3:9). As evidence of this, we only need to consider what is implied in the words of our text. When it is said that "except we repent we shall all perish," we may fairly take the converse of it to be true and conclude that they who do repent shall not perish. This blessed truth is confirmed by thousands of positive declarations.

Think of the instructive parable of the Prodigal Son which is always a source of comfort to every contrite soul. Reflect on the representation of God's love to penitents which is given to us by the prophet Jeremiah. With such you will need no other encouragement to turn to God with your whole hearts (Jeremiah 31:18-20). So then our parting exhortation to everyone is simply this: "Let the wicked forsake his way, and the unrighteous man his thoughts, and let him return unto the LORD, and he will have mercy upon him, and to our God, for he will abundantly pardon" (Isaiah 55:7).

SERMON 1258
THE MEANS OF EVANGELICAL REPENTANCE

*"I will pour upon the house of David, and
upon the inhabitants of Jerusalem, the spirit
of grace and of supplications; and they shall
look upon me whom they have pierced, and
they shall mourn for him, as one mourns for
his only son, and shall be in bitterness for
him, as one that is in bitterness for his
firstborn" (Zechariah 12:10).*

Repentance is a subject which everyone supposes he understands adequately, but which indeed is very rarely understood. The Scriptures speak of a repentance unto salvation, not to be repented of (2 Corinthians 7:10). By this is implied that there is a repentance which is not unto salvation, and which therefore itself needs to be repented of. In the light of this, this text deserves our deepest attention since it opens us to,

I. THE NATURE OF EVANGELICAL REPENTANCE

The sorrow that is produced in the heart by a true penitent is exceedingly deep. Nothing can be more pungent than the grief of a parent who has lost "his firstborn," "his only son" (Luke 7:12). Yet it is to this that the mourning of a penitent is twice compared. In both cases, the soul is greatly bowed down. It is indisposed to receive gratification from those vanities which once amused it. Instead, it loves to indulge in pensive solitude and in painful reflections. A parent's anguish may indeed be softened by the care of surviving friends. It may eventually lose its poignancy by the lapse of time.

But nothing can mitigate the pangs of a wounded spirit, and nothing can silence the accusations of a guilty conscience, until "the balm of Gilead," the blood of Jesus, is applied to it. Even then sin will never cease to grieve and burden the soul (Ezekiel 16:63).

But repentance can only be called "evangelical" when it has direct reference to Christ. Twice it is said in the text that men shall mourn "for him," that is, for Christ (compare John 19:37). It is not that the sufferings which Christ endured on the cross are the proper grounds of a penitent's sorrow. Rather, it is his grief that he has so dishonored Christ by his sins and that he has yet again and again "crucified him afresh" by continuing in sin. Many who are not really humbled are concerned for their sins as having subjected themselves to God's displeasure (Exodus 10:16, 17). But it is the true penitent alone who mourns for sin, as dishonoring Christ and as counteracting all the gracious purposes of his love.

This will appear more fully by considering,

II. THE MEANS BY WHICH IT IS TO BE ATTAINED

The outpouring of the Spirit is the primary means of producing penitence in our hearts. For the Holy Spirit is called "the Spirit of grace and of supplication" because he is the author and giver of all grace, and because it is through his agency alone that we are able to pray. It is this Spirit that Christ will "pour out" upon us. He has not only the right to send the Holy Spirit, as being God coequal with the Father, but in his mediatorial capacity he is authorized and empowered to send forth the Spirit, "having received of the Father the promise of the Holy Ghost," on purpose that he may impart to us out of his own immeasurable fullness. To him all must look for this blessing (Acts 5:31). All may look with an assurance of obtaining it, provided they truly and earnestly desire it (John 14:13-17). The great and the learned, "the house of David," must submit themselves to his influence. Nor shall the poorest or the most illiterate of "the inhabitants of Jerusalem" be destitute of this mercy, if they only ask for it of their heavenly Father (Luke 11:13). Also, not until this Spirit convinces us of our sin can any of us know our condition, so as to be suitably and permanently affected by it (John 16:7, 8).

As a secondary means, the Spirit turns our eyes to a crucified Savior. For nothing except a view of Christ dying for us can ever completely break our obdurate hearts. This has a powerful tendency to produce real sorrow, for while it shows us the awfulness of sin in its most dreadful colors, it reveals to us also the remedy provided for the expiation of sin. On the one hand, we are humbled by a sense of our extreme vileness. On the other, we are overwhelmed with a sense of the Redeemer's love. The combination of these two effects constitutes that real shame and sorrow which may be described as "evangelical repentance."

We may reinforce this subject for two reasons.

1. *For conviction.* All acknowledge that they need repentance and profess their intent to repent. But do not imagine that mere acknowledgments and faint purposes of amendment, which are usually made on dying beds, are sufficient. If the comparison in the text is just, nothing will suffice but a heart that is broken and contrite under a sense of sin. Such precisely is the view which the apostles also give of true repentance (2 Corinthians 7:11; James 4:9). O that we may never rest in anything short of such repentance, in case instead of looking on Christ with salutary contrition, we behold him hereafter (as we must do) with endless and unavailing sorrow (Revelation 1:7).

2. *For encouragement.* Because of the hardness and stubbornness of their hearts, many are discouraged. Indeed, we all feel that in spite of all that we may weep for day and night for our sins, and are seriously desirous to do this, rarely if ever can we bring our souls to any measure of tenderness and grief. But let us look more at Christ as dying for us, and do not confine our attention—as we often do—simply to our sins. Let us especially beg of Christ to pour out his Spirit upon us, and then the heart of stone will soon give way to a heart of flesh (Ezekiel 36:26). The Spirit of grace and of supplications will easily effect what, without his aid, is impossible for man to do. The heart of rock, once it is struck by him, will yield its penitential streams through all this dreary wilderness (allusion to Numbers 20:11).

Part V
PRACTICAL CHRISTIANITY

SERMON 2117
PRACTICAL CHRISTIANITY

"The fruit of the Spirit is in all goodness,
and righteousness, and truth"
(Ephesians 5:9).

M any people are prejudiced against the writings of the apostle
Paul, as though they contain nothing but dissertations
about predestination and election. It is as if all they were calcu-
lated to do was to drive people into a depression rather than to
improve their morals. But there are no writings in the whole of
Scripture that are more practical than his. It is true that he unfolds
the whole mystery of godliness more fully and deeply than the
others. He seems to have been raised up of God for that very end,
that the theory of religion might be more distinctly known. But in
all his epistles he has special regard to the interests of morality. He
sets a standard never known before, and for the practice of which
he adduces motives which have never been so appreciated. In not
one of his epistles does he maintain more strongly those doctrines
which are thought to be so objectionable than in this. Yet half of
the epistle is preoccupied with exhortations to holiness, in all its
different bearings and relations.

In the words we have before us, we have what I may call a *com-
pendium* or *summary* of Christian morals.

And that we may know what practical Christianity really is, I
will describe it as follows:

I. NOTE ITS DISTINCTIVE PURPOSES

Sanctification in both heart and life is the great end of the gospel. It is a vital part of what is revealed to us in redemption. Here he sets forth some of the things that it includes:

1. *Goodness*. This is the one all-comprehensive character of the Godhead. It shines forth in all his works. It meets us wherever we turn our eyes. "The earth is full of the goodness of the LORD" (Psalm 33:5). The effect of the gospel is to transform us into his image. It does this by creating the gospel in our hearts and calling it forth in our lives. Under the influence of this divine principle, we shall seek to promote the happiness of all around us. Whatever is kind and lovely and of good report, in such a spirit and temper of the mind we shall cultivate it utterly and exercise it always. There will be no trouble which we will not labor to alleviate. There is no need which we shall not endeavor to supply. To "be good, and do good," even like God himself (Psalm 119:68), will be the height of our ambition and the very end of our lives.

2. *Righteousness*. While goodness is spontaneous, acting irrespective of any particular claim which people may have upon us, "righteousness" has respect to the obligations which we have in order to "render unto all their dues." This is also the way in which the gospel forms within us. It stirs us up, both in word and deed, to act toward others as we, in a change of circumstances, should think it right for them to do to us. There is in the heart of man a selfishness which disposes him to see everything with partial eyes. It magnifies his own rights and overlooks the rights of others. This disposition the gospel will subdue and mortify. And in its place it will establish a principle of universal equity that will weigh the claims of others with exactness, and prompt us always rather to "suffer wrong than to do wrong."

3. *Truth*. This is the perfection of Christian morals, or rather the bond which keeps all the other graces in their place (Ephesians 6:14). Where the gospel has done its perfect work, there will be "a spirit that is without guile" (John 1:47). The Christian has a transparent character. He appears as he is, and is as he appears.

You will note that in the immediate context of our text, the apostle says, "Walk as children of the light. For the fruit of the Spirit is in all goodness and righteousness and truth." Now, these three graces mentioned in the text are represented as constituting light, or at least as comprehending all that is contained in that image. Now, of all things in the whole creation, light is the most pure (for it is incapable of defilement). It is the most innocent (for it injures nothing which has not, through its own weakness, an aversion to its rays). It is also the most beneficial (for there is nothing in the universe, whether animal or vegetable, which is not nourished and refreshed by it). Reverse the order of these statements and you see how light beams forth in our text. It embodies all the purity of truth, all the innocence of righteousness, and all the beneficence of active goodness.

But in order to understand Christianity properly we must,

II. Trace It to Its Source

It does not come from nature. For the natural man cannot attain to it. It is "the fruit of the Spirit," even of that very Spirit who raised up our Lord Jesus Christ himself from the dead (Ephesians 1:19, 20).

1. *It is the Spirit who alone infuses life into us.* We are by nature "dead in trespasses and sins." But it is the Spirit who quickens us, that we may live unto our God (Ephesians 2:1). It is true, indeed, that having been "baptized into Christ," we have become by profession branches of the living vine. But then we are only as dead and withered branches that can produce no fruit. We will shortly be broken off and cast into the fire (John 15:2, 6). It is the Spirit alone who engrafts us into Christ as living branches. He causes us to receive from Christ that divine energy, so that we are able to bring forth fruit to his glory. "Christ came that we might have life, and might have it more abundantly" (John 10:10). It is by the operation of his Spirit that we receive it. It is by the mighty working of that Spirit in our souls that we display its energies (Colossians 1:29).

2. *It is the Spirit who suggests to our mind those motives which alone can stimulate us to exertion.* He "reveals the Lord Jesus Christ in our hearts" (Galatians 1:15, 16). "He glorifies Christ within us, taking of the things which are his and showing them unto us" (John 16:14). "He sheds abroad in our hearts the love of

Christ" (Romans 5:5), which alone can constrain us to devote ourselves unreservedly to him (2 Corinthians 5:14). Until we receive this impulse, we are satisfied with formal services and a partial obedience. But when we are thus enabled "to comprehend something of the unbounded love of Christ, we can rest in nothing, until we are filled with all the fullness of God" (Ephesians 3:18, 19).

3. *It is the Spirit who assists us in all our endeavors.* Whatever we may have attained, we still have no sufficiency in ourselves. Indeed, we shall put our hands to the work, but we can accomplish nothing until the Holy Spirit "strengthens us with might in our inward man" (Colossians 1:11). Taking, as it were, one end of our burden to bear it with us, he "helps our infirmities" and gives us his own effectual aid (Romans 8:26). That is why these graces are properly called "the fruit of the Spirit." For they could not be produced without him, and are invariably the result of his agency in our souls. It is he who, as our church well expresses it, "works in us, that we may have a good will; and works with us when we have that good will" (Tenth Article).

It must be confessed, however, that there is a resemblance of this holiness found in those who have not the Holy Spirit. So it is necessary to,

III. DISTINGUISH IT FROM ALL COUNTERFEITS

It must be admitted that in many remarkable people there are found virtues they have naturally that resemble the graces described above. In some there is the quality of kindness or a sense of fairness or a high degree of integrity. Reasonably we can ask, "What distinguishes these traits from the 'fruit of the Spirit'?" The answer is that we can only look on the outward act, and externally they may be very difficult to distinguish. But to God, who sees the heart, they are as different from each other as light from darkness. For of these counterfeits I must say the following:

1. *They proceed from man, and man alone.* Man needs no particular communication of the Spirit to enable him to perform them. The light of reason points them out as commendable virtues, while the strength of a person's resolution is enough for per-

forming accordingly. Such people never need to pray to God for his Spirit, nor do they feel need of divine help. But the graces referred to in our text are "the fruit of the Spirit." They never were, nor ever can be produced in any other way than by his Almighty agency.

2. *They have respect to man, and to man alone.* The worldling, however virtuous, acts not to God, nor has any distinct desire to fulfill the will of God. He reckons that as a member of society, he has duties to perform. Therefore he performs them solely from a human perspective and context. He has no other perspective than that of an intelligent heathen. But the Christian aims at "*All* goodness, righteousness, and truth." He views them as the Lord Jesus Christ did, and makes the outward discharge of them, as the Lord Jesus Christ did, subservient to higher and nobler ends than man himself. As a servant of the Lord Jesus Christ, he has to advance Christ's interests in the salvation of men. So it is a less significant matter to exercise kindness to men as such, if he may not, according to his ability, also promote their spiritual and eternal welfare.

3. *They are done for man, and man alone.* A worldling is only concerned to please his fellow man, and for man alone. He wants to establish a good character before them. If he can do so, he is satisfied. Standing high in his own esteem, and in the esteem of others, is all he wants. But the Christian desires that God, and God alone, may be glorified. He does not seek the applause of men, but of God. He cherishes no conceit about himself and his imagined superiority. Much less does he go about trying to establish his own self-righteousness, by which to stand before God. Instead of self-admiration, he acknowledges that his attainments come from God, and gives glory to God. Indeed, the more he is able to do so, the more indebted he becomes to God. So he dare not "to sacrifice to his own net, or burn incense to his own drag." Rather he accounts himself, after all, as an unprofitable servant, saying, "not unto us, O LORD, not unto us, but unto your name be the praise."

Now whether we can discern the difference between these two attitudes in others or not, we can certainly distinguish them in ourselves. So we can easily discern "whose we are, and whom we serve." I cannot urge ourselves strongly enough to be jealous over ourselves, so that we do not make the terrible mistake of confusing the virtues of the flesh for the graces of the Spirit, in case having "a name to live we prove to be really dead" (Revelation 3:1).

For the cultivation of this subject, notice the three following points:

1. *How excellent is our religion!* Those who merely view Christianity as a system of doctrines, irrespective of what effects they should have upon us, have a very erroneous perspective. So I will readily grant that mysteries, however grand they may be, are of little value if they bring no sanctifying effect within us. But look at the change the Spirit can make in the life of the believer. See how such poor, selfish creatures can be transformed into the likeness of Jesus Christ, walking in the world as he walked. Go and look in the world, into the family situation, and into the privacy of his life, to see the dispositions and habits of the true Christian. How can one see this, if only with a glance, and not admire such a religion from which it flows? I charge you therefore not to be content with a partial view of Christianity, merely looking for doctrinal orthodoxy that may be also doctrinally speculative. No, rather see it in all its practical efficiency, and you will be ready to respect it with honor and love.

2. *How easily we may find out our true state before God!* We shall surely find out without much difficulty what our attitude and tempers really are. We shall know whether or not we are in the daily habit of imploring God to help us grow spiritually. Yet our natural temperaments differ so greatly that we cannot be absolutely certain whether someone is a natural or a spiritual person. This can only be learned from the struggles he has and the victories he achieves under the influence of the Holy Spirit. At all events, we may be sure that where there is no delight in doing good to the souls of men, where in our conduct toward others there is willful inconsistency or lack of simplicity and godly sincerity in our motives and principles, then we are not Christians. I pray you will use this test on yourselves (2 Corinthians 13:5). Do so, that in the end your hopes will not be disappointed (Psalm 139:23, 24).

3. *How wonderful is our allotted path!* I do not say that you will not have times of humiliation, for they come to the best of us. But for the daily course of your lives, you need only follow our text.

See the daily Christian in his daily walk. "Goodness, righteousness, and truth" are embodied in him. Like the sun's rays, he diffuses light and happiness all around him. This is what it means to "walk in the light, as God is in the light." This is to honor God. This is to adorn the gospel. This is to fulfill what Christ came himself to do in the world. This is to possess a meetness for the heavenly inheritance. So let those who do not possess true religion condemn it if they will. But I am certain that when viewed aright, "its ways are ways of pleasantness, and all its paths are peace."

SERMON 2240
THE SPIRIT OF VITAL
CHRISTIANITY

"God has not given to us the spirit of fear, but
of power, and of love, and of a sound mind"
(2 Timothy 1:7).

The real character of Christianity, as infused into the soul of
the believer and exhibited in his life, is by no means generally
understood. It forms a man of energy, but it is energy combined
with graciousness and regulated with discretion. Whoever has it
operates like a new creation. But it changes very considerably the
views, dispositions, habits of the soul, so that it gradually "transforms a man into the divine image in righteousness and true holiness." It does not so absorb men that they will be in all things the
same identity. Each will still remain in his unique original cast, so
that this leads to an endless diversity in the characteristic features
of different saints. Not all the grace that God ever bestowed would
produce a perfect identity of character between Peter and John:
but the principles which divine grace instills into the soul remain
the same in every age and in every place. Of all its subjects it may
be said, "God has given to us, not a spirit of fear, but of power, and
of love, and of a sound mind."

In order to expand and illustrate this wonderful promise, I will
endeavor to show:

I. THE SPIRIT WHICH GOD INFUSES INTO THE SOULS OF HIS PEOPLE

1. *It is not a spirit of fear.* Fear is taken from the soul that is truly given up to God. There may remain what we may call a *constitutional* fear. There are some whose piety cannot be doubted, but who have strange and unaccountable fears such as of this or that animal. And no depth of religious principle will prevent this happening. For its seat is in the imagination and not in the heart. But the fear of man, which has so great dominance over the worldly mind, will be dismissed, being subjected to (and if I may say so) swallowed up by the fear of God (Luke 12:4, 5).

2. *It is a spirit of power.* A holy resolve will be formed to serve the Lord and "to follow him fully." Nothing will deter the child of God from his purpose. Father, mother, brother, sister, houses, lands, yea, and life itself are regarded by him as of no account in comparison with his duty to God. In that sense he "hates them all" in comparison to his God and Savior (Luke 14:26). As for sin, it is an enemy which he pursues with unrelenting animosity, determined through grace that not a single lust will continue in him unmortified and unsubdued. Whatever his besetting sin may be is pursued by him with more than usual vigilance, if by any means he may prevail to bring it under subjection and to destroy it utterly (Hebrews 12:1). He will go from victory to victory, finding that however weak he is in himself, "through the strength communicated to him from above, he can do all things" (Philippians 4:13).

3. *However, this power is blended with a spirit of love.* The energy to which we have just referred could be unfriendly. So it needs intimate friends and family to deal with the issues of self-will and deplorable self-conceit. Therefore the believer must be particularly on his guard to avoid all such misunderstandings. His whole spirit must savor of love. He must show that whatever he does, he does from absolute necessity. And as far as love can operate in conformity to God's will, no one can exceed him in its nurture. Even toward those who persecute him, this must be an active and continual exercise. For it is his fixed determination "not to be overcome of evil, but to overcome evil with good" (Romans 12:21).

4. *Not even love must be left to operate except under the direction of a sound mind.* Enthusiasm is no part of true religion. Rather, it is in opposition to it and is always the offspring of an undisciplined mind. True religion is *wisdom*. God, when he gives it to the soul, gives us "sound wisdom" and discretion (Proverbs 2:7). Under the influence of divine grace, a man will pause before he acts, and he will weigh as in a balance the claims of duty as they may be affected by times and circumstances. He will distinguish carefully between the things which are necessary and those things that are only of subordinate importance. He will deal appropriately with what he judges to be necessary, and strip it of all needless offense in order to "cut off occasion from those who seek occasion against him." Both in the world and in the church, he will be anxious so to demean himself that all who see him will acknowledge that God is with him of a truth (1 Corinthians 10:32, 33). So he gives no needless offense in any way. But he will labor, with David, to "behave himself wisely in a perfect way" (Psalm 101:2).

But in order that we may better appreciate his spirit, let us note,

II. Its Importance in Christian Ministry

The words that we are looking at were specifically given to Timothy, who was a young and devout servant. They deserve therefore the special attention of all who are engaged in the ministry of the church.

1. *In such will be found no spirit of fear.* A minister is a standard-bearer. If he faints, what must be expected of others? So he must go with his life in his hand. He must "set his face as a flint" against the whole world (Isaiah 50:7). No intrigues, whether of men or devils, must appall him (Jeremiah 1:17; Ezekiel 2:6, 7). His spirit must be that described by the prophet: "Truly I am full of power by the Spirit of the LORD; and of judgment, and of might, to declare unto Jacob his transgression, and to Israel his sin" (Micah 3:8). In the midst of all the afflictions that may come upon him, he must say, "None of these things move me, neither count I my life dear unto myself, so that I may finish my course with joy, and the ministry which I have received of the Lord Jesus, to testify the gospel of the grace of God" (Acts 20:24).

2. Servants of God must have conspicuously a spirit of power. They have more difficulties to overcome than others. They stand in the forefront of the battle. They must be examples, not only to the world, but to the whole church of God. Speaking to Timothy while still a youth, it was said, "Be an example to the believers, in word, in conversation, in charity, in spirit, in faith, in purity" (1 Timothy 4:12). If a minister is overcome with any evil, the injury done to the church of God is incalculable. For then the whole ungodly world takes advantage of it to exult over him and to "blaspheme the very name of God himself" (Romans 2:24). Indeed, they will harden themselves in their own iniquities and impute to the gospel itself the evils which they see in him (2 Peter 2:2). So he must "be steadfast, immovable, always abounding in the work of the Lord; for then only shall his labor be not in vain in the Lord" (1 Corinthians 15:58).

3. Ministers must also more especially have a spirit of love. For nothing but love to immortal souls can enable them to sustain despite all their struggles and difficulties. They should therefore "have compassion on them that are ignorant and out of the way" (Hebrews 5:2). They should be able to "call God to witness that they have great heaviness and continual sorrow in their hearts" for their perishing fellow-creatures (Romans 9:1, 2). They should be ready to welcome even death itself, if it may be considered subservient to the spiritual welfare of their brethren (Philippians 2:17, 18). At the same time, their whole deportment should be controlled by this principle. Everything they do should come from it, and everything which they suffer should exercise it, and their whole walk should be like that of their divine Master, in a spirit of love.

4. In all their varied circumstances, they must show that they are under the influence of a sound mind. In nothing is wisdom more required than in the service of ministry. For if the circumstances of his service are more arduous, and his trials are more diversified than others, so the lack of judgment is more deeply felt by him than by any other. Indeed, the prejudices of many are reinforced by it, and the souls of many are hardened in their sins. So a minister must be particularly wise and have a well-disciplined mind. His views, both of truth and duty, must be clear. In regard to everything his judgment must be accurate and wisely formed.

He must be freed from every bias that might influence his mind and from every lust which might blind his eyes. He must be cool, considerate, prayerful. He must feel his entire dependence upon God to guide him aright. He must cry to him for that "wisdom, which is profitable to direct." So where God has really fitted a man for the ministry, there will be in differing degrees "a spirit of wisdom and understanding, a spirit of counsel and of might, a spirit of knowledge and of the fear of the LORD; all concurring to make him quick of understanding in the fear of the LORD" (Isaiah 11:2, 3).

Application—

1. To those of you who have not received this spirit, I would say, "seek it of the Lord". It is the gift of God, and cannot proceed from man. It may come to us through man, but it is really from God alone, even from him "from whom comes every good and perfect gift" (James 1:17). Whether we are ministers or laymen, this spirit is indispensable to our eternal well-being. No man can be saved without it. "The fearful" shall go into the lake of fire as certainly as "whoremongers or murderers" (Revelation 21:8). The man who for lack of strength draws back, "draws back to perdition" (Hebrews 10:39). The person destitute of love is no better than sounding brass or a tinkling symbol (1 Corinthians 13:1). And the man devoid of wisdom will perish (Proverbs 10:14). So I say then, seek this spirit; "so you shall have good understanding in the sight of both God and man" (Proverbs 3:4).

It is remarkable that when the apostle Paul is instructing Titus how to speak to both old and young, he specifies many things which he would insist upon with all. But with young men, everything that was essential was pinpointed on one thing: "Exhort young men to be sober-minded" (Titus 2:6). So this I would particularly insist upon. Every grace will flourish with sobriety of man. Without it no one can ever walk worthy of the gospel or adorn as he ought the doctrine of God our Savior.

2. To those who have received it, I would say "stir it up within you." This was a direction given to Timothy: "Stir up the gift of God that is in you." It is like a fire that is beginning to go out and needs to be stirred up. The fire which burned upon the altar came down from heaven, but it was to be kept alive by the care of man. Likewise the fire that is kindled in us must ever be kept burning on the altar of our hearts. We must "stir it up" by reading, meditation, and prayer. For the very opposition which is made to the gospel must call forth in us the greater energy to defend it.

Paul was now imprisoned for the sake of the gospel. This must have alarmed Timothy and induced him to draw back from that measure of activity and zeal which would bring similar vengeance upon his head. So the apostle says to him, "Do not be ashamed of the testimony of the Lord, nor of me his prisoner; but be a partaker of the afflictions of the gospel, according to the power of God" (v. 8). So I say to you, let "none of you be ashamed of the gospel of Christ." But rather account it an honor if you are called to bear in some measure those afflictions that are allotted to the followers of the Lamb. They will test your graces. But they will also tend to quicken them and make them burn with redoubled brightness. So let growth in grace be your grave concern. Whatever will encourage that, do it with diligence and welcome it with delight.

SERMON 1156
MERCY BEFORE SACRIFICE

*"I have desired mercy and not sacrifice; and
the knowledge of God more than burnt
offerings" (Hosea 6:6).*

There is a disposition in every one of us to substitute external observances for the devotion of the heart. It is the tendency to rest satisfied with rendering to God some easy service, while being utterly averse to those duties of self-denial, which are so much more difficult. But God cannot be deceived nor mocked. He will look at the heart and not at the outward appearance only. He is indignant with the partial obedience of the hypocrite no less than with the flagrant disobedience of the profane. It was thus he dealt with his people of old, "showing them by his prophets, and slaying them by the words of his mouth," because they rested in their sacrifices and burnt offerings when he desired the more acceptable services of faith and love.

Because of this the prophet shows in this text:

I. THE USE OF INSTITUTED ORDINANCES

The text does not suggest that God does not require sacrifices at all, but rather declares his specific preference for spiritual obedience. It is similar to our Lord's injunction "not to labor for the meat that perishes, but for that meat which endures unto eternal life" (John 6:27). This is not intended to prohibit the pursuit of earthly things, but only to enjoin a higher regard for the concerns of eternity.

God approves and loves the observance of his appointed ordinances. God appointed a great variety of ordinances to be observed. But the most important among them were "sacrifices and burnt-offerings." He honored these with many distinct tokens of his approval. It is not improbable that his acceptance of Abel's offering was marked by the descent of fire from heaven to consume it (Genesis 4:4). Certainly on many other occasions God vouchsafed to men this testimony of his regard; and in unnumbered instances he imparted grace and peace to the souls of his people while they presented their sacrifices before him.

Under the dispensation of the gospel, God has enjoined the public administration of his Word and sacraments. He has crowned the observance of these ordinances with the brightest displays of his glory and the richest communications of his love. He has promised his presence in them to the end of the world (Matthew 28:20). This is done in a manner and to a degree that we are not generally to expect on other occasions.

Thus under both the law and the gospel, God has clearly shown his regard for the ordinances of his own institution.

But the acceptance of such services depends on the manner in which they are performed. For God looks rather to the disposition of the worshiper than to the matter of his offering. If there is an absence of a contrite spirit, he values nothing that such a worshiper can offer. This is repeatedly and strongly declared (Isaiah 1:11-14; 66:23). It is as true under the gospel as under the Law (Psalm 51:16, 17; Matthew 15:8, 9). The Scriptures bear witness to all this. Balaam's answer to Balak (Micah 6:5-8), and Samuel's to Saul (1 Samuel 15:22), and the discreet scribe's to Christ (Mark 12:33) all concur in establishing this point beyond any doubt.

So these considerations may well prepare us to acknowledge:

II. THE SUPERIOR EXCELLENCE OF VITAL GODLINESS

The view given here of vital godliness deserves attention. For true religion, as it is experienced in the heart, consists in faith and love, or in such "knowledge of God" as produces "mercy" both to the bodies and souls of men. Our blessed Lord twice quotes the words of our text and explains them in this way. On one occasion he was vindicating the conduct of his disciples for plucking some ears of corn on the Sabbath. What they had done was certainly permissible on any other day, but not on the Sabbath, unless there had been some urgent reason. Such a necessity existed here. And if it was enough reason to vindicate David, it could also exonerate the disciples—if the Pharisees had only understood the text themselves (Matthew 12:1-7; 9:10- 13).

Such religion as is here described is far more excellent than any outward observances whatever.

1. *This is valuable in itself, whereas they are valuable only in relation to the ends for which they were instituted.* A knowledge of God and a delight in the exercise of mercy to the bodies and the souls of men render us conformable to the image of Christ; it constitutes our suitability for heaven, where both our knowledge and our love will be perfected. But the performance of ceremonies, as has already been shown, is worthless if it is not instrumental to the production of humiliation and trust, of purity and zeal. Duties which do not bring us to God, and God to us, are good for nothing.

2. *This argues real conversion, whereas they will remain in the most ungodly state.* No man can know God as reconciled to him in Christ Jesus, or love his fellow-creatures for Christ's sake, unless he be renewed in the spirit of his mind. He may possess carnal wisdom, together with humanity and compassion, while he is yet unregenerate; but if he have that faith and that love which are the essential constituents of vital godliness, he must have been born again. He could not have these things unless they had been given him from above. But any man may be observant of ceremonies; as the Pharisees themselves were, at the very same time that they were slaves of pride, of covetousness, and of hypocrisy.

3. *This invariably honors God, whereas men are often the means of greatly dishonoring him.* The exercises of faith and love are only very partially seen by human eyes. Their more sublime operations are only known to him who sees the secret of the soul. What is seen compels men to acknowledge the excellence of true religion. So even the enemies of God are constrained to reverence the godly and to admire the grace of God in them. But an attendance on ordinances is often substituted for the whole of

religion. It is as if God were no better than an idol, having neither discernment nor feeling regarding the dispositions of the heart. Can a greater insult than this be given to Jehovah? Or can anything reflect more dishonor upon him in the world? (Psalm 50:13, 14).

Let vital godliness be thus contrasted with outward observances and the text will be seen to have its full impact.

Address—

1. *Those who are regardless of even the forms of religion.* It is grievous to see how Sundays are profaned and the ordinances of the gospel neglected. But consider, brethren, what must be the consequence of defying God in this daring and contemptuous manner? O that you would lay it to heart, before it is too late!

2. *Those who are attentive to the form, but are regardless of the power of religion.* To those of this description our Lord says, "Go, and learn what that means, 'I will have mercy and not sacrifice.'" So we repeat his words, "Go, and learn this." A clear understanding of this passage will not deceive you. While you are destitute of faith and love or not living in the daily exercise of them, you differ little from those whom we have addressed above. They are open sepulchers that pour out their nauseous odors before all. You are "whited sepulchers" that while proper outside, retain all that is filthy and abominable inside. It is with such people that God himself classes you now (2 Timothy 3:1-5). If you repent not, it is with such that you will be numbered for all eternity.

3. *Those who possess vital religion in their hearts.* While the majority act as if form were all, you are to act as if form were nothing. In this regard there is a great fault among the professors of the present day. They are too apt to come late to the house of God, being irreverent in their postures during the divine worship, and sitting at their ease when they should either be devoutly kneeling in their supplications or standing up to sing the praises of Jehovah. It is this that gives occasion to the world to say of you, "They mind the sermon, but care not at all about the prayers." Beloved brethren, let there be no occasion of such censure amongst us. It is dishonorable to our profession. It casts a stumbling block in the way of the ungodly. And it is highly displeasing to our God.

Where real necessity prevents an early attendance on God's worship, or weakness of body requires an easy posture, the text applies in full force. But where these things do not exist, we must reverence the institutions of God and man. The more humility we have, the more we shall show it in the whole of our deportment.

SERMON 2390
LOVE TO THE BRETHREN

*"Seeing you have purified your souls in
obeying the truth through the Spirit unto
unfeigned love of the brethren, see that you
love one another with a pure heart
fervently" (1 Peter 1:22).*

As our Christian *profession* is our Christian witness and brings upon us distinct obligations to holiness, so our Christian *experience* should influence us to serve our God as much as possible. The more we have attained, the more we shall aspire after still further attainments. This is the effect of the apostle's exhortation to us. We may note,

I. WHAT HE TAKES FOR GRANTED WITH REGARD TO ALL TRUE CHRISTIANS

Writing to those who profess to be followers of Christ, the apostle gives them credit that they were indeed his disciples. So he takes the following for granted:

1. *That they had "obeyed the truth."* In Scripture, "to obey the truth" is the same thing as believing in the Lord Jesus Christ. The substance of the record is that in Christ Jesus is life, and we either have it or we are destitute of it, according as we possess or not the knowledge of God (1 John 5:11, 12). This is the true record of God, which we are enjoined to receive with all humility and gratitude. When we embrace it so as to found all our hopes of salvation entirely upon it, then we may properly be said to obey the truth. Now this every Christian does. He does not merely give his

assent to any propositions about Christ, but he "flees to Christ for refuge," relying upon him as his only Savior. So the apostle takes for granted that those to whom he was writing had so received Christ. However they might have been baptized into the faith of Christ, they would be no better than heathen if they had not truly believed in him.

2. *That in obeying the truth they had also "purified their souls".* Our outward conduct we may clean in various ways. If we are concerned about our reputation or appearing self-righteous before God, or have a spirit of pride and complacency, these are motives that will affect to some degree our outward behavior. But it is the property of faith alone to purify the heart (Acts 15:9). Here nothing but faith will prevail, so where it is it will inevitably produce this effect (1 John 3:3). But where faith has not this fruit, it is dead, and it will no more avail for our salvation than the faith of devils (James 2:19, 20). A good thing it is that the apostle takes it for granted that those to whom he wrote had experienced this effect of their faith, since it is the chief purpose of the gospel to produce it (Titus 2:11, 12).

3. *That they had so purified their souls as to have reached unfeigned love of the brethren.* As faith purifies the heart, so in a special way it "works by love" (Galatians 5:6). The love of the brethren was never, nor could be, found in an unrenewed soul. There may be a resemblance to it, or some partial attachment to our own group, or a worldly attachment to someone who is spiritually minded. But there can never be love of spiritual persons simply on account of their relation to Christ and their conformity to his image. Let the least amount of true grace be given to the soul, and instantly this love will spring up in the heart. Many things may impede its growth in the mind. Yet it may be taken for granted that this principle abides and operates in the heart of every true Christian. "He that loves him that begat, cannot but love those who are begotten of him" (1 John 5:1).

4. *That they had attained all this through the influence of the Holy Spirit.* Faith itself cannot exist in the heart until the Spirit of God has wrought it in us. For he must overcome our reluctance, and make us willing to obey the truth (Psalm 119:5). Nor can our hearts be purified except by the same almighty power. So faith in-

deed is the instrument whereby our sanctification is effected. But the Holy Spirit is the agent. Every progressive step of it must be done by him (Romans 8:13). Our love can flow from no other source. Wherever grace is exercised by us, he must be acknowledged as its author. "It is the same Spirit that works in all" (1 Corinthians 12:7-11).

II. THE EXHORTATION BASED UPON IT

"The end of the commandment," says the apostle, "is love." Our profession as Christians supposes that it exists and operates in our hearts. But care must be taken that it is exercised:

1. *With sincerity*. There can be a politeness and civility which is only a counterfeit of Christian love. It is not this that the text is referring to. We are indeed commanded in other parts of Scripture to be "courteous." But the love that is conjoined in the text is "unfeigned" love to all the saints, and which comes from their relationship to God and to ourselves. It must be an abiding principle in our hearts that operates consistently in the whole of our conduct toward others. It must lead us to exercise meekness, forbearance, and forgiveness, and to seek their material and spiritual welfare as occasion may arise (1 Corinthians 13:4-7). In brief, our love must be without dissimulation (Romans 12:9). It must not be in word and in tongue only, but in deed and in truth (1 John 3:18).

2. *With purity*. Even when there is considerable Christian love, it is still a mixed alloy. We may be influenced too much by selfish concerns. We may be seeking our own interests or honor while we imagine that we are giving a testimony of Christian love. Possibly our love was at first pure; but it easily degenerates into mere carnal affection. Great caution is required therefore, especially among young people, lest your hearts lead to indiscretion and Satan takes advantage of you to lead you into sin.

3. *With fervor*. An empty form of philanthropy is not enough to allay the wants of the poor. Nor is a cold expression of regard to the brethren a fulfillment of the sacred duty of love to them. Such love should know no bounds to those who are linked to the love of

Christ. Did he not love us to such an extent as to lay down his life for us? So we also ought to be ready to lay down our lives for the brethren (1 John 3:16). There is no service, however difficult or self-denying, which we should not give to them for good. We should love one another, as the Greek word means "intensely." To sum up in a word, we should love one another as Christ as loved us (Ephesians 5:1, 2; John 15:12).

Application—

Let us:

1. *Inquire whether the things that are taken for granted are found in us*. Have we indeed received the Holy Spirit? Through his almighty influence, have we believed in Christ, and purified our souls, and have this holy love within us? Do these attainments become so many motives to diligence and means of spiritual discernment? If we live in faith, our self-examination will increase our comfort. But if not, it may be a means of convincing the soul. Let us be assured that faith, love, and holiness universally characterize the Christian, and so our evidence of conversion will be consistent with our attainment in these things (John 13:35; Isaiah 61:9). So let us exercise these graces so that the Spirit's agent in us may be acknowledged by all (1 John 3:19).

2. *Endeavor to fulfill the duties that are required of us*. No more blessed command could possibly be given. To obey it is to enjoy heaven upon earth. Heaven is a sphere of ineffable, unceasing love. So the more we have of this divine principle, the happier we shall be. So let us seek to mortify whatever may hinder this growth in our souls. Let us beware lest through the abounding of iniquity it becomes cold. So let us strive to exercise it with all purity and fervor as those who are so highly privileged.

Part VI
WORSHIP

SERMON 536
THE WORSHIP OF GOD
IS DELIGHTFUL

*"LORD, I have loved the habitation of thy
house, and the place where thine honor
dwells" (Psalm 26:8).*

B etween the people of God and the men of this world there
is a much broader line of distinction than is generally
imagined. In the performance of outward duties there may be little
difference. But in their motives and principles they are as separated as heaven and earth, indeed (as I had almost said), as heaven
and hell. They have a completely different *taste*. The one finds
heavenly things to be their most delightful occupation. The other
finds them a constraint and feel themselves only in their element
when they are engaged in worldly company and carnal pursuits.
The faithful servant of God enjoys the testimony of his own conscience, and has no real delight in anything but doing God's will
and enjoying his presence. In this regard, David may serve as a
mirror where every real saint may see his own image. He could
appeal to God that he had found no pleasure in worldly company
and worldly pursuits. His only delight was entirely in communion
with his God and in the ordinances of God's grace (v. 2-5).
   In order to expand on this assertion before us, let me show,

I. THE REASONS HE HAD FOR SO LOVING THE
HOUSE OF GOD

   To describe all of them would be impossible. Let it suffice to
specify a few of those which had most conviction to him.

1. *It was the immediate residence of God.* "I have loved," he says, "the habitation of thy house, and the place where thine honor dwells." When Moses made the tabernacle, it pleased God to come down and honor it with his more immediate presence, and to reveal there his glory in the sight of all Israel (Exodus 40:34-38). There God promised, in a special way, to meet his people. He said, "You shall put the mercy-seat above and upon the Ark; and in the Ark you shall put the testimony that I shall give you. There will I meet with you; and I will commune with you from above the mercy-seat, and from between two cherubim which are upon the Ark of the testimony, of all things which I will give you in commandment to the children of Israel" (Exodus 25:21, 22). The same wonderful privilege was given to all Israel through the medium of their high priest, as long as the tabernacle and the temple stood.

On innumerable occasions David benefited from this condescending and merciful arrangement. Do we wonder, then, that he should love the house of God, where he was blessed with such a vast privilege and where such wonderful benefits were given to him? But we know from himself what his feelings were in regard to it: "One thing have I desired of the LORD, that I will seek after; that I may dwell in the house of the LORD all the days of my life, to behold the beauty of the LORD, and to inquire in his temple" (Psalm 27:4).

2. *There he was able to worship God in the way that God himself had appointed.* Although God might be worshiped acceptably in any place, yet it was at the tabernacle *only* that any sacrifice could be offered to him, or where full access to him could be enjoyed. There alone could a sinner be sprinkled with the blood of his offering and have the pardon of his sins thus sealed upon his soul. Hence, when David was driven from Jerusalem and forced to take refuge in a heathen land, this was the great subject of his complaint. It was not that he was separated from his friends, but that he was cut off from communion with his God in the established ordinances of his worship. Hear his sad complaint: "As the hart pants after the water-brooks, so pants my soul after thee, O God! My soul thirsts for God, for the living God: when shall I come and appear before God? My tears have been my meat day and night; while they continually say to me, 'Where is thy God?'

"When I remember these things, I pour out my soul in me: for I have gone with the multitude; I went with them to the house of God, with the voice of joy and praise, with a multitude that kept holy day—As with a sword in my bones, my enemies reproached me, while they say daily unto me, 'Where is thy God?'" (Psalm 42:1-4, 10).

3. *There he obtained those supplies of grace and peace which he daily needed.* The whole book of Psalms is little else than the record of answers to his prayers. "I waited patiently for the LORD; and he inclined to me, and heard my cry. He brought me up also out of a horrible pit, out of the miry clay, and set my feet upon a rock, and established my goings: and he has put a new song in my mouth, even praise unto our God" (Psalm 40:1-3). True, he might enjoy much of this in his own secret chamber. But it was chiefly in the house of God that he obtained these benefits. This he acknowledges himself: he assigns it as the reason for his ardent attachment to that holy place. "How amiable are thy tabernacles, O LORD of Hosts. My soul longs, yes, even faints, for the courts of the LORD: my heart and my flesh cry out for the living God. Yes, the sparrow has found a house, and the swallow a nest for herself, where she may lay her young; even thine altars, O LORD of Hosts, my King and my God. Blessed are they that dwell in thy house, they will still be praising thee—A day in thy courts is better than a thousand; I would rather be a door-keeper in the house of my God, than to dwell in tents of wickedness. For the LORD is a sun and shield: the LORD will give grace and glory: and no good thing will he withhold from them that walk uprightly" (Psalm 84:1, 10, 11).

This example is evidence enough to commend our devotion for the house of God. But I must proceed to add,

II. THE INCOMPARABLY GREATER REASONS WHICH WE HAVE FOR A SIMILAR DEVOTION TO HIS HOUSE

The dispensation which we are privileged to enjoy is of a more liberal kind than that under which David lived:

1. *Our access to God is more intimate.* Although David was a prophet and a king, yet he did not dare to enter into the most holy

place where God displayed his glory. Had he presumed to enter there, he would have been struck dead upon the spot. Not even the high priest could enter there, except one day in a year, and in a manner that God himself prescribed. But we are permitted to come even to his very throne and to behold him upon his mercy-seat. Yes indeed, the veil of the temple was, at the time of our Savior's death, rent in twain from the top to the bottom. From that instant a new way of access to him has been opened up for all sinners without exception.

This is the interpretation that was put on that event by the inspired apostle, who says, "Having therefore boldness to enter into the holiest, by the blood of Jesus, by a new and living way which he has consecrated for us through the veil, that is to say his flesh, and having an High Priest over the house of God, let us draw near with a true heart in full assurance of faith" (Hebrews 10:19-22). "The Holy Ghost himself," I say, has taught us this (Hebrews 9:7, 8). And is there no basis for love through the divine ordinances in all of this? Indeed, I think that the freedom that has been accorded to us should produce in us a corresponding freedom of mind in approaching God, with an exquisite joy in drawing near to him.

2. *Our views of God are clearer*. Even the high priest himself, when he was admitted into the sanctuary, could see nothing but a bright cloud that was on the ark between the cherubim. But we have access to the true tabernacle, the Lord Jesus Christ, "in whom dwells all the fullness of the Godhead bodily" (Colossians 2:9). "He is the image of the invisible God" (Colossians 1:15), "the brightness of his glory, and the express image of his person" (Hebrews 1:3). "In beholding him, we behold the Father himself" (John 14:9). Indeed, "as with an unveiled face we behold the glory" both of the Father and the Son (2 Corinthians 3:18). We see "God in Christ reconciling the world unto himself" (2 Corinthians 5:19), and are able to call him our father and our friend (Galatians 4:6).

Concerning the perfections of God, we have incomparably clearer views than were ever granted even to David himself. Indeed, he says that in God, "mercy and truth are met together, righteousness and peace have kissed each other" (Psalm 85:10). But he did not have such insight into that mystery as we can enjoy. The full discovery of God, as "a just God, and yet a justifier of ungodly men" (Romans 3:26) was reserved for us under the gospel dispensation. We see not only mercy, but faithfulness and justice engaged on our side and pledged for the forgiveness of our sins (1 John 1:9).

How marvelously are his purposes also revealed, and with what distinctiveness are they exhibited to our admiring eyes! Things which no eye ever saw, or ear heard, or heart conceived under the Jewish economy are now revealed to us by the Spirit. So from eternity to eternity we can behold the designs of God unfolding, first as they were originally focused between the Father and the Son, then actualized by Christ Jesus in his incarnate and glorified state. Lastly we see how they will be consummated at the day of judgment. Is it any wonder that we should delight in drawing near to God and have our souls filled with these heavenly contemplations? If the shadow of these things so endeared David to the house of God, what should the effect of them be on the substance upon our hearts?

3. *Our communications from God are more abundant.* No doubt David was most highly favored of the Lord. "God was very abundant toward him, both in faith and love" (1 Timothy 1:14). But we cannot yield to him, no, not even to him the privileges that we enjoy. The Holy Spirit was not then "poured out so abundantly" as he has since been upon the servants of the Lord (John 7:39; Titus 3:6). To us he is given as "a Spirit of adoption" (Romans 8:15) and as "a witness" testifies of that adoption (Romans 8:16). He is to us "a seal," to mark us for the Lord's peculiar treasure (Ephesians 1:13, 14). The servile spirit of the Law is completely banished from us, and we are "made free indeed" (John 8:36).

It is with such exalted views that we are sometimes blessed when we can see the Lord Jesus Christ actually bearing our sins in his own body on the tree. Then we can plead our cause at the right hand of God, and see that everything has been settled for our welfare, both in heaven and on earth. Then we can realize that a mansion in heaven is being prepared for us as he himself takes possession of it for us as our forerunner. Shortly he will come again in his own person to invest us with all the glory that he has purchased for us. We shall even share his own throne, his own kingdom, and his own glory. What we have now is but "an earnest" of heaven that has already begun in the soul.

All this is guaranteed to us constantly under the ministry of the Word and at the table of the Lord. If then we seem to be caught up, as it were, in third heavens, and scarcely know whether we are in the body or out of the body because of the brightness of such vistas and the blessedness of our souls, it is not surprising. I do not mean to say that this is the experience of all, nor of any at all times. But I do say that it is the privilege of all. It is our own fault if we do not actually possess it. But the hope of gratifying our taste with these wonderful realities cannot fail to enchant us with the house where this feast is provided for us (Isaiah 25:6-8).

In conclusion it is now profitable to ask:

1. **Why is it that this experience is so rare?** It must be confessed that there are only a few who have this kind of delight in the ordinances of God. Why is this? Would they not all be of similar value to all if all desire to make preparation for them? The truth is that most people only attend as a perfunctory form without any real consciousness of the ends for which they have been appointed. How would we view them if we thought of them like our mother's breast to which we were invited for the support and nourishment of our souls? Supposing we came to them, "desiring the sincere and unadulterated milk of the word, that we might grow thereby"? (1 Peter 2:2). Then indeed would we find such communications from the Lord Jesus as filling us with unutterable joy (John 4:10; 7:37, 38). But we do not feel our need of mercy. We have no real desire for the Savior. We are merely content with a "godliness which consists of mere form, without anything of power." No wonder that the house of God has no charms for us.

Indeed, people may be affected by the divine ordinances just as they might be moved by a splendid concert or on account of the eloquence of the director of the orchestra (Ezekiel 33:31, 32). Or they may set a high estimate on those that encourage them to have a high opinion of their own goodness (Isaiah 58:2). But as a means of access to God, and as the way of communion with him, they really have no true delight in these things. To enter into the experience of David, and to have the same mind as his, religion must be our one great and paramount concern. Once Christ becomes our supreme joy, whatever brings us close to him, and he near to us, will be "as marrow and fatness to our souls."

2. *What are the prospects of those who have found this experience?* They are indeed blessed among men. They no longer need to envy anybody else in the world. For they possess what is vastly superior to any delight of the senses. See someone at the footstool of the Most High. See even a poor publican who, aware of his own unworthiness, does not dare look up to heaven. Little does he realise how delighted God is, to see him, and how He delights to listen to his sighs, treasures up his tears in His vial, and blesses him in seeing the state of his soul, and of the prospects that lie before him? The fact is, that "as far as the east is from the west," so are his sins taken away from him; and "his name is written in the Lamb's book of life." For all such is prepared "a crown of glory, that fades not away." He now sees His God by faith: soon, he shall see Him face to face. Now he draws near to God in a temple made with hands; soon, he shall commune with Him in His temple above. Now he pours out his prayers and praises in the staccato of his weak and infirmed nature. Soon, he shall be eternally engaged without hindrance nor infirmity in praising God.

SERMON 866
ISAIAH'S VISION OF CHRIST

Then said I, Woe is me! For I am undone;
because I am a man of unclean lips, and I
dwell in the midst of a people of unclean lips;
for mine eyes have seen the King, the LORD
of hosts. Then flew one of the seraphim unto
me, having a live coal in his hand, which he
had taken with the tongs from off the altar;
and he laid it upon my mouth, and said, Lo,
this hath touched thy lips, and thine iniquity
is taken away, and thy sin purged
(Isaiah 6:5-7).

Previous to the full revelation of himself in the gospel, God was pleased to communicate his mind and will to men by dreams and visions, which since the completion of the sacred canon are no longer to be expected. But we must not therefore imagine that the revelations so made are less interesting to us than those which proceeded more immediately from the enlightening influence of the Holy Ghost. The same importance must be attached to everything which God has spoken, so far at least as the instruction which is intended to be conveyed is itself important. For instance, the vision of Isaiah seems to have been a peculiar favor granted to him; but still it contains valuable lessons for us. In this twofold view we will consider it,

I. AS PECULIAR FAVOR GRANTED TO HIM

That we may have a more distinct view of it, we shall notice in the following way:

1. *The vision granted.* The place where the prophet was supposed to be was the outer court of the temple. From there, the veil which separated it from the sanctuary being drawn aside, he beheld

Jehovah seated on his throne, and his train (like that of eastern monarchs) filled the temple. If no additional light had been cast on this vision in the New Testament, we should not have thought of inquiring more minutely about the glorious object whom he saw, and who is here so repeatedly designated by titles peculiar to the one Supreme God. But we are permitted to declare that the person whom he saw was the Lord Jesus Christ, even our "Immanuel, God with us" (John 12:41).

Around the throne were the "seraphim, the holy angels like flames of fire" (Psalm 104:4), in a posture of devout adoration. Each of them had six wings. With two he covered his face, as unworthy to behold the deity. With two others his feet were covered as unworthy to serve him. With the remaining two he flew with all possible activity to fulfill his will. In themselves they were perfect and spotless creatures. Yet conscious of being as nothing in the sight of a pure and holy God, they were filled with profoundest awe and served him with reverential fear.

In their worship of him they celebrated, in alternate and responsive songs, the holiness of his nature and the wonders of his grace. Whether in the repetition of the word "holy" there is any reference, as some have thought, to the Three Persons of the Godhead, we do not try to decide. But they evidently regarded the holiness of God as that attribute which comprises the glory and perfection of all the rest. Indeed, it is this attribute in which he is more especially glorious (Exodus 15:11), and at the remembrance of which the whole universe should give thanks (Psalm 30:4). Together with this glorious subject they evidently combined the wonders of redeeming love. It is in that view alone that "the earth" can be said to be "full of his glory." In the whole creation there is a marvelous display of wisdom and power. But in redemption alone are seen the mercy, truth, and faithfulness of our God. Although the seraphim are not interested in that work as we are, yet as exhibiting the full radiance of all the divine perfections in united splendor, they admire it, they sing of it, they glorify the Lord Jesus on account of it (compare Psalm 72:17-19, where the same person is spoken of and the same subject pursued).

At the sound of their voices, the doors of the temple were shaken and the house was filled with smoke. It is possible that this was designed to express the approval of God and his delight in that work which was the subject of their praise (2 Chronicles 5:13, 14;

6:1). But we rather suppose that it was intended to intimate the future abolition of the temple worship, when the time would arrive for the complete establishment of the Christian dispensation (Amos 9:1, compare Hebrews 12:27).

2. *The fear aroused.* In all the manifestations of God to men, the sight of his majesty has excited alarm and terror (Judges 13:22; Daniel 10:6-8; Revelation 1:17). A measure of this feeling we see in the prophet on this occasion. But with this, there was also a deep sense of humiliation and contrition. As Job on a similar occasion was led to exclaim, "I abhor myself, and repent in dust and ashes" (Job 42:6), so the prophet views himself and all around him in the light of God's holiness and accounted himself a leper in the midst of a leprous world. Whatever he might have judged of himself before, he was now dumb. As indeed, every human being must be in the presence of a holy God (Romans 3:19), since "we are all as an unclean thing, and all our righteousnesses are as filthy rags" (Isaiah 64:6). From that apprehension and terror we are freed by the gospel. But the humiliation and self-abasement should rather increase in proportion to the more exalted privileges we enjoy (Ezekiel 16:63).

3. *The consolation administered.* Instantly one of the seraphim flew to him to declare that his iniquities were all blotted out as a morning cloud through the atoning blood of Christ. This was symbolically represented to him by a coal taken from off the altar of burnt offering and applied to his lips. Doubtless the performance of this duty was a delightful service to the seraph, who would willingly forego for a season the more immediate vision of God himself for the honor of executing his will as a messenger of mercy to sinful men. But we hasten from this more restricted view of the subject to consider it,

II. AS AN INSTRUCTIVE LESSON TO US

While we acknowledge that such visions are not to be expected by us, we may contemplate this with great advantage to our souls. For we may learn from it:

1. *That a sight of Christ is the highest privilege we can enjoy.* What constitutes the joy of heaven? What is it that is the great

source of happiness to the seraphim around the throne? It is the sight of Christ enthroned in his glory. It was that sight afforded to the prophet in a vision that afterwards the apostle Paul was given immediate admission in heaven. Is there then no such vision to be enjoyed by us? To our bodily eyes there is not. Nor to our imagination will any such view of him be presented. But to the eye of faith the Lord Jesus is truly visible. The eyes of every believer may even now "behold the king in his beauty" (Isaiah 33:17). In the gospel he is fully revealed to us. There he appears as "the brightness of his Father's glory, and the express image of his person." We may "behold his glory, the glory as of the only-begotten of the Father, full of grace and truth."

We need not envy the prophet himself. For we may have even brighter views of Jesus than he ever enjoyed. We are told that John was greater than all the prophets. Yet "the least in the kingdom of heaven is greater than he" (Luke 7:26-28). How did he excel all others? Others prophesied of Christ, but he pointed him out. "Behold the Lamb of God which takes away the sin of the world." And how do we excel him? He beheld Jesus when he came to accomplish our redemption. We behold him after its accomplishment, seated on his throne of glory, and actually applied to millions of his people the full benefits of that redemption. So let those who embrace the gospel know their high privilege. Let the poor especially rejoice and be glad. It is not human learning or the strength of intellect that makes this discovery of Christ—it is *faith*. If we search the sacred records with a believing eye, then will "God shine into our hearts, to give us the light of the knowledge of the glory of God in the face of Jesus Christ."

2. *The more lowly we are in our own eyes, the richer communications we shall receive from him.* See how speedily the angel was sent to comfort the mind of the dejected prophet! This was a faithful evidence of the care which Jesus gives to all his afflicted people, especially when humbled in the dust before him. "He will not break the bruised reed, nor quench the smoking flax, until he bring forth judgment unto victory." Though he is "the high and lofty One that inhabits eternity, whose name is Holy, yet will he dwell with him that is of a contrite and humble spirit, to revive the spirit of the humble and to revive the heart of the contrite ones" (Isaiah 57:15; 66:2).

Does not his word universally test this blessed truth, that "while he who exalts himself should be abased, the man that humbles himself shall be exalted?" Do not be afraid, then, you who feel your own unworthiness. Do not give way to depression. Do not say, "Woe is me! I am undone." Do not follow the unbelieving example of Peter, who said, "Depart from me; for I am a sinful man, O Lord" (Luke 5:8). But know that if you feel yourselves lost, it was precisely such that he came to seek and to save (Luke 19:10). Know "that where sin abounded, his grace has much more abounded" (Romans 5:20, 21). If, like Mary, you are enabled to go behind him and wash his feet with your tears, he will before long say to you, "Your sins, which are many, are forgiven you." It is in this way that he is daily acting by the ministry of his word. He sends his servants to take his promises and apply them to the hearts and consciences of his people (1 Thessalonians 1:5). Thus he fills them with "a peace that passes understanding" and with "joy that is unspeakable and glorified."

3. *That a sense of his pardoning love should inspire us to surrender ourselves absolutely to him.* See the result which was instantly produced on the prophet's mind. God planned to send his messages of love and mercy to the Jews, yet he knew beforehand that they would prove ineffectual for their conversion. To carry such messages was a painful task. Yet when God asked, "Who will go for us?" the prophet did not hesitate for one moment to offer his services, saying, "Here am I, send me" (Isaiah 6:8).

This is how we should show our gratitude to God for all the mercies given to us through the Son of his love. We should not inquire whether the job is pleasant or whether it will advance our credit in the world. It should be enough for us to know that this is the will of the Lord. Then we should account it an honor to do it or suffer it. This especially applies to those who minister in holy things. If God says, "Who will go for me, to carry my gospel to the heathen?" we should not stop to ask whether the office will be lucrative or not, or whether the climate to which we are to go will be more or less healthy. No, we should stand forth and say, "Here am I, send me." O that we experience this holy zeal and that we do not so pathetically "confer with flesh and blood" when we are called to do it! When in fact it means that we leave even this vision of God himself in order to fill his will toward sinful man!

However, in whatever type of occupation we have, we should not be actuated by the same spirit around us. Rather, we should so feel the constraining influence of Christ's love that we live no longer to ourselves, but utterly unto him, who died for us and rose again (2 Corinthians 5:14, 15).

SERMON 1401
THE LORD'S SUPPER

*"I say unto you, I will not drink henceforth
of this fruit of the vine until that day when I
drink it new with you in my Father's
kingdom"* (Matthew 26:29).

The great object for commemoration under the Jewish dispensation was the redemption of that people out of Egypt. What occupies our minds is the infinitely greater redemption which has been granted to us from all the miseries of death and hell through the mediation of our Lord and Savior Jesus Christ. The one was typical of the other, both in the means and in the end. The deliverance of the Jewish firstborn from the sword of the destroying angel was effected by the blood of the paschal lamb sprinkled on the doors and lintels of their houses. What we experience is through the blood of God's only dear Son, shed for us and sprinkled on us. The Passover was instituted in remembrance of the former when the people ate the paschal lamb. The Lord's Supper was instituted in remembrance of the latter. We receive the consecrated bread and wine as memorials of the body and blood of Christ. These latter ordinances supersede the former. It will continue to the end of time in remembrance of our Redeemer's death. So to understand fully the passage before us we must notice the Lord's Supper,

I. AS INSTITUTED BY CHRIST

It was instituted at the close of the Passover feast, with a special reference to the circumstances with which that ordinance was administered. Without entering into minute details (for which we have only the authority of rabbis, and which are more curious than useful), we may observe that this Supper was instituted:

1. **As a commemorative sign.** Our blessed Lord was about to suffer and die for the sins of men. In order therefore that this mystery might never be forgotten, he broke the bread in token of "his body given for men," and poured out the wine in token of "his blood shed for them." He specifically commanded that in all future ages this ceremony should be observed "in remembrance of me" (Luke 22:19). It was to be "a showing forth of his death till he should come again" at the end of the world, to take all his redeemed people to himself (1 Corinthians 11:26). The one great end for which he died was also in this way to be made known to all succeeding generations.

The redemption of mankind was the subject of a covenant entered into between the Father and the Son. The Son committed his soul as an offering for sin. The Father pledged that when this was done, his Son would see a seed that would prolong their days. The pleasure of the Lord would prosper in his hands. Indeed, "He would see the travail of his soul, and would be satisfied" (Isaiah 53:10, 11). This covenant was ratified by the shedding of Christ's blood. The cup which was administered in remembrance of it was to be for all mankind a memorial, that on the Redeemer's part everything was effected for the salvation of man and that all who would embrace the covenant so ratified would assuredly be saved. "The cup was the New Testament in his blood"; or in other words, represented the New Covenant which that blood both ratified and sealed.

2. **As an instructive symbol.** The killing of the Passover lamb was not sufficient. The people must feed upon it in the way in which God himself had prescribed. So now there is sufficient that by the breaking of the bread and the pouring out of the wine, we commemorate the death of Christ. If the ordinance was merely commemorative, that would have answered the purpose. But it is intended symbolically to show forth the way in which we are to obtain an interest in the Redeemer's death. We must apply it, every one of us, to ourselves. We must feed upon it. And by doing so we declare our trust in it. We must show that as our bodies are nourished by bread and wine, so we hope to have our souls

nourished by this union and communion with our blessed and adorable Redeemer. Hence the command given to everyone is to eat the bread and to drink the cup. So there can be no more constructive ordinance than this. For it shows that it is by an actual fellowship with Christ in his death, and by that alone, that we can ever become partakers of the benefits which it has procured for us.

But my text leads me to notice the Lord's Supper more particularly,

II. As Still Honored with His Peculiar Presence

When our blessed Lord said that "he would no more drink of the fruit of the vine, until he should drink it new with his disciples in the kingdom of God," he intimated that there was to be at least some period when he would again hold communion with them in that blessed ordinance. He did not do this in his lifetime. For on the very day after he had instituted it, he was put to death. Nor did he at any time during the forty days of his continuance upon earth after the resurrection. For although it is true that "he ate and drank with his disciples after he was risen from the dead" (Acts 10:41), yet never again did he partake of the Passover or of the Lord's Supper. He merely ate and drank, in order to show that he was not only a spirit but possessed a body that was capable of performing all the proper functions of the body. Yet he had, and ever will have, communion with his people in that ordinance. For he has said, "Wherever two or three are gathered together in my name, there am I in the midst of them." Again he says, "Lo, I am with you always, even to the end of the world."

Properly speaking, his kingdom has now come. The Scriptures, both of the Old and New Testament, continually represent the Christian dispensation as the establishment of the Messiah's kingdom upon earth. This kingdom is called "the kingdom of God," and it is that which the Father establishes through the agency of the Holy Ghost. This is the kingdom spoken of in our text. For when Christ had accomplished the redemption of the world by his death and resurrection, *then* was all that had been typified in the redemption from Egypt, all that had been prefigured in the Passover feast, and all that was shadowed forth in the Supper of the Lord "fulfilled" (Luke 22:16, 18). Consequently, the time was come for the renewed manifestations of his presence in the sacred ordinance. True indeed, bodily he appears among us no longer; but spiritually he does. According to his promise, "he comes to us and makes his abode with us" (John 14:21, 23) and "sups with us" (Revelation 3:20).

Therefore now he executes what he gave us reason to expect. Spiritually he feasts with us when we are assembled around the table of the Lord. The first Christians observed it every day (Acts 2:42, 46), not only because of the command that the ordinance should be observed, but on account of the blessing which they obtained in its administration. And so has this continued to be the observance on the Sabbath day for ages since then (Acts 20:7). Although I am not aware of any specific promise of more than an ordinary manifestation of the Savior's presence in that sacred ordinance, yet I believe that he does seal it with a special blessing. I would appeal to the experience of many of you, whether he does not "draw near" to those who there draw near to him (James 4:8). Does he not again and again in a special measure "make himself known to them in the breaking of bread"? (Luke 24:35).

But we will not have a balanced view of the Lord's Supper unless we contemplate it,

III. AS REALIZED AND COMPLETED IN THE ETERNAL STATE

Then the whole mystery of redemption will be completed. Then will the kingdom of the Messiah, which is now established upon earth, "be delivered up to God, even the Father, that God may be all in all" (1 Corinthians 15:24, 28).

Then we shall spiritually renew this feast. Our Savior spoke of that time when he said, "I appoint unto you a kingdom, as my Father has appointed unto me; that you may eat and drink at my table in my kingdom, and sit on thrones, judging the twelve tribes of Israel" (Luke 22:29, 30). There we read that "Abraham, Isaac, and Jacob are sitting at the table" with all the myriads of the redeemed (Matthew 8:11). Lazarus is leaning there on his bosom (Luke 16:23), exactly as John leaned upon the bosom of the Lord Jesus at the Passover feast when this Supper was instituted (John 13:23, 25; 21:20). There shall all the redeemed of the Lord be in due time assembled. There will the great work of redemption occupy all their minds, precisely as it does when we surround the table of the Lord. There, at this moment, they are "singing a new song, saying, "Thou art worthy to take the book, and to open the seals thereof; for thou wast slain, and hast redeemed us to God by thy blood out of every kindred, and tongue, and people and nation; and hast made us unto our God kings and priests; and we shall reign on the earth" (Revelation 5:9, 10). By its reference to the redemption of the world, this may well be called "the Song of Moses and of the Lamb" (Revelation 15:3). To all eternity will "this wine be new" to those who drink it; the wonders of redeeming love be more and more unfolded to every admiring and adoring soul.

And will the Lord Jesus Christ partake of it with us? Indeed he will: "The very Lamb of God himself, who is in the midst of the throne, will feed us, and lead us to living fountains of waters: and God shall wipe away all tears from our eyes" (Revelation 7:17). Did he break the bread and administer the cup to his disciples when on earth? So will he also at the feast in heaven. As he himself has said, "He will gird himself, and make us sit down to meat, and himself come forth and serve us" (Luke 12:37). We know very little of the heavenly world, but this at all events we may say: He will appear there as "a Lamb as it has been slain" (Revelation 5:6). Under this character he will be the light, the joy, the glory of all the hosts of heaven (Revelation 21:23).

Upon this theme I would express the following advice:

1. *Seek a right view of this ordinance*. To those who despise it as a mere qualification for civil offices, I say nothing. I leave them to God and their own conscience. But they can be certain that I will say nothing in their favor, nor do I think that it is a light matter. But there are two mistakes which I would seek to rectify.

First, that the ordinance as an *act* recommends us to God. The other is that no one should venture to observe the ordinance until he has attained to the highest order in the religious life. The former of these errors leads to the indulgence of self-righteous hopes. The latter works to produce slavish fears.

Concerning the sanctity of this ordinance, I would not say a word that would diminish its importance. But we must remember what it is, and for what purpose it was appointed. It is precisely what the Passover feast was. As every child of Abraham partook of it, so everyone who truly believes in Christ partakes of this. In fact, the whole body of Christians has for many ages observed it. No one is at liberty to neglect it, nor should anyone be accounted a Christian if he has neglected it. So this shows that no one who desires to serve and honor God should abstain from it. They should come to it to express their gratitude to the Lord Jesus for what he has done for them, and to obtain fresh supplies of grace and peace at his hands.

Yet no one should think that the performance of this duty has any such charm in it as to recommend him to God and to conciliate divine favor, for it is Christ alone that can save us. Whether we seek him in this or any other ordinance, it is he alone that can reconcile us to God. So it is not the act of praying nor the act of communicating at his table that can form any legitimate basis of hope. It is on Christ, as apprehended by faith, that we must rely. So only so far as we exercise a simple faith in him can we justly hope for acceptance with our God. Let the ordinance be viewed correctly. It is a memorial of the death of Christ, and the medium of communion with Christ, whose body and blood we feed upon in the sacred elements and by whom we are strengthened for all holy obedience. So let the ordinance be observed in this way, and we shall find it a good preparation for heaven; yea, an earnest and foretaste of heaven itself.

2. *Seek to realize the great truths that are declared in it.* Here you see Christ giving himself for you. In the bread broken and the wine poured forth, you behold his agonies even unto death—even those agonies which have removed your guilt and obtained the remission of your sins. O let the sight fill you with holy joy and gratitude! Let it encourage your access to God, even though you had a thousand times greater guilt upon you than ever was contracted by any other human being! The death of Christ was the propitiation for the sins of the whole world. If every sinner in the universe would look to him, it would suffice to conciliate the divine favor on their behalf, and save them all without exception. In full confidence of this, take the sacred elements within your lips and expect from God all those blessings which his dear Son has purchased for you.

3. *Look forward to the feast that is prepared for you in heaven.* Soon, very soon, you shall be called to "the supper of the Lamb in

heaven," and there you will see the Redeemer and his redeemed all feasting together in endless bliss. Well may we say, "Blessed is he that shall eat bread in the kingdom of our God" (Luke 14:15). So anticipate this blessed day. Watch and pray for your summons there. Survey the glories that shall then encompass you on every side, and let it be your first priority *now* to get "the wedding garment" that shall qualify you to be acceptable guests at that table. Remember that "Christ, our Passover, was sacrificed for us" (1 Corinthians 5:7). Remember that even in this world it is your privilege to "keep the feast" from day to day. Be assured that the more constantly you feed on Christ here, the better you shall be prepared for the most intimate intercourse you can have with him above, and the fullest communication of all his blessings you will have now.

Part VII
PRAYER

SERMON 2167
PRAYER FOR GROWTH IN GRACE

(Colossians 1:9-13)

Wherever Christianity gains ascendancy, there benevolence begins to be seen everywhere. This is particularly seen in the prayers which the apostle offered for others. Their fervor and fullness clearly demonstrate this, that they proceeded from a heart that was full of love. They impress us with the excellence of those blessings given to us in the gospel. The apostle did not only confine his attention to the welfare of a few with whom he might happen to be, but it extended to the whole church—as much to those whom he had never seen as to those among whom he ministered. He only needed to be told that a work of grace was started in people, and he instantly felt a union of heart with them and took a lively interest in their concerns. This is well seen in the prayer before us. Paul had heard of the happy state of the Colossian church. From the moment that he had heard the good news about them, he began to remember them all in his prayers. So in the passage before us he tells them what he has prayed for on their behalf.

I. HE DESIRED THAT THEY MIGHT INCREASE IN THE KNOWLEDGE OF GOD'S WILL

"The knowledge of God's revealed will" is the foundation of all true obedience. Every Christian must have this to some extent.

179

But he is not satisfied that they should have a scanty measure of it. He wishes that they be "filled with it" so that it would engage all the faculties of the believer. Nor does he rest content with a theoretical view of divine truth, however clear or comprehensive it might be. He coveted that their knowledge would be practical and experiential. He desired that it would be a knowledge that diffuses "a spiritual savor" to enable the believer to conduct himself "with all wisdom," including all his secret conflicts with sin as well as his public exercises of duty to God and before man.

This was the apostle's first request for the converts at Colossae. He desired that as they already had some knowledge of God's will, so they might be "filled" with it, enjoying at the same time its sweet savor and its practical influence, "in all wisdom and spiritual understanding." Should that not be the prayer also for ourselves? Let us not forget that while we aspire after divine knowledge, we must chiefly seek that which brings a feast to the soul and which enhances it with a specific and accurate discernment of good and evil.

II. He Desired Their Obedience to His Commands

The more awareness the Christian has of divine truth, the more earnestly will he seek to fulfill the will of God. In his endeavors for wholeness, he will seek to make himself most docile and seek for the highest end. He will not limit himself merely to the rules prescribed by men. Nor will he merely aim at obtaining eternal happiness. But he will consider the relationship he has with God and the obligations he has received from him and the expectations which he has of future benefits. So he will endeavor to "walk worthy of" such a Father, such a Redeemer, such an unspeakable Benefactor. He will be like a dutiful and affectionate servant who does not merely consider what he *must* do in order to escape censure or to receive his wages, but what will *please* his Master. So he asks himself, "What will please my God?" That is the great object of his ambitions. That is the spring of his actions. With this in mind he will seek to be "fruitful," not only in some good works, but "in every good work," however difficult and self-denying.

This was the attitude the apostle had in his prayer. He longed that the Colossians might desire for themselves what he himself experienced, that "they might walk worthy of the Lord unto all pleasing, being fruitful in every good work." It is certain that to the measure that we attain such a knowledge of God's will, so we shall desire, both for ourselves and others, an increase of righteousness and true holiness.

III. HE ALSO DESIRED THAT THEY SHOULD INCREASE IN THE ENJOYMENT OF GOD'S PRESENCE

"The knowledge of God" seems to be different from "the knowledge of his will," which has been mentioned above. The former relates to a view of his truth, the latter to the enjoyment of his presence. In this sense, the latter is not a mere repetition, but a blessing that is intimately connected with a whole life. With whom will God meet, and to whom will he reveal himself but to "him that rejoices in working righteousness?" (Isaiah 64:5). Yes, these are the evidences of what such persons will receive, and such revelations that the world has no conception of (John 14.21, 23). God will "shed abroad his love in the heart" of his people. He will testify to them of their adoption into his family and seal them unto the day of redemption. How wonderful this is for every saint to receive! What a rich reward this is for any self-denial that he may exercise in the path of duty! Would to God that all professing Christians might experience this, that not a single day might ever pass in which they could not say with the beloved disciple, "Truly our fellowship is with the Father, and with his Son, Jesus Christ!" (1 John 1:3).

IV. HIS DESIRE THAT THEY INCREASE IN SUBMISSION TO HIS PURPOSES

The more anyone lives in the enjoyment of God and diligently seeks to perform his will, the more he may be expected to be hated and persecuted by the ungodly world. Yet under all his trials he must be "patient." For whatever length of time these may be extended, he must be "long-suffering." He must not merely possess his soul in patience, but he must qualify it with "joyfulness," regarding it as his privilege and blessing that he is counted worthy to suffer shame for his Redeemer's sake (Acts 5:41). But "who is sufficient for these things?" It is not possible for feeble man to maintain such behavior, unless he be "strengthened with all might" by the Holy Spirit. Yes, there must be such an exertion of divine power as will demonstrate "his glorious power." Nothing less can bring this work about.

So we see here the relevance of the apostle's prayer. If we cannot serve the Lord without sharing his cross, or sustain our trials in our own strength, then we may either abandon our calling or implore such help from God as shall make us more than conquerors.

V. HE DESIRES THAT THEY MIGHT INCREASE IN GRATITUDE TO GOD FOR HIS MERCY

There can be no condition, however trying, in which a Christian ought not to abound in thanksgiving to God. The Israelites, to whom God divided Canaan by lot, were unspeakably indebted to him. But how much more are they to whom he has given "an inheritance among the saints in light"! This is in heaven, where they dwell in the immediate presence of their God! For this purpose they are made "meek." For it is impossible that they should enjoy it if they do not possess the suitability for it. Their heavenly Father has "delivered them from the power of darkness," even as he did Lot from Sodom or the Israelites from Egypt, with a mighty hand and a stretched out arm. Moreover, he has "translated them into the kingdom of his dear Son," and brought them to a cheerful and unreserved obedience to his will. Must not they then give glory to their God? What if they are burnt at the stake? Ought they not to rejoice that God has rescued them from hell, and that they are entering into a state of uninterrupted, everlasting bliss?

Surely no Christian should be content with less than this. We should all unite in wrestling with our God until he pours out his Spirit upon us and transforms us to the model which is here proposed for the Colossian converts.

The inference of this is:

1. *How glorious are the Christian's privileges!* Did not the apostle incessantly ask God what he was not willing to bestow? No indeed. "If we opened our mouth wide, he would fill it." All these must the Christian be, in whom these things are found! O believer, do not be content with low objectives, but aspire after the highest measures of wisdom, purity, and joy.

2. *How dependent are we upon our God!* It is not only at the beginning of our religious life that we should depend upon God, but to the last hour of our lives. For we can have no knowledge, holiness, or joy but what we receive from him. So let us make our requests known to him, and depend upon him for all our relevant needs of grace and strength.

3. *How great is the benefit of intercession!* We are not sufficiently aware of this. But when we recollect the intercessions of Abraham for Sodom, of Lot for Zoar, and of Moses for Israel, how can we be so remiss in this duty! Let us incessantly plead for each other, knowing that the effectual fervent prayer of a righteous man avails much.

SERMON 2377
THE EFFICACY OF FERVENT PRAYER

*"The effectual, fervent prayer of a righteous
man avails much"* (James 5:16).

P rayer and intercession are generally considered as duties. But
when seen aright, they may rather be regarded as privileges,
seeing that they are the way of obtaining for ourselves and others
those blessings which no created being can bestow. From this perspective, the passage before us, together with the preceding context, gives us the greatest possible encouragement. It is to be re-
gretted, however, how some have misinterpreted and abused this
passage.

On the direction given "to pray over a sick person, and anoint
him with oil in order for his recovery" (James 5:14, 15), they have
founded an ordinance to be observed when someone is past recovery. What was designed by God as symbolic only of a miraculous power, given at that time for the restoration of bodily health,
they have used as the essential means in all ages of saving the immortal soul.

Again, because the saints are encouraged to "confess their faults
one to another" to deepen their mutual sympathy and direct them
in their mutual intercessions (v. 16), these deceivers have required the laity to confess their sins to the clergy in order to obtain
forgiveness from them at the hands of God. In contrast, the
apostle James (who makes no such reference regarding any particular order of men) says that confession is as much required from
the clergy to the laity as from the laity to the clergy.

185

However, we will not stop to notice these grievous errors, but pass on to what more immediately concerns us. I want to point out to you,

I. THE IMPORTANCE OF THIS ASSERTION

The preceding context suggests chiefly the work of intercession. But it is also said, "Is any afflicted, let him pray" (v. 13); and so we must not confine our attention to prayer as offered for others, but also notice that it is offered for ourselves. So we say that when "a righteous man" draws near to God, and presents before him prayers which are inspired and dictated by the Holy Ghost, he shall prevail. For it is his distinct office to "help our infirmities" in prayer (Romans 8:26) and to "make intercession for us" (Romans 8:27). Such an intercessor will prevail . . .

1. *For others*. There are numerous instances of this, so we can only be selective. We begin with Moses who, when God was very angry with his people for making and worshiping the golden calf, set himself to pray and intercede on behalf of his people. As I may say in human terms, God, seeing the impossibility of resisting the importunity of his servants, "Let me alone that my wrath may wax hot against them, that I may consume them . . . and if you think my covenant with Abraham will thus be broken, I assure you it will not. For I shall make of you a great nation" (Exodus 32:10). But Moses would not "let him alone," but pled for them with all earnestness. Consequently the Lord repented of the evil he had intended to do to his people (Exodus 32:14).

Joshua is my next example. Desirous that his enemies the Amorites would be utterly destroyed, he prayed that neither the sun nor moon would continue on the course but instead give him the light he needed to pursue them relentlessly until his mission was accomplished. Thus the whole universe was arrested in its course—enough to threaten its own dissolution. For whatever stood in the way of his prayer, he was bold enough to challenge: "'Sun, stand still upon Gibeon, and Moon likewise in the valley of Ajalon, until this people have avenged themselves of their enemies.' And so the sun stood still in the heavens for a whole day. There was no day like it in the history of Israel, or indeed afterwards, that the Lord so heard the voice of a man" (Joshua 10:12-14).

While in this instance the material creation stopped by the voice of prayer, in another instance heaven itself was moved by the voice of two of God's servants when an angel was sent. It was when Jerusalem was besieged, and was quite unable to hold out against the enemy that had come against it. But Hezekiah and Isaiah took to prayer. And what was the result? An angel was sent from heaven to destroy *in a single night* one hundred and eighty-five thousand of the besieging enemy. The blaspheming monarch, who had boasted that nothing could withstand him, was forced to return immediately to his country where he was slain by his own sons while in the very act of worshiping the senseless idol in which he had trusted for his success. The historian records how "Hezekiah the king, and the prophet Isaiah, son of Amoz, prayed and cried unto heaven. And the LORD sent an angel, which cut off all the mighty men of valor, and the leaders and captains in the camp of the king of Assyria. So he returned with shame to his own land. And when he entered into the house of his god, his own sons slew him there with the sword" (2 Chronicles 32:20, 21).

Daniel is another example I will mention to show how immediately the prayer of a righteous man succeeds. From the prophecies of Jeremiah, Daniel understood that the close of the Babylonian captivity was near. So he sought to find out more specific instruction from God about it so that he could take advantage of it for his people. "I set my face," he says, "to the LORD God, to seek by prayer and supplications, with fasting and sackcloth and ashes; and I prayed to the LORD my God." See the result! "While I was speaking in prayer, and confessing my sin, and the sin of my people Israel . . . indeed, in the very act of prayer, the man Gabriel, whom I had previously seen in a vision, flew past me, and touched me about the time of the evening oblation, and informed me, saying, 'O Daniel, I am come to give you skill and understanding. At the beginning of your supplications the command was issued; and I am here to show you all that you have asked'" (Daniel 9:3, 4, 20-23). See how expeditiously God gave an answer to prayer, to let him know right at the beginning of his petition that his prayer was answered.

2.*For ourselves*. I mention this last because it is, in fact, the greatest. For prayers on behalf of others prevail only for temporal blessings, since they cannot avail for the salvation of their souls. If they could, no creature would ever perish. When Stephen prayed, "Lord, lay not this sin to their charge," it probably prevailed on behalf of Saul and some others, but it cannot conceivably have been effective for them all. But a man's own prayer is sure to prevail. There are no limits to the benefits which he shall receive, provided he only ask according to the will of God. He may not be answered in the way he would like, just as the cup that Jesus asked earnestly to be removed was not taken from his hands. Nor was the thorn taken away from Paul when he cried in such importunity. But both he and his divine Master were answered in a way far more consonant with the purpose of Jehovah.

So likewise, in some way—indeed, the best way—prayer will most certainly be answered for all who cry to God in sincerity and truth (Jeremiah 29:13). Whatever they ask in Christ's name shall be given them (John 14:13, 14; 15:7). They may exhaust all the powers of language in asking, but they shall have all; indeed, "exceedingly abundantly above all that they can ask or think" (Ephesians 3:20). While the assertion of our text should be seriously considered for its own sake, yet much more because of,

II. THE INSIGHT IT GIVES US INTO:

1. *The character of God*. We generally think of God as a Being of infinite majesty who (unless in very special matters) does not trouble himself with human affairs. So when someone claims to have received answers to prayer, he is looked upon as wild, visionary, and presumptuous. Yet when God is viewed as our text shows him to be, there he is shown to have the deepest concern for the least of his children. He attends to their every cry and treasures up every tear in his vials (Psalm 56:8). Not a single breath of theirs passes unnoticed, nor any desire of theirs of which he is unconscious (Psalm 145:18, 19). He is as concerned for the lowliest Lazarus as he may be for the highest archangel. He is concerned for every individual as if he were the only one in his universe. So even a mother's love is a very poor image of the character of his condescension and grace (Isaiah 49:15).

2. *The Christian's state.* Outwardly, there is no difference between a child of God and anyone else. But as seen by God, they are vastly different. In one, God beholds his own image; but in the other, the image of the evil one. On the former he looks with pleasure and rest; but on the latter he sees afar off, with utter disdain (Psalm 138:6). He is open to every request of the former, but the latter he sees as an abomination (Proverbs 15:8). This is illustrated by Abraham, the friend of God, whom God heard in his distress; whereas God "laughs at their calamity, and mocks at their fear" (Proverbs 1:24) who know not God. Ungodly men may think it is vain conceit that some should claim God hears prayer. But in spite of all their blindness, the Jews could recognize the difference. "We know," they said, "that God hears not sinners: but if any man be a worshiper of God, and do his will, him he hears" (John 9:31). Whether you believe it or not, there is this fundamental contrast between the children of light and of darkness (2 Corinthians 6:14-16).

3. *The use and excellency of the gospel.* It is the gospel alone that can bring someone into this happy state. Nothing else can make him acceptable before God. To be reconciled with God we need a Savior, so that we can be "made one spirit with him" (1 Corinthians 6:17) and be entitled to participate in all he possesses, namely "of the love wherewith the Father loves him" (John 17:23), "the joy with which his soul is filled" (John 17:13), and "of the glory which the Father has given him" (John 17:22).

Here then is the true secret of the difference we have spoken about. The believer is viewed as *in Christ*, washed in his blood, clothed in his righteousness, and altogether "one with him, even as the Father and Christ are one" (John 17:21). So I urge you to receive the gospel without delay, seeing that through that alone you can have access to God, obtaining that fellowship with him which is your privilege to enjoy.

To conclude: Remember to whom these privileges belong, exclusively to "the righteous man." The ungodly and the hypocrite have no part in them. Seek to have the character of the righteous, seeking it in faith in the Lord Jesus, "by whose obedience you shall be made righteous" (Romans 5:19), and by whose all-powerful grace you shall be "renewed after the divine image in righteousness and true holiness" (Ephesians 4:24). Then all these blessings shall be yours, and you shall be "a people near unto God" (Psalm 148:14). Indeed, you shall "have power with God, and shall prevail" (Hosea 12:3,4) in all your supplications. For others you will prevail to a great extent; but for yourself, you shall obtain all the blessings, both of grace and of glory.

Part VIII
THE HOLY SCRIPTURES

SERMON 1630
CHRIST'S APPEAL
TO THE SCRIPTURES

"Search the Scriptures; for in them you think you have eternal life: and they are they which testify of me" (John 5:39).

When our Lord confessed himself to be the promised Messiah, claiming an authority equal to that of Almighty God, he needed to show abundant evidence of his divine mission. He needed to prove, by testimonies of the most unquestionable kind, his title to the honor he assumed. Nor was he backward to give all the proof which was required. He appealed to the testimony of John the Baptist, whom the whole Jewish nation considered a prophet, and whose evidence therefore ought to have great weight with them. He appealed also to his own miracles, which were so great and numerous as to be in themselves an indubitable evidence that God was with him. He appealed further to the testimony that the heavenly Father also had given him at his baptism, both by an audible voice from heaven and by the visible descent of the Holy Spirit upon him. Finally, he appealed to the Holy Scriptures, which the Jews themselves received as the Word of God and which bore testimony to him in a way that agreed exactly in every respect with his person and character. As these had existed for centuries and might be compared with all that he had either done or taught, their testimony is unique and must carry conviction to everyone.

From the words before us we shall notice,

I. THE TRANSCENDENT EXCELLENCE OF THE HOLY SCRIPTURES

Two things are spoken in this text concerning them:

1. *They reveal eternal life to us*. Reason alone could never suffice to discover the immortality of the soul. Philosophy has never enabled any man to establish the certainty of a future state or to make it an article of general belief or to produce any considerable influence on the minds of those around him. Many have reasoned well on this subject and spoken approximately to the truth. But they could never with certainty affirm a future state of rewards and punishments; much less could they tell us how to avoid the one and retain the other. But the Scriptures have taken aside the veil and shown us that this present world is introductory to another, in which men shall exist to all eternity. True, the Old Testament speaks only darkly on this subject. Yet it was sufficiently clear to impress the Jewish nation at large that the souls and bodies of men would live in a future state of existence.

The Sadducees, the free-thinkers of their day, were exceptions to this general rule. But the national creed accorded with what was more fully revealed under the Christian dispensation. "By the gospel, life and immortality have been fully brought to light"; yea, and the way of salvation has been clearly revealed so that we who live under its benign influence do not merely think, but *know* that there is for those who believe in Christ a salvation that is treasured up, "salvation with eternal glory." So in this respect even a child among us is better instructed than all the wisest philosophers of Greece and Rome.

2. *They testify of Christ Jesus our Lord*. "The testimony of Christ," we are told, was "the Spirit of prophecy" from first to last. The testimony which the Scriptures have borne to Christ is clear. Unlike the ambiguous answers of heathen oracles, they are clear and precise, incapable of any other interpretation than that which they profess. For example, take the prophecy relating to the time and place of our Savior's birth. It was as much understood before his advent as afterwards, even by those who did not have the grace to welcome his arrival. It was also copious, so that nothing that could be desired was omitted to designate the Messiah's advent. His person, his work, his offices, were all described and shadowed

forth. The nature of his salvation was fully delineated and the extent of his kingdom declared. It was in the highest possible measure convincing.

The prophecies concerning him were so detailed that they could never have entered into the mind of an uninspired man, nor could possibly have been accomplished by any contrivance or conspiracy of men. Although a Jew, our Lord Jesus was to die, not a Jewish but a Roman death, the death of the cross. Yet in his crucifixion he was not to suffer all that was usually associated with that punishment; for "not a bone of him was to be broken." On the other hand, there were to be inflicted on him indignities that were never associated with that punishment. He was to be scourged before his crucifixion and to be pierced to the heart with a spear after it. The very taunts with which he was to be insulted on the cross were accurately and literally foretold. Also the cruelty in offering him vinegar in the midst of all his torments was also foretold. The division of one of his garments and the casting of lots for the other were among the circumstances which no human being could have divined and which no imposter would have ventured to predict.

Who would ever have imagined that one so shamefully treated in his death should yet "have his grave with the rich"? The very price which was to be paid for his blood, as well as the subsequent application in the purchase of a potter's field and the untimely death of the one who betrayed him, these and other circumstances equally detailed prove beyond a doubt that Jesus was the person testified about, and that the testimony borne of him was divine.

Had the different witnesses lived at the same time, it might have been speculated that all of these were devised and executed by some raw-concerted conspiracy. But the witnesses lived in ages and places far apart from each other, even many hundreds of years apart. Yet all the prophets so harmonized with each other in their various predictions that there is no room left for doubt that while wholly unconnected with each other, they were altogether under the direction and influence of the Spirit of God. Thus we consider the testimony itself, or the witnesses by whom it was delivered, and can have no doubt that Jesus is the Christ, the Son of the living God.

Since such is the excellence of the Scriptures, let us contemplate,

II. Our Duty in Regard to Them

This is clear and obvious:

1. *We must search the Scriptures for ourselves.* As we possess these divine records, we should apply ourselves diligently to their study. We should search them with simplicity of mind, desiring to learn from them the will and mind of God, and determining through grace to obey them in every way so that we receive implicitly whatever they declare, obeying without reserve whatever they command. Instead of being prejudiced in judging them, or limiting them by our own passions, we must come to them with the simplicity of a little child, submitting our own wisdom to the wisdom of our God and our own will to the will of God. Indeed, we must desire to know God's will in order that we may do it. Like Samuel, we must lend to every word of God a willing and obedient ear, saying, "Speak, Lord, for your servant hears."

We have a most instructive example in the conduct of the blind man whom Jesus healed. Jesus asked him, "Do you believe in the Son of God?" The man immediately replied, "Who is he, Lord, that I may believe on him?" His whole bias was toward his God. His desire for instruction was the only purpose of glorifying God by the strictest possible conformity to his holy will. If we are like him, we are assured that we shall be enabled "to know of every doctrine whether it be of God" (John 7:17).

Of course, we must pursue our search with all diligence. The very word *search* suggests that we sift every word, like miners will excavate the earth in the search of precious jewels, and use all our faculties as animals may pursue their prey. A casual and cursory stroll through the Scriptures is of little use. Even a formal habit of reading such as the Psalms and lessons for the day will not do. But instead we must examine every attitude and implore God to impress upon our minds its true import. Diligence of itself will not help for a full understanding of the Scriptures. Rather, we must have the eyes of our understanding opened by the Spirit of God. His aid will only be given to us as a result of fervent prayer.

In fact, we must never approach the Scriptures without the petition of David, "Open thou mine eyes, O LORD, that I may behold wondrous things out of thy law." Hence these two things, diligence and prayer, are united by Solomon as both being necessary to attain this divine knowledge: "If you apply your heart to understanding, yea, if you cry after knowledge and lift up your voice for understanding; if you seek her as silver, and search for her as for hid treasures; then you will understand the fear of the LORD, and find the knowledge of God. For the LORD gives wisdom: out of his mouth come knowledge and understanding" (Proverbs 2:2-6).

But especially we must search the Scriptures with a more specific purpose—in order to know Christ. As they testify of him, so it should be our greatest concern to see and learn what they really testify. Merely critical knowledge of Scripture, although it may be good, has no saving benefit. Nor does a historical knowledge of Scripture, nor even a speculative knowledge of its doctrines and precepts, help us at all. It is the knowledge of Christ, and that alone, that conveys to our souls the blessing of salvation. "This is life eternal, to know you the only true God, and Jesus Christ, whom you have sent."

In the great mystery of a crucified Savior "are hid all the treasures of wisdom and knowledge." "In comprehending the height and depth and length and breadth of the love of Christ as revealed in that mystery, we shall be filled with all the fullness of God."

My dear friends, even good people do not fully bear this in mind. People will go into the country to pursue some object. For one it may be to obtain health, or another for pleasure. But it is only the botanist who really will acquire the science of plants. Likewise, in perusing the holy Scriptures, whatever else people may obtain, none will find the knowledge of Christ in all the glory of his person or the extent of his love or the fullness and excellence of his salvation, except those who go with this express purpose, and stretch themselves utterly toward it. You will remember that the cherubim upon the mercy-seat were in a bent posture, looking down upon the Ark, that peculiar symbol of the Lord Jesus Christ as mediating between God and us. The apostle Peter explains this to us in declaring all the wonders of salvation that are revealed to us in the Scriptures, that "the angels are desiring to look into them" (1 Peter 1:12).

So then, brethren, be in this attitude whenever you take the sacred volume into your hands. Like the apostle Paul, seek to your dying day to know more and more of Christ, "the power of his resurrection, and the fellowship of his sufferings." For according to the measure that "you behold the glory of Christ, you shall be changed into the same image from glory to glory, even as by the Spirit of the Lord" (2 Corinthians 3:18).

2. *Endeavor to spread the knowledge of them as much as you can.* The command "to search them" evidently implies the duty to promote the knowledge of them with other people. In this respect the Christian world has done well in spreading the Holy Scriptures both at home and abroad to an extent quite unprecedented. In the work of translating the holy Scriptures and sending out missionaries to spread the knowledge of them, this age has excelled all that have ever gone before it.

But who would have ever thought that a great part of the Christian world should set itself against the circulation of the Scriptures, and even prohibit their people from reading them? Yet this is done in every part of the world. Some will not permit the Word of God to be read, except by their special permission, and with their corrupt glosses, which in many instances obscure and falsify its meaning. What can we say about this, except to be amazed at such conduct in a church professing itself to be the Church of Christ. I do not know which is the greater, the impiety or the cruelty of such an attitude.

The Lord Jesus Christ says, "Search the Scriptures." "No," say these evil men: "You shall not search them; I will not even allow you to have them in your possession. If they are given to you I will take them from you." If it is replied, "In them we have eternal life," these men retort, "We do not care about that. You shall perish rather than let us allow you to read that Book." "But Christ has said, 'They testify of me'; so I want to know what they testify." "I do not care about that," is the reply. "I will not allow you to know what they testify unless it is interpreted, or rather corrupted and falsified, by me." What such men will have to answer for at the bar of judgment, God alone knows. But I fear that their doom will be terrible, seeing that they will have to answer for the souls of thousands whom they have kept in sorrow's bondage and blinded to their eternal ruin.

So judge, my friends, whether you should not try to counteract this impious tyranny and to diffuse the knowledge of salvation to the perishing millions of your fellow men. I do not suggest that you should do this in a spirit of opposition, but rather in a spirit of love. And as the legislation at their request has made them partakers with you in all civil and political privileges, so you should labor to impart to them the full enjoyment of your spiritual privileges, in the knowledge of Christ, and of his salvation.

(Preached for the Society of Scripture Readers in Dublin, March, 1830).

SERMON 2257
THE EXCELLENCY
OF THE SCRIPTURES

*"All Scripture is given by inspiration of
God, and is profitable for doctrine, for
reproof, for correction, for instruction in
righteousness: that the man of God may be
perfect, thoroughly furnished unto all good
works" (2 Timothy 3:16, 17).*

Little do people realize how indebted they are to God for the
possession of the holy Scriptures. This was the exclusive possession of the Jewish people for fifteen hundred years, and it raised
them above all other peoples of the earth. As the apostle Paul saw,
their great advantage was that "unto them were committed the
oracles of God." In the knowledge of them Timothy was early instructed, and "by these he was made wise unto salvation." The
whole Mosaic dispensation taught him this great lesson, that he
must be saved by vicarious sacrifice. All the prophets directed his
views to that great sacrifice, which eventually was to be made by
our Lord Jesus Christ. It is of these Scriptures that the apostle Paul
speaks in our text. In his commendation of them, we see,

I. THEIR TRUE ORIGIN

The Scriptures of the Old Testament were "given by inspiration
of God"; of this there is abundant evidence in the very nature of
the things which they contain. What could Moses have known of
the creation of the world, of the fall of man, and of the Flood, if
they had not been revealed to him? What could he have known of
the perfections of God or the means of fallen man being restored
before God or of the prophet who should in due time be raised up

from among his brethren to be like him, a Mediator, Lawgiver, Redeemer, and Governor? How could he ever have given such a perfect code of laws as the Ten Commandments? How could he ever have constructed such a complicated series of ceremonial laws that so fully reflected later on the work and office of the Messiah?

If he was a good man, how could he ever have deceived the world with his own invention of them all? And if he were evil, how could he ever have given such a holy framework of law? Likewise, we cannot gainsay that the prophets were also inspired of God, since it was impossible for them to have invented so minutely and harmoniously the predictions of things that actually came to pass later. The same might be said of the writers of the New Testament.

While the apostles and the evangelists are of one voice in declaring the Old Testament was inspired of God, in their own writings they were also "moved by the Holy Ghost" (2 Peter 1:19-21). They professed to be inspired by the same Spirit in all that they declare. Each expressed himself in his own style, as any other writer would do, but in the matter of *what* they wrote they were inspired by God. And in the manner of expressing it they were preserved from any error or mistake. So we may affirm that God is the Author of all the Scriptures, and that every part of them is "given by inspiration from him."

The apostle proceeds to declare,

II. THEIR PRIMARY USE

This is expressed in four differing terms, which may be summarized in two ways. The Scriptures are profitable:

1. *For the establishment of sound doctrine*. They declare all that is needful for us to know. They lay down with all precision all that we need to know. They enable us to "reprove," or to "refute," in the most convincing way all error which ignorance or pride might raise. There is such perfect unity in the system of revelation that you cannot overthrow one part without overturning the whole. Deny the divinity of Christ and you also entirely destroy the doctrine of the atonement. Deny the influences of the Holy Spirit and

you lose the possibility of the transformation of the soul into the divine image. Maintain the merit of good works and you annihilate the whole covenant of grace. Whatever is of fundamental importance, we find in Scripture the most abundant means of discovering the truth and of refuting error. So we must always abide by Scripture and appeal to it on all occasions.

2. *For the securing of a holy practice.* Innumerable evils occur in the world. But all of them are condemned in the Word, while at the same time the ways of true piety are pointed out with clarity to all who desire to walk in them. There is no secret evil of the heart that is not exposed by the Word, nor any attainment of true righteousness for which there are not explicit instructions. The "works of the flesh" and the "fruit of the Spirit" are set over against each other, and are described so clearly that there is no room for ignorance in the Scriptures, nor any possibility of mistake for a truly upright man before God.

From these immediate uses of Scripture, we may easily discern,

III. Their Ultimate Design

This is to render men "perfect," as the great object of God in all that he has revealed. It is *this* which the Scriptures are admirably designed to effect. They lack nothing:

1. *For their instruction.* We cannot conceive of any good work which anyone instructed by the Scriptures is not fitted to carry out. From them he will learn to be "a man of God." In his secret walk with God, he will also learn there all he needs. In his conduct with his fellows, he will also be instructed in his duties. Whether as parent or child, husband or wife, master or servant, he will learn all that is necessary to please God and be approved by his fellow men.

2. *For their encouragement.* There is not a human motive that is not dealt with by the Scriptures. Not only are the tremendous sanctions of heaven and hell portrayed, but all the wonders of redeeming love are displayed in such majesty and splendor. The promises of God are also richly outlined so none can be added that are not already there. In whatever circumstances one is in, there

is all there for one's encouragement and support so that one is "thoroughly furnished for every good work." When called upon to act, he is "able to do all things through Christ who strengthens him." Or if he is called to suffer, he is made "more than conqueror through him who strengthens him."

Since such is the excellency of the Holy Scriptures, let everyone set himself to discharge his duties in relation to them:

1. *Refer everything to them as your standard.* Rely not on the opinions of men, but bring them to the law and the testimony. For if they speak not according to this Word, there is no light in them (Isaiah 8:20). Test your views of yourself and of Christ by Scripture. See if your life and conduct be that of the apostles. For you can readily deceive yourself, but you can never deceive God. "Examine yourselves, whether you be in the faith: prove your own selves." Then you will have the testimony of a good conscience and of acceptance with God.

2. *Consult them in all things as your guide.* Difficulties will often arise, and if you go to men for counsel, you may easily be led astray, since none but those who have imbibed the Scriptures can inculcate what they have learned of their principles. So study daily the holy Scriptures to direct you in your conduct. "Instructed by them, you will be wiser than your teachers" (Psalm 119:99, 100). Then you will be able to "walk wisely before God in a perfect way" (Psalm 101:2).

3. *Ask God, having revealed them to the world, to reveal them also in your heart.* For plain as the Scriptures are, yet they are still a "sealed book" to all whose eyes have not been enlightened by the Spirit of God. The natural man cannot discern what requires spiritual insight. Even the apostles, in spite of all they received in both public and private from their divine master for over three years, still needed "their understandings opened by him, that they might understand the Scriptures." So do we need the teachings of God's Spirit, without which we remain in darkness. Pray, then, like David: "Open thou my eyes, that I may behold wondrous things out of thy law!" Then you will be guided into all truth, finding the Scriptures fully adequate for all the gracious ends for which they have been revealed.

Part IX

THE CHRISTIAN'S EXPERIENCES
OF DEPRESSION AND SUFFERING

SERMON 574
CAUSES AND REMEDY
OF DEPRESSION

*"Why are you cast down, O my soul? And
why are you disquieted within me? Hope in
God, for I shall yet praise him, who is the
health of my countenance, and my God"*
(Psalm 43:5).

God has allowed many of his most distinguished servants to be
in trouble, and to record their experience for our benefit, so
that when we are in similar circumstances, we may know that we
are not walking an untrodden path. We will then be sure how to
behave ourselves in such a situation. The Psalmist was well aware
of afflictions of every kind. In the preceding psalm, which seems
to have been penned during his flight from Absalom, he gives us a
very melancholy picture of his condition. Tears were his meat day
and night, while his enemies gloried over him. They said continually, "Where is now your God?" (Psalm 42:3, 10). "His soul was
cast down within him." For while "the waves and billows
threatened to overwhelm him, the water-spouts threatened to
burst upon him. So deep called unto deep" (Psalm 42:6, 7) to
bring about his ruin. It seemed as if all the powers of heaven and
earth were combined against him. In complaining of these things,
he sometimes argues with God.

"Why have you forgotten me?" (Psalm 42:9). At other times he
checks himself, and as it were, reproves his soul for its disquietude
and despondency (Psalm 42:5, 11). The psalm before us was evidently written on the same occasion. It contains the same complaints (compare 42:9 with 43:2). It ends like the former, with a
third time condemning his own impatience and encouraging his
soul to trust in God.

His words lead us to consider,

211

I. THE SOURCES OF DEPRESSION

It cannot be doubted that temporal afflictions will produce a very great dejection of mind. Although sometimes grace will enable a person to triumph over them as of small consequence, yet more frequently our frail condition is left to feel its weakness. The effect of grace is to reconcile us to the ways of Providence, and to make them work for our good. But although we are saints, we cease not to be men. So it often happens that heavy and accumulated troubles will so weaken our bodily frame as ultimately to enfeeble the mind also, and to render it susceptible of fears; to which, in its unbroken state, it was a complete stranger. The depression of the Psalmist himself arose in some measure from this source. Therefore we must not wonder if heavy losses and cruel treatment from our near friends, or troubles of any other kind, should weigh down the spirits of those who have made less attainments in the divine life. But we shall confine our attention principally to spiritual troubles. And among these we shall find many fruitful sources of depression.

1. **Relapses into sin.** By far the greatest part of our sorrows originates here. A close and steady walk with God is productive of peace. But relapses from him bring guilt upon the conscience, together with many other associated evils. And if those professors of religion who complain so much of their doubts and fears would examine faithfully the causes of their disquiet, they might trace it back to secret neglects of duty or to some lust that is still harbored and indulged.

2. **The temptations of Satan.** Undoubtedly this wicked fiend is the occasion of much trouble to the people of God. Otherwise his temptations would not be characterized as "fiery darts" (Ephesians 6:16), which suddenly pierce and inflame the soul. We may judge in some measure how terrible his assaults are when we see the apostle, who was unmoved by all that man could do against him (Acts 20:24), crying out with such agony and distress under the buffetings of Satan (2 Corinthians 12:7, 8). We shall have a yet more formidable idea of him if we consider that the Lord of Glory himself, when conflicting with the powers of darkness, sweat great drops of blood from every pore of his body through the agony of his

soul. Can we wonder then if the saints are sometimes dejected through the agency of that subtle enemy?

3. *The hidings of God's face.* We do not think that God often hides his face from men without some immediate cause. But we dare not say that he never does, for he is sovereign in the disposal of his gifts. And we know the example of when he withdrew the light of his countenance from Job without any flagrant transgression on the part of his servant to deserve it. It is scarcely necessary to observe how painful that must have been for those who love God. Our blessed Lord, who bore the cruelties of men without a complaint, was constrained to cry out bitterly under his dereliction from his heavenly Father: "My God, my God, why have you forsaken me?" And certainly this is the most distressing of all events: "The spirit of a man, when strengthened from above, may sustain any infirmity, but a wounded spirit, wounded too by such a hand, who can bear?" (Proverbs 18:14).

Having traced out the sources of depression, let us inquire after,

II. THE REMEDY

The great remedy for every temporal or spiritual affliction is faith. This, and this alone, is adequate for our necessities. The efficacy of this principle for the space of three thousand, six hundred years is declared in the eleventh chapter to the Hebrews. Toward the close of that chapter, we are told what it enabled them to do (Hebrews 11:33, 34) and what to suffer (Hebrews 11:36, 37). It was that which the Psalmist prescribed to himself as the cure of his disquietude.

1. *Hope in God.* We are too apt in our troubles to flee to other creatures for help (Hosea 5:13). But it is God who sends our troubles. "They spring not out of the dust" (Job 5:6); and he only can remove them. We should therefore look unto him and put our trust in him. This is the direction which God himself gives to us. He reminds us of his wisdom and power to overrule our trials for good; and exhorts us, when weary and fainting, to wait on him as our all-sufficient Helper (Isaiah 40:28-31).

2. *Expect deliverance from him*. To what end has God given us such "exceeding great and precious promises" if we do not rest upon them and expect their accomplishment? The refiner does not put his vessels into the furnace to leave them there, but he takes them out again when they are fitted for his use. And it is to purify us as "vessels of honor" that God subjects us to the fiery trial. We should say therefore with Job, "When he has tried me, I shall come forth as gold" (Job 23:10). It was this expectation that supported David. "I had fainted," he says, "unless I had believed to see the goodness of the Lord in the land of the living" (Psalm 27:13).

We are told that "light is sown for the righteous" (Psalm 97:11). That is sufficient for us. Between seed-time and harvest there may be a long and dreary winter. Still, every day brings forward the appointed time of harvest. So the husbandman waits in the assured expectation of its arrival (James 5:7). Thus should we wait, however long the promise may seem to tarry (Habakkuk 2:3). And as those who are now in heaven were once in great tribulation like ourselves (Revelation 7:14), so we shall in due season be with them, freed from all remains of sin and sorrow. In our darkest hours we should hold fast this confidence, "I shall yet praise him" (compare this text with Psalm 118:17, 18).

3. *View him in his covenant relation to you*. It is noticeable that our Lord in the midst of his dereliction addressed his Father, "My God, my God!" Now, this is what we should do. For God is the God of all his people. Yes, he dwells in them (2 Corinthians 6:16), and is, as it were, the very life of their souls (Colossians 3:4). However distressed then we may be, we should see him as "the health of our countenance and our God." What a foundation of hope did the remembrance of God's fatherly relation to them afford to the church of old! (see Isaiah 63:15, 16). What a sweet assurance God himself teaches us also to derive from this same source! (see Isaiah 49:14-16). If we wholeheartedly desire to be his, we have every cause to believe that we are his; and if we be his, he will never suffer any to pluck us out of his hand (John 10:27, 28). Therefore hold fast to this as to the anchor of the soul, and it shall keep you steadfast amid all the storms and tempests that can possibly attack you.

Address—

1. *Those who are in a drooping and despondent state of mind.*
We cannot advise you better than what has been suggested by the
example of David.

Inquire, first, into the reasons of your depression. If it proceeds
from material causes, recollect that they are rather tokens of God's
love than of his hatred. For "whom he loves he chastens" (Hebrews 12:6). If it arises from the temptations of Satan, do not take
all the blame upon yourselves. Recognize that a good part of it at
least comes from him from whom they proceed. If you are troubled
about the hidings of God's face, ask God to return and lift you up
once more before the light of his countenance. And if, as is most
probable, "your own sins have hid his face from you," humble
yourself for them, and implore his grace that you may be in the
future enabled to mortify and subdue them. At all events, having
once searched out the cause, you will know better how to apply
the remedy.

But in the next place, it is right to check these desponding
fears. The text is not a mere inquiry, but an expostulation. It is
the kind of complaint that you should address to your own souls.
And what is the benefit of such an attitude? It only weakens your
own condition, it discourages your heart, and it dishonors your
God. We do not say that there are not just occasions for depression. But we do say this—that instead of continuing in a dejected
state, you should return instantly to God, who would "give you
beauty for ashes, the oil of joy for mourning, and the garment of
praise for the spirit of heaviness" (Isaiah 61:3).

Above all, "encourage yourself in God." This is what David did
in the text, and on another most significant occasion as well
(1 Samuel 30:1-6). While there is an all-sufficient God on whom
to rely, you need not fear although earth and hell should be combined against you (Psalm 11:1, 4; 27:1, 3; 125:1).

2. *Those who are entire strangers to depression and dejection.*
We are far from congratulating you on your exemption from all
such feelings. On the contrary, we would suggest to you in reference to that exemption the very same things as we have recommended to others in their distresses.

First, inquire into the reason of your never having experienced such feelings. "Why are you not cast down, O my soul? And why are you not disquieted within me?" May it not proceed from an ignorance of your real state, and from an unconcern about what kind of account you must soon give of yourself at the judgment seat of Christ?

Next, expostulate with yourself: "O my soul, why are you thus callous and insensible? Will not your contempt of God's judgments bring about your ruin? It must not, and by the grace of God it shall not. But you have neglected your own eternal interests long enough. So God helping you, you will now direct all your attention to them from this time on. For if you are summoned before your God in your present state, it would be better for me that I had never been born."

Also, no less than those who are depressed, you must find your hopes in God. All your expectation must be from him, "with whom there is mercy and plenteous redemption." If you will only turn to him in earnest, you will have nothing to fear. For his Word assures you, "Let the wicked forsake his way, and the unrighteous man his thoughts; and let him return unto the LORD, and he will have mercy upon him; and to our God, for he will abundantly pardon."

SERMON 2336
AFFLICTIONS, THE
FRUIT OF GOD'S LOVE

*"My son, despise not the chastening of the
Lord, nor faint when you are rebuked of
him: for whom the Lord loves he chastens,
and scourges every son whom he receives"
(Hebrews 12:4-13).*

P ersecution for righteousness' sake is what every child of God
must expect. When faith is in living exercise, it will be sustained without murmuring. This is amply shown in the preceding
chapter (Hebrews 11:35-38). But when faith languishes, the trial
which believers are called to endure will appear almost insupport-
able. Such was the state of many of the Hebrews to whom the
apostle wrote. They were in danger of becoming weary and faint
in their minds through the greatness and long continuance of their
sufferings. On this account, the apostle Paul, having shown them
the power of a living faith to support them, brings before them a
number of considerations.

I. FOR THEIR CONSOLATION AND SUPPORT

The patience of Christ under his sufferings is beyond all comparison the strongest incentive to resignation under ours; since
ours fall so infinitely short of his. This the apostle first propounds
for their consideration, and then goes on in the words which we
have just read to offer other suggestions which also are of great
weight to reconcile the mind to trials, of whatever kind they may
be. Also from them, when bowed down in affliction, we may learn
to support them manfully.

217

1. *They are far less than we have pledged ourselves willingly to endure.* The very terms on which we come to Christ are that we should be ready to die for him at any time and in any way that he shall see fit. We are plainly warned by our Lord himself that if we will not lay down our lives for him, we cannot be his disciples. "If we love our lives, we shall lose them; but if we lose them for his sake, then shall we find them to life eternal." But what is the loss of temporal good when compared with that of life? Be it granted that, like the Hebrews, we have suffered much (Hebrews 10:32-34). Yet our persecutors have stopped far short of what they might have afflicted, and may for ought we know be yet permitted to inflict. We have not yet "resisted unto blood, striving against sin." Instead therefore of complaining of the heaviness of our trials, we have reason rather to be thankful for their lightness. If we faint when they are so light, how shall we support them when they come upon us with unrestrained force? "If we have run with footmen and they wearied us, how shall we contend with horses?" (Jeremiah 12:5). In our "strivings then against sin" and Satan, let us prepare for yet greater extremities. Then, when we are prepared for the worst that can come upon us, all that stops short of that will appear light and easy to be borne.

2. *They are all the fruits of paternal love.* In the Old Testament God had exhorted his people to regard their trials in this way, as sent by a loving Father to his children. They were to receive them with truly filial gratitude, "neither despising them" as though they came only by chance, "nor fainting under them" as though they had been sent in anger (Proverbs 3:11, 12). The apostle fixes our attention particularly on the tender and affectionate terms with which our God addresses us: "My son, despise not." We should not overlook such endearing expressions, which if duly attended to would reconcile us even to the most afflictive circumstances. The truth is that man is only an instrument in God's hands. The very afflictions which men lay upon us for our excess of piety, God lays upon us for our defects or for the further advancement of his work within us. Paul's thorn in the flesh was ordained of God to prevent his being too much elated by the revelations which had been given to him (2 Corinthians 12:7).

Our state in this world is then a state of discipline. We are still children that need correction on account of our many errors and faults. It is a correction that will gradually bring us to the exercise of true wisdom. This is found universally. No wise father will not occasionally correct his child. A man who sees children that are unconnected with him acting amiss takes no notice of them, but leaves to others the painful task of correcting them. His own children he corrects because of his particular interest in them and his love toward them. Would we then have God treat us as bastards that have no real relation to him? Would we not rather be dealt with by him as his beloved children, in whose welfare he takes the deepest interest? So whatever may be our affliction, bodily or mental, personal or family, or with whatever view it may be inflicted on us by others, let us see the hand of a Father in it, and say with Eli, "It is the Lord; let him do what seems good to him" (1 Samuel 3:18). Let us "hear the rod, and he who has appointed it" (Micah 6:9). And let us take advantage of it for the good of our souls.

3. *If we submit patiently to the rebukes of our earthly parents, how much more we should to those of our heavenly Father.* Earthly parents do not always correct as justly or as temperately as they ought. Sometimes their rebukes are nothing else than a projection of their own bad temper. Yet we have submitted to their corrections without presuming to question the wisdom, justice, or love that inflicted the punishment upon us. This is part of that honor which children were enjoined by God's law to pay to those who were fathers of their flesh. If they refused obstinately to do so they were, by God's own appointment, to be stoned to death (Deuteronomy 21:18-21). But this submission is due to an infinitely higher authority, for he is the father of *our spirits*. If we refuse to allow him to discipline us, a far worse death assuredly awaits us in the world to come. For he never inflicts any evil upon us that is not for our greater good, even that we may become to a greater degree "partakers of his holiness." Shall we then refuse the corrections of our heavenly Father while we pay submission to our earthly parents? "Shall we not much rather be in subjection to him and live?" Surely this is our truest wisdom and our highest privilege.

4. *However grievous our sufferings may appear now, they are all sent for our eternal good.* As long as we have human feelings, chastening of any kind will always be grievous to us. But after it

has produced its proper effects, "it yields the peaceable fruits of righteousness to them that are exercised thereby." At first, tribulation works impatience. But when the soul has been well disciplined by a continuance or recurrence of it, a better spirit is produced. Through the sanctifying operations of the Holy Spirit upon the soul, a different process results. "Tribulation works patience, and patience experience, and experience hope; even a hope that does not make ashamed" (Romans 5:3-5).

Shall we then complain of what is sent for such a purpose? Shall the vine grumble about the pruning knife, which cuts only with the purpose of increasing its fruitfulness? Shall the vessel complain of the furnace in which it is put in order to effect its suitability for the Master's use? So let us look to the end. There we shall never grumble at the means which infinite wisdom has purposed for its attainment. If we be "in heaviness through manifold temptations, let us not forget that there is a fit occasion for them; and that the trial of our faith, which is infinitely more precious than that which purifies gold, will be found to the praise and honor and glory of our God, and to our own selves also, at the appearing of Jesus Christ" (1 Peter 1:6, 7). If we are made "partakers of his holiness," we shall never complain of the means which were used to bring us to its attainment.

5. *Walk so as to encourage others by your example.* The influence of example is far greater than we may imagine. In order to avoid the displeasure of the Judaizing Christians, Peter had recourse to deception. Here I may observe that if an apostle swerved grievously from the path of duty through his carnal reasoning, who has not reason to take heed lest he also fall? What was the effect of this on others? "The whole Church dissembled with him; insomuch that even Barnabas himself was carried away with their dissimulation" (Galatians 2:13, 14). On the other hand, see the influence of the good example of the apostle Paul. He was imprisoned for the truth's sake, and retained his fidelity undaunted and undiminished; insomuch that "his bonds for Christ's sake became a matter of notoriety throughout Caesar's palace and in all other places." And what was the effect of this? We are told that "many of the brethren in the Lord, waxing confident by his bonds," and by what they heard of his fortitude in supporting them, "were much bolder to speak the word without fear," so that "the gospel

was furthered" by the very means which his enemies used to obstruct its progress (Philippians 1:12-14).

Similar effects will, to a greater or lesser extent, follow from our conduct under our afflictions. There are in every place many who may be considered as "lame" who will be stumbled and weakened and discouraged if they see us faint. On the other hand, they will be encouraged and made bold to go forward if they behold us following resolutely the path of duty and supporting manfully the trials that come upon us. So let us remember the probable influence of our conduct on those around us. Let us think how much good or evil we may do, according as we approve ourselves to God, or do not, in the discharge of our duty. There is a high purpose which we should pursue as the apostle prayed on behalf of the Colossians, to be "strengthened with all might, according to God's glorious power, unto all patience, and long-suffering, with joyfulness—giving thanks unto the Father who has made us meet to be partakers of the inheritance of the saints in light" (Colossians 1:11, 12).

Do not think that such a purpose as this should betray any arrogance in you. For Timothy was only a youth, and yet he was directed to be an example not only to the world, but to believers as well, in all that was good (1 Timothy 4:12). So it is the duty of each one of us, whether layman or minister, "so to let his light shine before men, that all who behold it may be led to glorify their Father which is in heaven" (Matthew 5:16). In short, let us all endeavor to walk so that we may say with the apostle Paul, "Whatsoever you have heard and seen in me, do; and the God of peace shall be with you" (Colossians 4:9).

Having instructed the Hebrews in the true nature and end of their sufferings, the apostle suggests some further considerations,

II. For Their Direction and Guidance

We shall also consider this as it is addressed to us. Like them, we are all sufferers in our time. And therefore:

1. *Yield not to depression*. Troubles, whether they are felt or feared, are apt to depress and to weaken the person. This we see clearly in the case of the prophet Ezekiel. "Sigh," says God to him,

"sigh, you son of man, with the breaking of your loins, and with bitterness sigh before their eyes. And it shall be, when they say to you, 'Why do you sigh?' that you shall answer, 'For the tidings: because it comes, and every heart shall melt, and all hands shall be feeble, and every spirit shall faint, and all knees shall be weak as water'" (Ezekiel 21:7). But whatever may happen to us and whatever trials we may have or how we may be threatened, remember that they are all ordered by a wise and gracious God, who controls and limits all according to his own sovereign will. For without his permission not a hair of our head can be touched.

Our enemies, unconscious of their dependence upon God, may plot and threaten our destruction. But see what the Psalmist says concerning them: "The wicked plots against the just, and gnashes upon him with his teeth: but the LORD shall laugh at him" (Psalm 37:12, 13) as a poor, impotent, and malignant worm, that only exists through his forbearance and tender mercy. Now I ask, shall God laugh at him, and we cry? Should we not rather set this poor impotent worm at defiance? But see what the Psalmist adds further: "The wicked have drawn out the sword, and have bent their bow, to cast down the poor and the needy, and to slay such as be of upright conversation." What is the issue of all this? "Their sword shall enter into their own heart, and their bows shall be broken" (Psalm 37:14, 15). "Say not then, 'A confederacy,' like those who are crying out, 'A confederacy'; neither fear you their fear, nor be afraid: but sanctify the Lord of hosts himself; and let him be your fear, and let him be your dread: and he shall be to you for a sanctuary" (Isaiah 8:12-14).

When others would alarm you with the supposed power of your persecutors, let your answer be, "The LORD is in his holy temple; the LORD's throne is in heaven" (Psalm 11:1-4). Even the greatest of all your adversaries, Satan himself, could not even enter into the pigs without permission. How then shall he, or any of his confederates, hurt a child of God without permission? (1 Peter 3:13). So you may laugh them all to scorn and shake your head at them (Isaiah 37:22). With God on your side, there are a million times "more for you than are against you." Only "be strong in the Lord" (Ephesians 6:10), and you will be more than conqueror over all.

2. *Swerve not from the path of duty*. Fear, unbelief, and impatience "will make our ways crooked" (Isaiah 59:8). The

contrivances which under their influence we seek to adopt to avoid difficulties will only increase our difficulties a hundredfold. The way to "make straight paths for our feet" is simply to fulfill the will of God and leave events to him. If Daniel and the Hebrew youths had attempted to avoid the trials which threatened them, they might have done so; but they would also have involved their souls in the deepest guilt. Instead, they followed a straight course, neither moving to the right hand nor to the left to avoid the den of lions or the fiery furnace. This was *right*. And this is the very direction given to us also by God himself: "Ponder the path of your feet; and let all your ways be established: Turn not to the right hand, nor to the left; but remove your feet from evil" (Proverbs 4:26, 27).

Make this the principle of your life that you will never leave: "I must obey my God." If the whole world combines to divert you from it, reply, "Whether it is right to hearken to you more than unto God, judge yourselves." It is this that will keep you from endless perplexity. It will make every path for you clear and straight. "If your eye be evil," and the film of worldly hopes or fears be over it, "your whole body will be full of darkness." "If your eye be single," however, and you have no other purpose than to love and honor God, "your whole body will be full of light" (Matthew 6:22, 23). Then your steps will be directed in a way in which you will neither err nor stumble.

Part X

EXEMPLARS OF FAITH

SERMON 20
ABRAM'S JOURNEY TO CANAAN

*"They went forth to go into the land of
Canaan; and into the land of Canaan they
came" (Genesis 12:5).*

The call of Abraham is one of the most instructive subjects
that can occupy the human mind. This is because it most
gloriously displays in it the perfections of almighty God; and because of it he showed himself one of the brightest patterns of
obedience that the world ever beheld.

Abram had a revelation from God while yet he was at Ur in the
land of the Chaldees. By that he was directed to leave his native
country, which was immersed (as he and his father also were) in
idolatry (Joshua 24:2). At Haran (or as it is also called, Charran)
he abode until his father's death. Then he received from God a
further direction to go into Canaan, with the express assurance
that the whole land of Canaan would be given to him and his
posterity for an inheritance, and that in his seed all the nations of
the earth would be blessed (Genesis 12:1-4). He complied with
this direction. He took his wife and family and all that he possessed and set out upon the journey. As the words before us say:
"They went forth to go into the land of Canaan; and into the land
of Canaan they came."

This call of Abram is very instructive for us, for it not only displays the glorious perfections of God who called him, but also
exhibits the distinguished virtues of him who obeyed the call.

This is how I propose to illustrate this subject, by setting before
you:

227

I. The Perfections of God for Your Admiration

This is drawn to our attention by Stephen in his words, "The God of glory appeared unto our father Abraham." Observe then three things:

1. *His sovereignty*. Why was Abram distinguished above all other of the sons of men to be so blessed in himself and to be such a blessing to the world? He and all his family were idolaters, as also were all around him. Yet was he selected by almighty God from among them and made a friend and favorite of heaven? What can account for this? Can it be traced to anything but the sovereign will and pleasure of Jehovah? However adverse any man may be to the idea of God's sovereignty in the dispensation of his blessings, he cannot deny nor can he question the matter in this instance. Yet this is really what is done in the conversion of every soul to God. The almighty Sovereign of the universe "has saved us, and called us with an holy calling, not according to our works, but according to his own purpose and grace which was given us in Christ Jesus before the world began" (2 Timothy 1:9). "It is God, and God alone, that has made any of us to differ" from our fellows (1 Corinthians 4:7). Everything, whether in heaven or in earth, must say: "By the grace of God I am what I am" (1 Corinthians 15:10).

2. *His power*. Nothing less than omnipotence could have effected such a sudden and total change in the heart of Abram as was brought about at this time. Nor indeed could anything else than omnipotence have sufficed to accomplish for him all that was now promised. And is less power required for the "turning of any man from darkness into light, and from the power of Satan unto God"? It is a new creation, and is expressly called so by God himself (Ephesians 2:10). It is compared by the apostle Paul to the power which the Father exercised in raising his Son Jesus Christ from the dead and exalting him to glory far above all the principalities and powers, whether of heaven or hell (Ephesians 1:19-21). From the first awakening of a sinner to his final exaltation to glory, he must say in reference to the whole work, "He that has wrought me to this self-same thing is God" (2 Corinthians 5:5).

3. *His faithfulness*. Abram did not have a single foot of ground. Indeed, for twenty-five years after the promise was made to him, he did not have one child to whom the promises were made. The

time was past in which according to the course of nature it was possible for him and Sarah to have a child. Yet the child was given to him and to his posterity in all the land of Canaan. In due time also, the seed in whom all the nations of the earth were to be blessed was given. Thus in a similar manner are all the promises fulfilled to everyone who believes in Christ. There is not one jot or tittle of God's word that is ever allowed to fail (Joshua 23:14). "The promises of God in Christ are, not yea and nay, but yea and amen, to the glory of God" (2 Corinthians 1:20), and to the everlasting salvation of all who rely upon them. However numerous their dangers may be, or however great their difficulties, "they shall never be plucked out of God's hands" (John 10:29). But they shall be "kept by his power unto full and complete salvation" (1 Peter 1:5).

Let us now set before you what is no less obvious in our text.

II. THE VIRTUES OF ABRAHAM ARE GIVEN FOR YOUR IMITATION

We are told on divine authority that if we be Abram's seed, we shall do the works of Abram. So note then five things:

1. *His simple faith.* He received implicitly all that God spoke to him. To whatever it referred, and however improbable humanly speaking, the accomplishment of it was that he never for one moment doubted the truth of God's word, "nor ever staggered at any promise through unbelief." Now, in this most particularly he is set forth as an example to us, who are required to "walk in the steps of that faith of our father Abraham, which he had while he was yet uncircumcised" (Romans 4:12). And more especially are we to imitate him in relation to the faith which he exercised on the Lord Jesus Christ, whom he beheld at a distance of two thousand years as the Savior of the world. If any person could ever be justified by his works, Abraham could certainly have claimed that honor. But eminent as his obedience to the divine mandates was, he had nothing whereof to glory before God; and aware of his own utter unworthiness, he believed in the Lord Jesus Christ for righteousness and was justified solely by faith in him (Romans 4:1-3). Why is this so minutely recorded concerning him? Was it not for his

sake, that he might be honored? No, it was entirely for our sakes, that we might know how we also are to be justified, and may look simply to Christ as our all in all (Romans 4:22-25).

2. *His prompt decision.* It is said concerning Abram that "when he was called to go out into a place which he should after receive for an inheritance, he obeyed." There was in him no hesitation, no delay. And in this way must we also obey the divine when bidden to "forsake all and follow Christ." We must "not confer with flesh and blood" (Galatians 1:16); but must, like the disciples with their nets and Matthew at the receipt of custom, leave all for Christ. We must be on our guard against specious excuses—"Lord, let me go home and bury my father," or "take leave of my friends." We must not be looking for "a more convenient season"; our obedience must be prompt, our decision firm and unchangeable. While it is called today, we must avail ourselves of the opportunity that is afforded us to do the will of God. To hesitate is treason. To delay is death. "What our hand finds to do, we must do it instantly, and with all our might."

3. *His self-denying zeal.* No doubt Abram felt the same attachment which men usually do to their native land. He found it painful to turn his back upon all his friends and to forsake all the comforts which he enjoyed in affluence and ease. No doubt, too, he had much to struggle with amongst his friends and acquaintances. For he was leaving his native country, and yet "he knew not where he was going." How strange this must have appeared! Yes, what folly and absurdity! But "he knew in whom he had believed," and had no fear that the Lord Jehovah, who had called him, would fail to guide his feet or to keep him in all his ways.

And shall not we also have much to contend with if we obey the call of God in his gospel? To renounce the world is "to mortify our members upon earth, to cut off our right hand, to pluck out our right eye, to crucify the flesh with the affections and lust." This is no easy task. The very terms in which these duties are expressed sufficiently declare what self-denial is necessary for the discharge of them. For without it our difficulties will be increased. We shall have foes without number to obstruct our way. And most of all, "those of our own household." Hence our blessed Lord warned his followers, saying: "If any man will be my disciple, let him deny himself, and take up his cross daily and follow me." In

truth, "if we hate not father and mother, houses and land, yea and
our own lives also in comparison with him, we cannot be his disciples." Let not this appear a hard saying, but obey it like
Abraham. And like him, you shall find it "a light burden and an
easy yoke."

4. *His prudent care.* Abram collected together all the substance
which he could conveniently carry with him, and took it along
with him for his support. To have acted otherwise, without necessity, would have been to tempt God rather than to trust in him.
He had many dependent on him. It became him, as far as with
propriety he could, to provide for their support. And the same prudent care becomes us also. It is one thing to improve the means we
possess, and another to trust in them. We must never say to gold,
"You are my hope; or to the fine gold, You are my confidence." At
the same time, we are to employ the talents which God has committed to us, that we may support ourselves and not be chargeable
to others. That is a remarkable expression of Solomon, "I, wisdom, dwell with prudence" (Proverbs 8:12). Prudent attention to
our worldly circumstances tends rather to honor than to disgrace
true religion. Abram, as the head of a family, provided for his
own, and he did right in this. Yes, if he had not done it, he would
have "denied the faith, and been worse than an infidel." Whatever your situation, in your determination through grace be like
David: "I will behave myself wisely in a perfect way" (Psalm
101:2).

5. *His persevering diligence.* In stopping at Haran until his
father's death, I suppose he judged that to be (or rather that it was
for the time) his proper destination. But afterwards being directed
to go to Canaan, he went forth, and did not turn aside until he
came there. There he abode for many years. Indeed, to the very
end of his life he held on in the good way which God had directed
him to pursue. And thus it is that we also must approve ourselves
to God. We must "not turn back, for if we do, God's soul will have
no pleasure in us." If we "turn back" at any time, it is to certain
"perdition." Let us "remember Lot's wife." In fact, it were better
for us never to have "known the way of righteousness, than after
having known it, to depart from it." Go on then, like Abraham,
"as pilgrims and sojourners here," "showing plainly that you are
seeking a better country" (Hebrews 11:9, 10, 13-16). And be

assured that "if, by patient continuation in well-doing, you seek for glory and honor and immortality, you shall in the end attain eternal life" (Romans 2:9).

SERMON 491
JOB, AN EXAMPLE OF
TRUE HUMILIATION

"Behold, I am vile!" (Job 40:4)

These are the words of a man whom God has described "perfect and upright." As a fallen descendant of Adam, he partook of the corruption of our common nature. But as a child of God, he was one of the most eminent of all the human race. It may be thought, indeed, that this confession of his proved him to have been guilty of some enormous crime. But it came as the expression of his great growth in the divine life and of his utter abhorrence of all evil. Doubtless there was a particular occasion for this confession, because he had transgressed with his lips in questioning the conduct of the provident care of God toward him. But if they were applicable to his own situation, how much more are they to all who possess not his high moral attainments. So we shall consider the words as expressing,

I. A DISCOVERY THEN MADE

Job had certainly low views of himself generally (Job 9:20, 30, 31). Yet he had exaggerated the vindication of his own character (Job 10:6,7; 16:17). Elihu had brought to his remembrance instances of this (Job 32:2; 33:8-12; 35:2). God himself testified against Job in this matter (Job 38:2; 40:2, 8). Job had repeatedly expressed the wish to confront God directly. He had also expressed his confidence that he could maintain his cause before him (Job 23:1-5; 31:35-37). God now interrupted him, for he saw how much he had erred and that all his former confidence was sheer presumption. So he now saw:

1. *That his conduct had been sinful.* Being conscious of the integrity of his heart in relation to the things which his friends had charged him with, he had done right in maintaining his innocence before them. But he had erred in maintaining it to the extent he did. He had erred in imagining that he had not merited at God's hands the calamities inflicted on him. Above all, he had erred in complaining of God as acting unjustly and cruelly toward him. These outworkings of his heart he now saw to be exceeding sinful, as betraying too high thoughts of himself and great irreverence toward the God of heaven and earth, "in whose sight the very heavens are not clean, and who charges his angels with folly." This was the sin therefore that he now began bitterly to bewail.

2. *That his whole heart was sinful.* He did not see his character as a mere isolated act, but he took occasion, from the fruit which had been produced, to examine the root from which it all sprang. He now traced the bitter waters to their fountainhead and discovered as a result the bitterness in the spring from which they flowed. This was a completely new discovery to him. He had had no idea how desperately wicked his heart really was, nor the evils that he had committed that could break forth with ten thousand times greater violence if they had not been restrained by the grace of God. The rebellion of which he had been guilty now proved obvious to him; he was as prone to sin as any other member of the human race. If he differed from the vilest of men, it was nothing to boast of, since he had not made himself different, nor could he possess anything which he had not received without the gift of God (1 Corinthians 4:7). This is the true way of recognizing any individual sin (Psalm 51:3, 5; Mark 7:21, 23).

But we must further view his words as expressing,

II. AN ACKNOWLEDGMENT OF THE TRUTH DISCOVERED

"Out of the abundance of his heart his mouth speaks." Feeling his sinfulness, it was a relief rather than a further hardship for him to confess it before God and man. And so we see here:

1. *The frankness of his confession.* There were no excuses made, no suggestions offered that might extenuate his guilt. He might have pleaded the weight of his sufferings or the falsity of the accusations brought against him. He saw that he had no excuse about sin. Whatever palliatives might be adduced to lessen its enormity in the sight of man, it was most hateful in the sight of God. This alone ought to abase us in the dust before our Lord. That Job's sin on this occasion was an exception to his general conduct did not in any way change his own estimation of the awfulness of it. On the contrary, the enormity of it would appear in proportion to the mercies that he had received before and to the exercise of piety that he had maintained before.

This is how we also should acknowledge our vileness before God. Doubtless there may be circumstances which may greatly aggravate our transgressions. These we at all times should certainly recognize. But it is never wise to look on the side that leads to a palliation of sin. Self-love is so rooted in our hearts that we shall always be in danger of framing a more favorable judgment about ourselves. The humiliation of the publican is what at all times befits us. Nor can we ever be in a more becoming state than when, like Job, we "repent and abhor ourselves in dust and ashes."

2. *The attitudes with which such confession is associated.* Job submitted to reproof. He acknowledged himself guilty in relation to the very thing that was laid against him. This is a good test of true and genuine repentance, for it is easy to acknowledge the sinfulness of our nature, but after a man has long and strenuously maintained his integrity, to confess his fault before the very people who have so vehemently accused him is no small achievement. Yet Job did confess that he had repeatedly offended, both in justifying himself and in condemning God. Also, he declared his resolution that with God's help he would offend no more (v. 5). In this way he showed without a doubt the reality and depth of his repentance. Of what use is that penitence that does not inspire us with a fixed purpose to sin no more? Humiliation without change is of no avail: "The repentance which is not to be repented of" produces such an indignation against sin as will never leave us under the power of it any longer (2 Corinthians 7:10, 11). May

we always remember this, and by the entire change of our conduct "approve ourselves in all things to be clear in this matter!"

Address—

1. *To those who have a high opinion of themselves*. How is it possible that you do this? Are you better than Job, who is represented by the prophet as one of the most perfect characters that ever existed upon earth? (Ezekiel 14:14, 20). Or if you were tested with the same trials, would you endure with more patience than he, of whom the apostle speaks with admiration, saying, "You have heard of the patience of Job"? Realize, then, that while you are indulging in a self-righteous and a self-complacent spirit, you are revealing your utter ignorance of your true state and character, and are altogether destitute of true repentance. It is you to whom the gospel is of no avail. For you only warrant a physician when you are sick; so if you are not lost, what is the use of a Savior? O put away from you your Laodicean pride, in case you are rejected by God with indignation and abhorrence (Revelation 3:7, 18). But if in spite of this warning you are determined to maintain your own confidence, then think whether "you will be strong in the day that God shall deal with you," or be able to stand before him as your Accuser and your Judge? Be sure of this, that if Job could not answer his God in this world, how much less will you be able to do it in the world to come.

2. *To those who are humbled under a sense of their vileness*. We bless God if you have been brought with sincerity of heart to say, "Behold, I am vile." If you feel your unworthiness as you ought to do, then will all the promises of the gospel appeal to you exactly as suited to your condition, and Christ will be truly precious to your souls. Whom does he invite to come to him but those that are weary and heavy laden? What was the end for which he died upon the cross? Was it not to save sinners, even the chief? Yes, indeed, "It is a faithful saying, and worthy of all acceptance" (1 Timothy 1:15).

But while we would encourage all to come and wash away their sins in the fountain of his blood, we would caution all against turning the grace of God into licentiousness. Many, in acknowledging the depravity of their nature, also make it an excuse for their sins.

Their acknowledgments may be sincere, but they are attended with no real tenderness of spirit, no deep contrition, no real self-loathing and self-abhorrence. Brethren, above all things guard this state of affairs. While you are ignorant of your vileness, there is hope that your eyes may be opened to see it and your heart be humbled under a sense of it. But to acknowledge it and yet remain obdurate is a fearful anticipation of that final impenitence that is everlasting ruin (Revelation. 16:9, 11, 21). If you would be right, you must stand equally remote from all presumption and despondency. Your vileness must drive you not away from Christ, but to him. And when you are most confident of your acceptance with him, you must walk softly before him all the days of your life.

SERMON 723
DAVID'S WAITING UPON GOD

*"I wait for the LORD, my soul waits, and in
his word do I hope. My soul waits for the
LORD more than they that watch for the
morning; I say, more than they that watch
for the morning" (Psalm 130:5, 6).*

Many of God's people are sometimes reduced to great straits,
either because of the violence of persecution or by the force
of temptation. So under such circumstances, what is the refuge
that they can have except in God? It is futile for them to look to
any creaturely help. It sometimes does not appear to them to even
wait upon God, because the desired relief seems so long in coming.
Under delays of just this kind, David was sometimes discouraged.
But whatever were the depths into which he had fallen, it is clear
that he cast himself upon the mercy of his God and was determined to "hold fast by God" and to maintain his confidence in him
even to the end.

I. THE EXPERIENCE OF DAVID

He describes it in few words: "He waited upon God." The comparison by which he illustrates his attitudes gives us a clue to really
understand the full import of his words. He is possibly referring to
watchmen who after a long and tedious night wait for the morning
when they will be released from their fatigues and retire to rest.
But I think rather he is referring to the priests and Levites whom
he had appointed to watch nightly in the tabernacle (Psalm

239

134:1), and who if they were not filled with a spirit of devotion by which they might enjoy communion with their God, would earnestly long for the morning to come so that their irksome task might be over. But more than they longed, David longed for the return of God to his soul.

1. *He waited for God with earnest desire.* No temporal distress can compare with what is spiritual. The troubles of an awakened or tempted soul are very heavy. The depths to which it is plunged in apprehending God's wrath are terrible. No wonder that David "panted after the LORD, as the hart after the water-brooks" (Psalm 42:1-3). No wonder when God's answers to his prayers were delayed, he cried, "How long, O LORD! How long?" (Psalm 6:3; 13:1, 2). But God does not disapprove of such importunity. On the contrary, he would have us "cry day and night to him" (Luke 18:7) and give him no rest until he arises and comes to our relief (Isaiah 62:6, 7).

2. *He waited with patient hope.* Although earnest in prayer, he was willing to wait the Lord's leisure. He would not attempt to use any wrong means for his own relief. Repeatedly it was in his power to slay Saul. But he would never perpetrate the act himself nor allow others to do so. Instead, he committed his cause to God, to whom vengeance alone belongs. So in reference to the mercies that he desired at God's hands, he was willing to wait. He evidenced his earnestness in that he says repeatedly, "My soul waits." It was not merely a wish that he entertained for relief, but a most intense desire. Yet he was as far from impatience as he was from indifference. He rested upon the Word of God: "In his Word," he says, "I hope." It was quite sufficient for him to know that God had promised to help his tempted people. And whatever apparent contradictions there might be between his actions and his word, the Psalmist had no doubt that they would all be cleared up in due time, and that not a jot or tittle of God's Word would pass away until all were fulfilled.

3. *He waited with confidence.* A watchman knows that eventually the morning will come. So instead of abandoning his post, he waits until the proper time for his relief. Thus David assured himself that God would come to him at last, and reveal himself to him out of the abundance of his grace and love. The verses that follow

my text show this to have been the real experience of his soul. So this affords me an opportunity to,

II. COMMEND IT TO YOUR IMITATIONS

Not only in this context, but in other places we find David calling upon us to imitate his example. He encourages us to avail ourselves of his experience for the comfort and direction of our own souls. "I had fainted," he says, "unless I had believed to see the goodness of the LORD in the land of the living. Wait on the LORD, be of good courage, and he shall strengthen your heart. Wait, I say, on the LORD" (Psalm 27:13, 14). So I would now urge you to look at the attitude of David's soul in this time of trial.

1. *Consider how it is relevant to every one of you.* You may not have committed David's sins or have been subject to David's trials. But which of us is not a sinner before God? Who among us does not need mercy? Who cannot find his consolation entirely in the contemplation of God? Can we not say with David, "If thou, LORD, should mark iniquities, O LORD, who shall stand? But there is forgiveness with thee, that thou may be feared"? (Psalm 130:3, 4). So it is plain that this spirit of waiting should mark us also. Indeed, in a spirit of repentance you should cry to God, "LORD, hear my voice, let thine ear be attentive to the voice of my supplications!" (Psalm 130:2).

However long God may defer his answer to your prayers, you should wait with meekness and patience. "If the eyes of a servant are to the hand of his master, and the eyes of a maiden to the hand of her mistress, should not your eyes be unto the LORD your God until he have mercy upon you?" (Psalm 123:2). Surely you should be as observant of God as you expect your colleagues to be of you. Think how long God has waited upon you. He has called, but you would not hear. He has entreated, but you would not regard him. Will you then be impatient if he does not come at the moment that you call? And this especially when you are urged by nothing but a fear of his wrath which you richly deserve? Know, every one of you, that it becomes you to await his appointed time. Be content if the morning never comes until the very moment of your departure from this world of woe.

2. *See what honor this does to God.* A meek, patient, and submissive spirit honors every perfection of the Godhead, for they express a confidence in his wisdom as alone discerning the right time to appear on your behalf. It demonstrates the reality of his goodness, which does not willingly afflict you, but orders everything for your greatest good, even to humble you the more deeply and to prepare you for a richer appreciation of his mercy whenever it is granted to you. It also honors his power, as able to bring relief whenever his wisdom and goodness judge that it is expedient to confer this. Above all, it glorifies God's truth and faithfulness, since it makes the written Word a ground of hope—indeed, an assured hope that whatever God has promised he will perform.

So I ask then, is it not desirable that you should be found in an attitude by which God is so honored and with which he cannot but be pleased? So let every one of you be able to make the statement to God, "I have waited for thy salvation, O LORD" (Genesis 49:18).

3. *See what benefit it gives to the waiting soul.* It is justly said, "The LORD is good to them that wait for him, to the soul that seeks him. It is good that a man should both hope and quietly wait for the salvation of the LORD" (Lamentations 3:25, 26). Let us hear the psalmist's own experience: "I waited patiently for the LORD, and he inclined unto me and heard my cry. He brought me up also out of an horrible pit, out of the miry clay, and set my feet upon a rock and established my goings: and he has put a new song into my mouth, even praise unto our God" (Psalm 40:1-3).

And who is there, even though he should not have been delivered to the same extent, that must not also say, "It is good for me to draw near to God"? (Psalm 73:28). I urge you then to adopt this resolution of the psalmist, "I will wait on thy name; for it is good before thy saints" (Psalm 52:9). So if at any time your mind is disturbed by reason of delay, check and chide your soul as David did: "Why are you cast down, O my soul? and why are you disquieted within me? Hope in God: for I shall yet praise him, who is the health of my countenance and my God" (Psalm 42:11). You must never forget that appeal which God himself makes to the whole world, "I said not to the seed of Jacob, 'Seek you me in vain'" (Isaiah 45:19). Even in this world you may be sure that God will accept and bless you. For he has said, "They that wait upon the LORD shall renew their strength; they shall mount up with wings as eagles; they shall run and not be weary; they shall walk and not faint" (Isaiah 40:31).

But in the world to come, can anyone doubt the acceptance of a penitent, contrite, and believing soul? You might as well doubt the existence of God himself. For he has said that "we shall reap if we faint not" (Galatians 6:9). To all his believing Israel he has pledged that "they shall be saved in the LORD with an everlasting salvation, and shall not be ashamed nor confounded, world without end" (Isaiah 45:17).

SERMON 1131
THE CHARACTER OF DANIEL

*"Then these men said, We shall not find any
occasion against this Daniel, except we find
it against him concerning the law of his
God" (Daniel 6:5).*

A mong the many things which Solomon denounces as "vanity
and vexation of spirit" is this: that "for every right work, a
man is envied of his neighbor" (Ecclesiastes 4:4). For no consideration, either of the intrinsic worth of virtue or the benefits that
result from it to the world, will abate the malignant expressions of
an envious mind. For many years, as a minister of state, Daniel
had conferred great blessings on the Babylonian empire (Daniel
2:48, 49). Now, after conquering Babylon, the Medo-Persian
monarch Darius became convinced of Daniel's outstanding abilities and placed him next to himself in power and authority over
his empire. Such had been the wisdom and integrity of Daniel in
the discharge of his high office, that those most capable of finding
any fault in his administration—and indeed those most intent on
making such a discovery, if ever it could be found—were
incapable of pointing the finger at anything at all.

But were they grateful to him for his services? Not at all. They
were envious of his talents, his virtues, and his honors, and labored with all their might to destroy him. "Then the presidents
and princes sought to find occasion against Daniel concerning the
kingdom; but they could find no occasion nor fault. For he was
faithful, and there was no error or fault found in him" (v. 4). They
were forced to admit this at the very time that they conspired to
take away his life. "Then these men said, 'We shall not find any

occasion against this Daniel, except we find it against him concerning the law of his God.'" Thus they not only acknowledged the astonishing excellence of his character, but they actually found in it their hope of prevailing against him. As it was only by putting in direct opposition to each other the commands of God and those of man, they hoped to involve him in something that would give occasion of complaint against him.

I shall take no further notice of their intense envy. For it is the character of Daniel that I want to draw to your attention. It is a character all the more remarkable since it has been drawn, not by friends, but by foes. And it was not for the sake of commendation, but for the sake only of finding out the best way of destroying him.

In the establishment of such a character as this, there must have been a very rare combination of virtues in Daniel. So let us, in order to clearly understand his character, be stirred up to each seek for himself the same attendant. Let me therefore,

I. DESCRIBE TO YOU THE TRAITS OF HIS CHARACTER

First we see in combined and continual exercise:

1. *Piety*. Undoubtedly this was at the heart of it all. And how deeply rooted it was in him his own enemies declared, for it was upon his piety that their hopes of winning against him were based—since if his piety was not sufficient to expose him, then their plot (as far as a violation of human laws was concerned) would have been defeated.

It is from this principle alone that any real good can come, for nothing but piety can produce consistency of conduct. For the corruptions of human nature are too strong to be overcome by anything but the grace of God. A man may be wise and experienced as a statesman, and yet fail in the practice of religion and virtue. But no one can maintain for a long period, and under every possible condition or difficulties, a conduct which is not open to some measure of censure, especially to those who "watch and wait for his halting." This can only be if he is assisted from on high and is in the habit of walking in the presence of the omniscient God.

This, then, is the first thing which is essential if human effort is to be profitable. Let your hearts be right with God. Come to him as sinners in the name of his dear Son. Experience from him a sense of his acceptance and a confidence that you are reconciled in him to God and the Father. Ask him to write his law upon your hearts so that you may have a consistent standard to which you will refer every emotion and thought. Look to him for the assistance of his good Spirit under all difficulties. Make it your constant aim to please him. Then you will have within you an Associate who will enable you to find your way in safety through this trackless wilderness. When your eye is directed to his law as your rule, and his glory as your end, then you are safe.

2. **Wisdom.** He also excelled remarkably in this. Otherwise he could not have conducted himself so exceptionally as he did for so many years throughout circumstances that were so complex and rigorous. The report of the Queen of Babylon to King Belshazzar about him was, "There is a man in your kingdom, in whom is the spirit of the holy gods; and in the days of your father light, understanding, and wisdom like the wisdom of the gods was found in him" (Daniel 5:10, 11). Ezekiel, a contemporary of Daniel, spoke of him as eminently distinguished in this regard (Ezekiel 28:3). Indeed, this was the reason that preference was given to him by the King of Persia above all the native princes: "He was preferred above the presidents and princes because an excellent spirit was in him" (v. 3).

This, too, should be found in us. Nor can we ever hope to be held in such esteem except by a few kind and partial friends. To those who are enemies of religion we shall only give disgust, unless our piety is wisely directed and controlled. It is certain that many well-meaning people give great offense by their unwise behavior. Indeed, they involve themselves in too many troubles which by more wisdom they could have avoided. So our Lord warns us about this: "Do not give that which is holy to the dogs, nor cast your pearls before swine; lest they trample them under their feet, and turn again and rend you" (Matthew 7:6). There may indeed be a carnal wisdom to which we should not listen. For flesh and blood are blind counselors to confer with (Galatians 1:16). But there is also sound wisdom and discretion, which is highly commendable and greatly conducive to good. So the apostle Paul says, "Walk in wisdom toward them that are without" (Colossians 4:5). So I cannot but recommend to all who are devout to take heed how they exercise it. For they can in their weakness and folly make religion itself to be looked upon as foolish, and involve in common reproach all who profess to serve their God. So the resolve of Daniel should be that of each one of us: "I will behave myself wisely in a perfect way" (Psalm 101:2).

3. *Consistency*. Clearly Daniel attended to all his duties, both those in the affairs of men, but especially those with reference to God. What a happy situation it would be if the same focus prevailed among religious professors today! But too often religious people set the two tables of law in opposition to each other. It is as if the fulfillment of the one meant the preclusion of the other. How common it is for young people to rebel against parental authority, under the idea that obedience to God must swallow up every other consideration. They certainly must do this with regard to authority that is directly opposed to God. But many concessions may be made, and indeed should be, in those things where there is no moral guilt involved nor direct opposition to a divine command. So where the path of duty is clear, sensitivity should be shown to the feelings and prejudices of a parent in pursuit of them. Indeed, filial obedience in God's estimate stands second only to that which we owe to him.

It is a common fault in servants who neglect their duties from a pretended regard for God. So instead of exercising a becoming respect for their masters, they are petulant and impatient of reproof and all too quick to "answer again." So in the conduct of masters there is also much to blame. For it is easy in the pursuit of religious duties (as they are called) to develop carelessness in personal and domestic affairs. All of this gives cause for offense, and so it must be carefully avoided by all who would maintain a consistent conduct and adorn the doctrine of God our Savior.

4. *Firmness*. The enemies of Daniel especially depended on this. They gave him credit for his piety, believing that not even the terror of a den of lions would induce him to violate his conscience and offend his God. In the affairs of state they could find no occasion against him. But in what concerned the law of his God, they were confident that they could find some basis of accusation against him. They were right in this. For he not only would not withhold from God his accustomed times of prayer and praise, but he would not even appear to do this. So he did not even shut his

window in case in appearance he gave them some ground of triumph over him. So he persisted as before to worship God in his accustomed way and to avow publicly his determined adherence to his conscience and faith.

He offers us an admirable example. We must expect "persecution from men, if we will live godly in Christ Jesus." No piety, no wisdom, no consistency can remove prejudice or suppress envy. Rather, we must expect opposition in proportion as our light shines before men. No one was as blameless as our blessed Lord. Yet no one was more persecuted with such general and unrelenting animosity. But our hearts must be fixed. We must be willing to sacrifice all that we have, including life itself, rather than dishonor God or violate his commands. So others should know beforehand where our path of duty lies, even though the whole world turns against us. This we should seek in all circumstances and have the same reply upon our lips: "Whether it be right to hearken to you more than unto God, judge you."

II. SEEK TO HAVE THIS CHARACTER

1. *Consider how it honors God.* Indeed, such conduct as Daniel's was never seen on earth, except among the servants of the Lord. Nothing but God's grace can possibly produce it. But wherever his grace operates, to the measure that it is found, this character is seen. No one can ever "behold such light" as Daniel reflected, but he will be immediately constrained to "glorify our Father which is in heaven." Man can as soon create a world as to form this new creation. So wherever it is found, one is forced to acknowledge, "He that has wrought us to the self-same thing is God."

2. *Consider how it disarms prejudice.* Lack of piety, wisdom, or consistency in a believer causes "the real truth to be evil spoken of" and "God himself to be blasphemed." But devout and consistent behavior forces the very enemies of God to acknowledge "the righteous is more excellent than his neighbor." So Paul, exhorting Titus "to show himself in all things a pattern of good works," adds "that he that is on the contrary part will be ashamed, having no evil thing to say of you" (Titus 2:7, 8). I well know that no blameless conduct can conciliate an ungodly man. For as long as he loves

darkness rather than light, he must hate you. But at least you can hope "to put to silence the ignorance of foolish men" (1 Peter 2:12, 15), and to "make those ashamed who falsely accuse your good conversation in Christ" (1 Peter 3:16).

3. *Consider how it benefits your own soul.* Doubtless your eternal reward will be in the light of your present attainments. So he "that builds on the good foundation nothing but wood, hay, stubble, will suffer loss, and if saved at all, be saved only as by fire" (1 Corinthians 3:12-15). But whoever encompasses in his mind and illustrates in his life the whole of his duties to God and man will have an entrance given to him abundantly into the kingdom of our Lord and Savior Jesus Christ (2 Peter 1:5-11). The more we improve our gifts, the richer will be the recompense. The more we improve our talents, the richer will be our reward for faithfulness. We may not have such a deliverance on our behalf as Daniel had in the lion's den. Nor may we see the vengeance of God executed upon our adversaries. But we shall have strength given to us to sustain our trials, and the weight of glory will be awarded to us. So go on then, "strong in the Lord, and in the power of his might." "Hold fast your confidence firm to the end." Then "your labor shall not be in vain in the Lord." For "if you suffer with him you shall also be glorified together" (Romans 8:17).

Part XI
THE MARKS OF A REAL CHRISTIAN

SERMON 709
THE TRUE TEST OF
RELIGION IN THE SOUL

"I esteem all thy precepts concerning all
things to be right; and I hate every false
way" (Psalm 119:128).

Religion is the same in every age. The doctrines of it, although they have been more fully and clearly revealed under the Christian dispensation, have never varied in substance. Nor has the practice of it ever changed except in the observance of rites and ceremonies. To love God with all our heart and mind and soul and strength, and our neighbor as ourselves, was the essence of true religion in the days of Abraham and of Moses. And so it is today. Doubtless there can be no true religion where the gospel is set at naught and despised. But the gospel may be highly approved as a system while the heart is far from being right with God. It is not by their profession of any principles that we are to judge of the condition of men, but by the practical effects of those principles on their hearts and lives. Our blessed Lord has established this as the only true criterion, the only adequate test: "By their fruits ye shall know them."

The genuine fruit of piety is as clearly exhibited in the words before us as in any other part of Scripture. The passage is especially worthy of our attention because the writer of it combines the fullest conviction of understanding together with the strongest affections of the heart. In his judgment, "He esteemed God's precepts to be right," and in his heart "he hated" everything that was opposed to them.

May God in his infinite mercy inspire us with the same

heavenly sentiments while we consider these two things: the Christian character as here portrayed, and the light which it reflects upon the gospel of Christ.

I. THE CHRISTIAN CHARACTER AS HERE PORTRAYED

In the text there is drawn a broad distinction between the child of God and every other person under heaven. For Christians are either nominal or real. Each class has gradations, from the highest to the lowest. But between the two classes there is an immense gulf which separates them as far as the east is from the west. To find out to which of the two we belong is of infinite importance. But self-love blinds our eyes and renders the discovery of it extremely difficult. This Scripture holds up, as it were, a mirror before us. If we look steadfastly into it, we may discern with great precision what manner of persons we really are.

The difference between the two classes is this: The nominal Christian, however eminent he may be in appearance, is partial in his regard for God's precepts (Malachi 2:9). But the true Christian approves and loves them all without exception (Psalm 119:6).

The nominal Christian, we say, is partial in his regard for God's precepts. He may esteem those who favor his own particular party. The Catholic, for instance, and the Protestant, will each glory in those passages of Scripture which seem to justify their adherence to their own respective modes of worship, and to afford them ground for believing that theirs is the more scriptural and apostolic church. The various classes of Protestants also will show an ardent zeal for what supports their respective tenets, and will be ready almost to anathematize each other in not giving sufficient weight to their particular passages on which they have found their respective differences. They not only esteem their own grounds of faith "to be right," but they "hate" the opinions opposed to them "as erroneous and false." The nominal Christian may also love those precepts which do not materially condemn him. The man who is sober, chaste, honest, just, temperate, and benevolent may take real pleasure in such passages of Scripture as inculcate the virtues in which he supposes that he himself has excelled. He may feel indignation against the ways in which such precepts are grossly violated.

He may further delight in such precepts as, according to his interpretation of them, afford him ground for rejecting the gospel. No passages in all the Word of God are more delightful to him than such as these: "Be not righteous overmuch"; "What does the Lord thy God require of you, but to do justly, and to love mercy, and to walk humbly with your God?" He is not afraid that he may not be righteous enough. Nor is he very anxious to inquire what is implied in walking humbly with God. For it is sufficient for him that these passages are, in his eyes, opposed to what he calls "enthusiasm." At the same time he will set aside the necessity of faith in the Lord Jesus and of a life of entire devotedness to his service. His hatred of all passages that bear an opposite aspect is in exact proportion to his zeal for these (that he has selected).

But while such portions of Scripture are approved by him, does he love all that the inspired volume contains? Does he love those precepts which are most sublime and spiritual? No. It is no pleasure to him to hear of "setting his affections on things above," or of having "his conversation in heaven." Nor does it give him any gratification to be told that the measure of holiness which he must aspire after is what was exhibited in the Lord Jesus, whose example he is to follow in the whole of his spirit and temper, his conversation and conduct, "walking in all things as he walked."

Nor is he much impressed with those precepts which "require much self-denial." "To crucify the flesh with the affections and lusts," and to root out from his soul every evil, although it be dear to him "as a right eye," or necessary to him "as a right hand," or to comply with those precepts as his only alternative between that and experiencing his portion in "hell-fire" is no attractive sound to his ears, although it proceeds from the meek and lowly Jesus (Mark 9:42-48).

Least of all is he pleased with precepts that strike at his besetting sin. The proud man does not have any pleasure in hearing about the workings of pride. Nor is the covetous man happy to have the sins of covetousness described. Likewise the gay and the dissipated dislike the ways of their folly being exposed. Nor is the self-righteous man pleased to know about the delusion of his hopes. No, they are all ready to deride the statements that will condemn their ways, just as the Pharisees derided our Lord when he exposed their covetous and hypocritical devices. "The Pharisees were covetous [it is said], and they derided him." The hearts of such rise against all such doctrines. With a great deal of bitterness they exclaimed, "In so saying, you reproach us" (Luke 11:45).

On the contrary, the true Christian approves and loves all the commands of God; both those which are evangelical, and those which are moral.

He loves those which are evangelical. It is no grief to him to be told that he must renounce all dependence on his own righteousness and rely entirely on the righteousness of the Lord Jesus Christ. Rather it is with heartfelt delight that he hears those gracious commands: "Look unto me, and be saved"; "Come unto me, and I will give you rest"; "Believe on me, and have everlasting life." "He esteems these precepts to be right," for he feels that they are suited exactly to his own need. He knows that his own righteousness is "as filthy rags." He knows that without the robe of Christ's righteousness, it is impossible for him to stand in the presence of a holy God. So whatever opposes this way of salvation, "he hates"; indeed, he shudders at the very thought of claiming anything on the ground of his own worthiness, saying: "God forbid that I should glory, save in the cross of our Lord Jesus Christ." Thankfully he traces all his mercies back to the covenant made from all eternity between the Father and the Son; and to that covenant he looks, as "ordered in all things, and sure." From his inmost soul he says of it, "This is all my salvation, and all my desire."

As is the need to come to Christ, so is there the need of "living altogether by faith in Christ" as the need of abiding in him as the branches of the living vine. There alone he receives from God's fullness continual supplies of grace and strength, and of "growing up into him in all things as our living Head." He sees the need of making him "our wisdom, our righteousness, our sanctification, our redemption," our *all*, and a glorifying in *him*, and in him alone. All of this is heard by the true Christian with utmost delight. For he desires that Christ should have all the glory. He sees that it is "right" that he who came down from heaven, and died upon the cross to save him, and ascended up on high, and has all fullness treasured up in him for the use of his church, dwells in them "as their very life." I repeat, he sees it "right" that this adorable Savior should be "exalted, and extolled, and be very high." He sees that he should be on earth as he is in heaven, the one object of our adoration and the continual theme of our praise.

While the blind and ignorant world is ready to blame his zeal for the Redeemer's glory as being carried to excess, his own constant grief is that he cannot love him more and serve him better.

Nor is the true Christian less delighted with the moral precepts, not one of which he would desire to have relaxed or moderated in the smallest degree. Instead of wishing them to be lowered to the standard of his attainments, or regarding them as grievous on account of their purity, he loves them for their purity (Psalm 119:140). He would esteem it his highest privilege to be conformed to them. He is well persuaded that they are all "holy and just and good." He loves them as perfective of his nature and conducive to his happiness.

He loves them, I repeat, as perfective of his nature. For what is holiness but a conformity to the divine image, as sin is to the image of the devil? It was by transgression that man lost that resemblance to the deity which was stamped upon him at his first creation. But it is by the new-creating influence of the Spirit, quickening him to a course of holy obedience, that this resemblance is gradually restored. Conscious of this, he longs for holiness, desiring to "be changed into his Redeemer's image from glory to glory by the Spirit of the Lord."

Nor does he love them less as conducive to his happiness. For sin and misery are as inseparable as holiness and true happiness. What is the language of every precept in the Decalogue? It is this: "Be holy and be happy." Of this he is convinced; and he finds by daily experience that "in keeping God's commandments there is great reward." He finds that "Wisdom's ways are indeed ways of pleasantness and peace."

At the same time, "he hates every false way." Every deviation from the perfect rule of righteousness is painful to him. He "hates it" and hates himself on account of it. Just as touch which might be scarcely felt on any other part of the body will occasion the severest pain to the eye, so those thoughts or feelings which would be completely unnoticed by other men inflict a wound on his conscience and cause him to go mournfully before the Lord of Hosts. Ask him on such an occasion, what is it that has caused him to moan and weep? Is it that his God has required so much? No: but that he himself has attained so little. He wants to "be sanctified wholly to the Lord, in body, soul, and spirit." If he could accomplish the desire of his heart, he would "stand perfect and complete in all the will of God." This is the object of his highest ambition. When he finds that in spite of all his efforts he still falls short of it, he groans inwardly and says with the apostle, "O wretched man that I am! Who shall deliver me from this body of sin and death?"

This, then, is the Christian's character. To a superficial observer he may not appear to differ much from others. But to those who have had opportunities to discover the real desires of his soul, he is a perfect contrast with the whole ungodly world. The very best of nominal Christians are content with low attainments and plead for indulgences in those things which are agreeable to their corrupt nature. The more sublime in spiritual precepts they soften down to the standard of their own practice. They rather applaud themselves for their excellencies, rather than loathe themselves for their defects.

The true Christian, in contrast, admits of no standard that is not that of absolute perfection. And in all that he falls short of it, he does his very best to loathe and "abhor himself in dust and ashes." Nor does he have any hope of acceptance with God other than in the light of the atonement which was once offered for him upon the cross, and of the blood which the Lord Jesus Christ once shed on Calvary to cleanse him from his sins. We do not mean to say that these defects are subversive of all the Christian's peace. For if that were the case, who could possess any peace at all? The Christian, in spite of his imperfections, has "comfort and the testimony of a good conscience," and an assurance that his God will "not be extreme to mark what he has done amiss." But he does not on this account allow himself any sin whatever. The use he makes of his own corruptions is to cleave the more steadfastly to Christ as his only hope, and to watch and pray the more diligently, that he may be preserved from evil and be enabled by divine grace to endure unto the end.

Now this description of the Christian's character leads me to show,

II. THE LIGHT IT REFLECTS ON THE GOSPEL OF CHRIST

Three things it suggests to us:

1. *An answer to those who misrepresent the gospel*
2. *A reproof to those who would abuse the gospel*
3. *A direction to those who would adorn the gospel*

First, we may derive from this an answer to those who misrepresent the gospel. It has in all ages been a favorite argument against the gospel that it supersedes the necessity of good works and opens the flood-gates of licentiousness. This was argued repeatedly against the apostle Paul himself. On that account he set himself to answer it with all imaginable care: "Shall we continue in sin that grace may abound?" And again, "Shall we sin because we are not under the law, but under grace?" To both these questions he answers with holy indignation: "God forbid!" When his enemies went so far as to affirm that he gave men a license to sin, saying, "Let us do evil that good may come," he scorned to return any answer other than this: "Their damnation is just."

It would be greatly wished that those who now so confidently repeat these accusations against the followers of the apostle would reflect on the guilt that they incur and the danger to which by such calumnies they expose themselves. Until now the same objections are made to all those statements which resemble Paul's. If we deny to good works the office of justifying the soul, we are represented as denying the necessity of them altogether. Although these objections have been refuted a thousand times, and should be refuted ten thousand times more, the enemies of the gospel will still repeat them with as much confidence as ever.

Let them, however, look into our text and see what David's principles were. For of all the Old Testament's saints, there is no one who more determinedly sought to be justified by the righteousness of Christ without any works of his own than he. Hear what is said of him by the apostle Paul, in confirming the very sentiments which Paul himself maintained: "To him that works not, but believes in him who justifies the ungodly, his faith is counted for righteousness." Likewise David describes the blessing of the man to whom God imputes righteousness without works, saying: "Blessed are those whose iniquities are forgiven, and whose sins are covered; blessed is the man to whom the Lord will not impute sin" (Romans 4:5-8). Here we have a full exposition of David's views respecting the gospel. And how did these views operate on his soul? Did the idea of being justified by a righteousness not his own, a righteousness without works, a righteousness imputed to him and apprehended solely by faith—did this, I say, make him regardless of good works? No. Look at the text and be convinced, you objector. Look at the text, you condemner, and blush.

Next, look at the writings of the apostle Paul and see whether there is any difference between them and David. Was there in theory? No. The apostle affirms that "the grace of God which brings salvation teaches us that, denying ungodliness and worldly lust, we should live righteously, soberly, and godly in this present world." Was there in practice? No, neither David nor any other saint ever made higher attainments in holiness than the apostle Paul. "He was not a wit behind the very chiefest apostles."

Perhaps it will be said that the professed followers of the apostle Paul differ from him in this respect: that while in speculation they adopt his doctrine, in practice they deny its sanctifying efficacy. That there are antinomians in the world, we confess: There were in the days of Christ and his apostles; some who called Christ, "'Lord! Lord!' while yet they did not the things which he commanded." And there were some who "professed to know God, but in works denied him." It is to be expected that corrupt as human nature is, such characters will be found in every age. But is such conduct the necessary result of these principles? Was it so in the apostles' days or is it so at this day? If justification by faith alone is the necessary cause of laxity in morals, how is it that a higher tone of morality is universally expected from those who maintain that doctrine than from others? Why is it that the smallest sins in such persons are more severely recognized than the most licentious lives of the ungodly world?

To all who misrepresent the gospel, we would give this answer: Look at David and see what effect the gospel had on him. Look at Paul and contemplate its effects upon him. Look at the insistent declarations of Scripture and see what was the life of all the primitive believers. Nay, look only at the expectations which you yourselves have formed. For if you see a professor of the gospel act unworthy of his profession, you deem him inconsistent. This is evidence that both the obligation to holiness is acknowledged on his part and the performance of it is expected on yours. Consequently the gospel is, by your mutual consent, "a doctrine according to godliness."

From the passage before us, we may in the next place offer a reproof to those who would abuse the gospel. We have already admitted—and with great grief we confess it—that there are some persons professedly of antinomian principles who are so occupied with contemplating what Christ has wrought out *for* them that they cannot give a moment's thought to what he has engaged to work *in* them. To speak of holiness, or any duty, they will look down upon as legalism. Indeed, they think that Christ has by his own obedience to the law superseded the necessity of holiness in us. They see the whole work of salvation as so finished by him that there remains nothing to be done by us, no repentance for sin, no obedience to God's commands, but merely to maintain confidence in the provisions of God's everlasting covenant and to rejoice in God as our portion.

Shocking as these thoughts are, they have been professed recently to a very large extent; and many have been deceived by them. To see how unscriptural they are, we need only refer to the character of David as depicted in the words of our text: Does he discard the law as a rule of life? Does he pour contempt upon the precepts of God as unworthy of his notice? No, throughout all his Psalms he speaks of them as objects of his supreme delight: "O how I love your law! All the day long is my study in it." "I love your precepts above gold; they are sweeter to me than honey on the honeycomb." Similarly Paul also says: "I consent unto the law that it is good"; and again, "I delight in the law of God after the inward man!" It is true that he does speak of himself as "dead to the law." Also he speaks of the law as dead with respect to himself. What use does he teach us to make of this liberty? Does he speak of it as freeing us from all moral obligations and restraints? No, but there is a reason for our giving up ourselves henceforth in a marriage union to Christ as our second husband, that we may bring forth fruit unto God (Romans 7:1-4; Galatians 2:19).

Now then, we would ask, were David and Paul right? If so, what must we think of the sentiments of these deluded people? Are they more spiritual than David? Or have they a deeper insight into the gospel than Paul? The very circumstance of their discarding all the exhortations of Paul and casting behind them all his practical instructions demonstrates that they are for the present, at least, "given up to a delusion, to believe a lie." Some of them, we trust, do not practically live according to these principles. And if this is so, we hope that God in his mercy will sooner or later give them to see their errors. For if they practically carry into effect these ideas, they will have reason to curse the day that ever they were born.

Let me particularly address the young people with some hints on this important subject.

When you go into the world, you will be in danger of being ensnared by people of this kind. There is something very imposing in the idea of glorifying the Lord Jesus Christ and of making him "all in all." The devout mind is delighted with this thought. So it is easily induced to regard jealously anything that may be supposed to interfere with it. But do not be wiser than what is written; and let nothing tempt you to imagine that you can honor Christ by setting aside any of his commandments. It is by your love to his commandments that you are to prove yourself to be his disciple. However delighted you may be with the visions of Mount Tabor, you must never forget that you have work also to do with the plain (Luke 9:33, 37).

We are far from wishing anyone to be working for self-righteous principles or in a legal spirit. Nor would we say a thing to discourage the fullest confidence in God. It is our privilege, doubtless, to trace all our mercies back to his everlasting love and to view them all as secured to us by covenant and by oath (Hebrews 6:17, 18). But then it is no less our privilege to fulfill God's will and to be like the holy angels, of whom it is said, that "they do his commandments, hearkening to the voice of his Word." So beware lest you ever be led away from this ground. Rejoice in the Lord Jesus Christ as the propitiation for your sins, as your all-prevailing advocate, and as your living Head. But while you believe in him and love him and rejoice in him, let your faith and love and joy stimulate you to a holy and unreserved obedience. If he has "set your heart at liberty," let the effect be to "make you run with more enlargement the way of his commandments."

Lastly, we would find from our text a direction to those who would adorn the gospel. "Esteem all God's precepts to be right, and hate every false way." If God has enjoined anything, do not ask whether the world approves of it. If he has forbidden anything, do not inquire of the world whether you should abstain from it. The world is an inadequate judge of Christian morality, as indeed it is of Christian principles. Both the one and the other are "foolishness to the natural man." Of all the more sublime precepts, whether evangelical or moral, they are ready to say, "This is a hard saying, who can hear it?" But let no true Christian "consult with flesh and blood." Rather let him say with David, "Away from me you wicked: I will keep the commandments of my God."

Does God call you to "live no longer to yourselves but unto him"? Does the Lord Jesus Christ bid you "follow him without the camp, bearing his reproach"? Are you ready to "lay down your lives for his sake"? Do not let these commandments be grievous in your eyes. Rather, "rejoice that you are counted worthy to suffer for his sake." If at any time you are being urged to turn aside from the path of duty, do not let the maxims or the habits of the world bias you one moment. You are "not to follow a multitude to do evil." If a thing is right, you should love it and cleave to it although the whole world should be against you. Do this just as Noah, Daniel, and Elijah did. And if a thing is evil, you must not do it, though it causes the loss of all things—even of life itself—as a test of your integrity. It were far better to go into a fiery furnace for your steadfastness than to save yourselves by an undue compliance.

Doubtless this holy walk and conversation will involve you in the charge of being peculiar. But whose fault is it if this conduct makes you appear so? Is it yours? Is it not rather theirs, who will not yield obedience to the precepts of their God? We mean not by this to justify anyone who would effect a needless peculiarity. Far from it. It is only where the world is wrong that we should recommend any severance from them. Wherever they are wrong, there you must "quit yourselves like men" and show them by your example a more perfect way. In fundamental matters, the whole universe should not shake your resolution. Where duty evidently calls, you must be firm and "faithful unto death." It is certainly "a strait and narrow way" in which you tread.

SERMON 1714
THE IMPORTANCE
OF UNITY AMONG CHRISTIANS

*"Neither do I pray for these alone, but for them also
which shall believe on me through their word; that
they all may be one as thou, Father, art in me, and I
in thee, that they also may be one in us: that the
world may believe that thou hast sent me"
(John 17:20, 21).*

I n the preceding part of this chapter, our Lord has been inter-
ceding especially for his own disciples. But here he intercedes
for all his people to the end of time. Who the particular persons
were is known only when the Word of God reaches their hearts
and they are made obedient to the faith of Christ. But the substance of the petition is clearly most important, because the Lord
had before made the same request on behalf of his own disciples.
Now he repeats it more strongly in the two verses following our
text.

We will try to show,

I. WHAT IS THAT UNION WHICH CHRIST
PRAYED FOR ON OUR BEHALF

If we interpret the union spoken of in verse 11 as relating only
to the testimony which the apostles were to bear concerning
Christ, still we cannot possibly limit the import of the text to that
sense. For the terms are too varied and too strong to admit of such
a limitation. The comparison instituted between Christ's union
with the Father and ours with each other in him leads our thoughts
into a far different channel; a channel mysterious indeed, but
deeply fraught with the richest instruction. Christ is one with the

Father, in essence and in operation; being "the brightness of his Father's glory and the express image of his person," and at the same time acting in everything in perfect concert with the Father. Having no will but his, he speaks nothing but according to his commands, doing nothing but his direction and seeking only the glory of his name.

This fitly illustrates the union which his people have with each other in and through him:

1. **They are formed into one body.** Sometimes they are represented as a temple, composed of living stones and having a living stone for its foundation, even Jesus Christ himself. They are built as a habitation for God himself (1 Peter 2:4, 5; Ephesians 2:20-22). At other times they are spoken of as a body, of which Christ is the Head and all the different individuals are members (1 Corinthians 12:12, 13, 27). Thus, while they are united with each other, they are also united with the Father and the Son: "The Father is in Christ, and Christ is in them; and thus they are made perfect in one," ever "growing up into Christ as their Head," and contributing to each other's perfection until they arrive at "the full measure of the stature of Christ" (Ephesians 4:13, 15, 16).

How earnestly the Lord Jesus Christ desired this may be gathered from the frequent repetition of it already noticed. Well might he plead for it in this way, since its accomplishment was the chief purpose of his death (John 11:51, 52). It was the great end of God the Father in the whole economy of redemption (Ephesians 1:9, 10).

2. **They are all animated by one spirit.** "He that is joined to the Lord," says the apostle, "is one Spirit" (1 Corinthians 6:17). This is true of every individual and of the whole collective body of believers. "Christ dwells in all of them," and "as Christ himself lived by the Father, so do they live by him" (Ephesians 3:17; Colossians 3:4; John 6:56, 57). Hence there is no distraction in the body, but in consequence of its being under the control of one living, governing principle, its powers are all exerted harmoniously for the attainment of the same objective. So the members of Christ's mystical body are one in sentiment, in affection, and in the scope and tenor of their lives.

In *sentiment* they are one. Although in matters of little consequence there may be a wide difference between them, yet in the fundamentals—such as our fall in Adam, our recovery by Christ, our renovation by the Spirit, the evil of sin, the beauty of holiness, the security of believers, and many other points connected with the spiritual life—there is no difference. All that are taught of God agree on these things. But if they differ a little in an argument, they agree completely when they come upon their knees before God. This shows that their differences are more imaginary than real. For there is "a unity of faith" to which they all come (Ephesians 4:13). The uneducated Indian attains as easily to this as the most learned philosopher. For it is learned by the heart rather than by the head. It is God alone that can guide us to the knowledge of it (1 Corinthians 2:14).

In *affection* they are also one, being "kindly affectioned one to another with brotherly love," and "loving one another with a pure heart fervently." They are all "taught of God to do so" (1 Thessalonians 4:9). What the real tendency is of Christianity may be seen in the effects produced on the first Christians (Acts 2:44, 45; 4:32). If there is not the same measure of love among Christians today, it is not because of any lack of efficacy in the grace of God, but to the meager measure in which it is possessed. For in proportion as the grace of Christ abounds in the soul, so there will be the measure of our faith and love (1 Timothy 1:14).

Moreover, in the *scope and tenor of their lives* they are also one. They all acknowledge the Scriptures as the one directory which they are to follow. According to their several attainments, "they walk by the same rule" (Philippians 3:16; Galatians 6:16). Without this, all other "unity," whether "in the faith" or "in the Spirit," is of no avail.

This "holding of the Head" by faith, this ministering to each other by love, and this progressive increase of the whole body in the ways of holiness constitutes that true union which the gospel produces and which our Lord so earnestly desired on our behalf (Colossians 2:19).

Let us now consider,

II. Its Unspeakable Importance

Clearly it is of utmost importance. For on it depends:

1. *The honor of Christ.* In the days of the apostles, the Messiah-ship of Christ was abundantly proved by the most remarkable miracles that were wrought in confirmation of it. But it was the design of God that when Christianity was once established, it should carry its own evidence along with it, convincing men by producing such effects in the world as would demonstrate to all its divine origin. The perfect consistency which there was in the testimony of all the apostles and of the first teachers of Christianity shows that they must have been inspired by the same Spirit. He kept them from all error and guided them into all truth. In the whole apostolic age we only read of one point of difference that arose. This was whether the believing Gentiles should be required to submit to circumcision or not. Even that was discussed not for the dissatisfaction of any of the apostles, but only for some of the less enlightened converts. The agreement which there was in doctrine was made more obvious by the wonderful unity which was shown in the life and conversation of the whole church.

There were indeed spots and blemishes in many. But these were approved by the authorized teachers of religion, and served to illustrate more clearly the proper efficacy of the gospel (1 Corinthians 11:19). Twice our Lord suggests that this union of his people would confirm the truth of his mission (Compare v. 23 with the text). It is certain that the same effects are produced by it at this time. Where should we look for such a union of feeling, of affection, and of conduct as is to be found in the Church of Christ?

Because of this, believers are distinguished as a peculiar people. The very peculiarity which pervades the church of God makes an impression on the hearts of thousands, who if they could instantly attain to a measure of peace and holiness which they see in the true believer, would willingly sacrifice all that they have in the world for it. But because of the intrinsic corruptions which they have, they are determined to go on in sin, though they are constrained to acknowledge that the gospel of Christ is a faithful saying, worthy of all acceptation.

2. *The credit of the church.* God the Father "loves his people, even as he loves his only dear Son" (see v. 23). But how is it to be known that he loves them? Who can look into their hearts and see those evidences which he makes of himself there, as he does

not to the world? When "he sheds abroad his love there," who can discern it but the people themselves? As Solomon expresses it, who can "interfere with their joy"? It is only to be discerned by the effects it produces in their lives, just as the radiant countenance of Moses attested to the intercourse that he had had with God. So where the piety of anyone is of an exalted kind, it carries with it a conviction to the minds of others. It makes religion itself appear to be honorable and induces many to say, "We will go with you; for we perceive that God is with you and the truth."

3. *The welfare of the world generally.* In general, the world "hates the light, and will not come to it, lest its deeds should be reproved." But Christians, when they live truly exemplary lives, are living witnesses for God. They are epistles of Christ, known and read of all men. Their whole spirit and conduct is a sermon to all around them. The apostle Peter tells us that many unbelieving people who utterly despise the Word of God are "won by the good conversation" and conduct of their devout friends. On the other hand, we know that divisions and scandals in the church are the way of casting a stumbling-block before many, over which they fall to their eternal ruin. So what can more strongly evidence the importance of union in the church than such serious considerations? Surely if the welfare of the world so much depends on it, no wonder our Lord offered such repeated supplications for it on our behalf. Nor should we ever cease in our exertions for the advancement of it in the church of God.

From this subject we see:

1. *The duty of the world to be united to the church.* The church is represented as "one fold under one Shepherd." We must be gathered to that fold. Nor must we decline that open profession that shows us to be his sheep. If we are ashamed of Christ and his people, Christ will be ashamed of us. We must not only "believe with our hearts unto righteousness, but make confession with our mouths unto salvation." As Judah and Israel are to become one at that latter day, like two sticks in the prophet's hand (Ezekiel 37:16-22), so are Jews and Gentiles, rich and poor, to be all one in Christ Jesus (Galatians 3:28). Therefore I call on all "to give themselves to us" as the apostle Paul expresses it, but first to "give up their whole selves to the Lord" (2 Corinthians 8:5).

2. *The duty of the church to be united with itself.* Whoever hears the pleading of our blessed Lord so earnestly for this objective, how can he doubt what his duty is? If any doubt remains, let the apostle Paul determine it. This objective was so desirable in his eyes that it seems as if he never could be sufficiently urgent with his converts to cultivate it with all their hearts (1 Corinthians 1:10; Philippians 2:1-4). So let us ask God to "give us one heart and one way." Thus the sweetest fellowship will be given, not only with each other, but with the Father and with Christ. Then "the blood of Jesus Christ his Son shall cleanse us from all sin" (1 John 1:3,7).

SERMON 2235
GODLINESS WITH CONTENTMENT

"Godliness with contentment is great gain"
(1 Timothy 6:6).

To the great dishonor of Christianity, there are many professors, and even teachers, who are more content on promoting their own temporal interests or the interests of their party, than on advancing practical religion in the world. It is of such that the apostle Paul is speaking in the context. He enjoins to withdraw himself from them, as from those who disgrace the name of Christ, by giving reason for people to conclude that "they supposed gain to be godliness." In contrast to such characters, the apostle contradicts their opinion. He declares that although gain was not godliness, godliness was gain—indeed, "great gain"—if they linked it "with contentment."

To support this view, let us:

I. UNDERSTAND WHAT WE MEAN BY "GODLINESS"

The mindset which we may concede angels enjoy in no way suits us. For we are sinners, redeemed sinners. Therefore "godliness" must include such a frame of mind as becomes our condition. In view of this, it implies:

1. **A trust in God through Christ.** This is the basis of all true religion. Whatever a man may possess without this leaves him without a particle of real godliness. If we could imagine him to be as

273

just and honest, as kind and friendly, as devout and fervent as any man ever was, yet even if he did not have the heart of a sinner— that is to say a sinner justly condemned and delivered solely from condemnation by the blood of Christ—he would be utterly without true religion.

2. *A devotedness to God in Christ.* This must come from the former. For although faith and practice differ from each other, just as the root of a tree does from the fruit that it bears, yet we must in no way try to separate them, since they are equally essential to real godliness. A reformation of external conduct, or a partial surrender of the heart to God, will not do. If we would be approved by God, we must have "our whole selves, body, soul, and spirit, sanctified" to his service. And as Christ is the only Mediator through whom we approach God, so must Christ, that is to say God in Christ, be our only Lord and Ruler.

When we have such views of the nature of godliness then we see:

II. THE CONNECTION OF GODLINESS WITH CONTENTMENT

Such godliness as we have described must bring contentment with it, since all who possess it must feel:

1. *A consciousness that they deserve the miseries of hell.* No one can have a true union with God through Christ unless he has felt his desert of God's wrath and indignation. Can such a one be discontented with any lot that may be his? Must he not, even in the greatest suffering, say, "Shall a living man complain, a man for the punishment of his sins?" Will he not call every affliction light indeed, in comparison with the misery he deserves? Will he not under the pressure of the heaviest calamities thank God that he is not in hell?

2. *A sense of infinite obligation to God for mercies received.* One who has within him the elements of real godliness must see himself to be infinitely indebted to God for the gift of his dear Son, for the knowledge of salvation by him, and for the prospect of everlasting glory. A sense of these mercies cannot but be heightened also by the consideration that they were never offered to fallen angels,

nor accepted by the great majority of those to whom they have been offered. Can such a one grumble that he has a less measure of health, or riches, or material advantages than others, when he is so far exalted above them in things which matter infinitely more?

3. *A willingness to be conformed to the image of Christ.* No true disciple of Christ expects or wishes to be in a situation different from what his Lord and Master experienced when on earth. What was the condition of Jesus in the world? Did he live in ease, affluence, and honor? Indeed not: "He was despised and rejected of men, a man of sorrows and acquainted with grief." Often he had to depend upon the kind support of his friends and followers. But often he had not even "a place where to lay his head." Reflecting on this, who among us could ever grumble, since we know nothing about the poverty and persecution that awaited him? Should we not curb the first signs of discontent with this obvious reflection, "the disciple cannot be above his Lord. It is sufficient for the disciple that he be as his Lord."

The link between godliness and contentment being clear, let us now consider:

III. The Advantage of This Connection

The apostle Paul tells us that "godliness is profitable unto all things, having the promise of the life that now is, and of that which is to come." Let us see it then:

1. *In reference to this life.* Money is often conceived of with the exclusive title of "gain." But godliness has an incomparably greater right to that title. There are three chief ways in which money is considered valuable: to provide present gratification, to secure against future troubles, and to benefit our children, our dependents.

But in all these respects it cannot for one moment compete with godliness, for with godliness there is contentment. Suppose money was to afford every gratification one could conceive of— and that is a wild generalization—yet it will not pardon sin, give peace of conscience or enjoyment of the divine presence. Will these not far outweigh all such gratification? Suppose we assume money does give effective relief to our troubles, although it cannot assuage our pain either of mind or body; yet what consolations can equal those which come from godliness and contentment? The utmost that money can do is to provide some outward relief, whereas the piety described above will convert every cross into a comfort and every trouble into a fountain of joy. We are quite willing to admit that money has its uses, and very important uses too, but it can also be more of a curse to our children and dependents than a benefit. But it is still far inferior to true religion. For the godly and contented man will instruct his children and dependents in those principles which he has found so beneficial to himself. And is not the legacy of many prayers far better than thousands of coins of silver and gold we may give them? So however money may be coveted, godliness with contentment is a richer portion.

2. *In reference to the world to come*. The most blind man of the world is not foolish enough to think that "riches will profit him in the day of wrath." For the words that follow our text establish beyond all contradiction: "For we brought nothing into this world, and it is certain that we can carry nothing out." Here all competition ceases, and "gain" is seen to belong exclusively to the godly and contented mind.

Address—

1. *Those who boast of contentment, while they are destitute of godliness*. We readily admit that there are people who feel content while enjoying all that they wish. But we have no real contentment unless we can be contented with any change of circumstances which God might see fit to give us. Nor indeed can this fruit come from anything but real godliness. So the complacency which many take in their own fancied contentment, while they are unaffected by vital godliness, is really only a delusion, which if not rectified, in time will result in the most fearful disappointment and misery.

2. *Those who profess godliness, but show a worldly or discontented spirit*. The tree must be judged by its fruits. It is in vain to have the highest pretensions to Christian experience if we are not dead to the world and resigned to the will of God. O brothers, how many professors of godliness have, "through a desire to be rich, fallen into snares and temptations, and into foolish and hurtful

lusts, which have drowned them in destruction and perdition" (vv. 9-11). Remember that "the love of money is the root of all evil, which while some have coveted after, they have pierced themselves through with many sorrows. But you, O man of God, flee these things, and seek rather to be rich toward God."

3. *Those who profess both godliness and contentment.* Know that you have a richer portion than crowns or kingdoms. You never can have any cause to envy anyone. Only seek to grow in these divine graces. Give yourselves up wholly to God, and "having food and raiment, be therewith content" (v. 8). Godliness is "durable riches." One grain of contentment is worth a talent of gold. So let it be seen, beloved, that you live under the full persuasion of these things. Then your ardor in pursuit of heaven will be accompanied with a proportionate indifference about the things of time and sense.

SERMON 702
TRUE FREEDOM

"I will walk at liberty;
for I seek thy precepts" (Psalm 119:45).

Civil liberty is justly appreciated among us. Yet there are few who have any real understanding of what that liberty is in regard to morality and religion. Everyone realizes that unrestrained freedom is licentiousness. But not everyone knows that a perfect obedience to God's holy Word is the most perfect freedom that man can enjoy. Yet this is plainly intimated in the passage before us; from which I will take the occasion to show:

I. THAT THE UNGODLY ARE STRANGERS TO TRUE FREEDOM

They may boast of freedom and "promise to give it to all who conform to their ways. But they are altogether in a state of bondage" (2 Peter 2:19).

1. *To the world.* The tastes of men will differ according to their age and the sphere in which they live. For every age and every social rank are subject to the laws of custom which they dare not infringe. Even the religion of men must be conformed to this standard. God's commandments must be related to the scale at which men have established customs for their own lives. So if one is told what God requires, he immediately thinks to himself, "What will this person say, or that person do, if I submit to such

279

requirements that are so alien to the habits of those around me? Will they not scorn my oddness and set themselves to oppose my insufferable attitude?" So to justify their conduct, people will put the Scriptures entirely aside as an out-of-date book whose dictates have been superseded by wiser and more practical maxims of the current way of life—which yet is "philosophy, falsely so called." Indeed, of all unconverted people it is declared that they "walk according to the course of this world" (Ephesians 2:2). They "gaze strangely at anyone who presumes to choose for himself a holier path" (1 Peter 4:4).

2. To the flesh. There are different degrees to which people will yield to the impulse of their corrupt appetites. But everyone has "a law in his members warring against the law of his mind, and bringing him into captivity to the law of sin which is in his members" (Romans 7:23). In fact, there is no one so ignorant that even to his unenlightened mind a better path than he pursues cannot be prescribed. Look around and see what are the attitudes and habits of those around us. Are they not all "fulfilling the desires of the flesh and of the mind" (Ephesians 2:3) without affecting anything higher than the gratification of their own corrupt appetites? We are told that "they who are after the flesh do mind the things of the flesh" (Romans 8:5). From infallible authority we know that to whomever we yield ourselves servants to obey, his servants we are to whom we obey" (Romans 6:16). Indeed, to our dying hour these conflicts with this tyrannical master will continue. Even the apostle Paul himself complained, "O wretched man that I am! Who shall deliver me from the body of this death?" (Romans 7:24).

3. To the devil. No wonder Satan is called "the god of this world: for he works in all the children of disobedience" (Ephesians 2:2). Ever since he seduced our first parents in Paradise, he has subjected the whole race of man to his dominion, "taking them in his snares and leading them captive at his will" (2 Timothy 2:26). Men may deny the agency and even the existence of this enemy, but this is only evidence to the extent to which they are "blinded by him" (2 Corinthians 4:4), and how effectually he has lulled them to sleep in his arms. No doubt it is very humiliating to think of ourselves as his slaves. But this is the true condition of every unconverted person. Even the saints themselves are not delivered from his influence, but only through the mighty power of Jehovah himself as a result of fervent and believing prayer (Ephesians 4:12-18, James 4:7).

But the Psalmist's reference to freedom leads us to see more clearly:

II. HOW TRUE FREEDOM IS GREATLY ENJOYED BY THOSE WHO LOVE AND SERVE GOD

David saw that his service for God was perfect freedom. Indeed, it is so for the man whom "the truth of the gospel has made free" (John 8:32) and who "looks to God's precepts" as his or her only rule of conduct.

1. *He walks according to his own judgment.* For he has insight into the mind and will of God and so clearly discerns that there is not in all the Scriptures a command which does not lead to the happiness of all who obey it. His own mind and conscience go along with the Word of God. They set their seal to the truth and excellency of all that is contained in the Word. "Not one commandment appears to him to be grievous" (1 John 5:3). The whole law of God is esteemed by such as "holy, just, and good" (Romans 7:12, Psalm 119:128). To "love God with all his heart and soul and strength, and his neighbor as himself" does not seem to him any hardship, but rather the fulfillment of his true nature and the completion of his happiness. In no way would he allow one single part of this law to be canceled or mitigated to the slightest extent. For his own judgment tells him that this is no less than his privilege as well as his duty to be "holy, as God is holy," and "perfect, as his Father who is in heaven is perfect."

2. *It is also agreeable to his own inclination of will.* He is neither drawn nor driven against his own will. He is indeed "made willing in the day of God's power" (Psalm 110:3). "He is drawn with the cords of a man, and with the bands of love" (Hosea 11:4). He does not all that he would do. Indeed, in too many ways "he does what he would not" (Romans 7:15). But this very thing shows that it is rather strength than inclination that he lacks (Romans 7:16-20). If he did have the desire of his heart, he would leave no sin unmortified and no duty unfulfilled. He is like one who is running in a

race or "fighting a fight," but he has the will to complete the race and to conquer his opponent and knows "that death itself, his last enemy, will be swallowed up in victory."

3. *He desires to exercise his affections wholly for God.* For he has real delight in God. He does not observe the duties of prayer and praise through any fear of hell, but rather from the real pleasure which he feels in coming near to God. It is his privilege to call him by the endearing name of Father, and he would walk in communion with him all the day long. Think of Adam before his fall. There you have an image of those who through the tender mercy of God are restored. True, they still have "the flesh lusting against the Spirit, as well as the Spirit lusting against the flesh, so that they neither do, nor can they do, all that they would" (Galatians 5:17). But their taste is the very same as that of angels. The joy of angels is begun in them. For their life so far as they have really attained is both a preparation for heaven and a foretaste of heaven in their souls.

In conclusion, let me commend this freedom to your acceptance.

Do not think, my brethren, that the gospel is a mere system of restraints. No, it is a "perfect law of liberty" (James 1:25). "All who are made free by Christ are become free indeed" (John 8:36). O that religion were understood from this perspective! No prisoner would have more delight to shake off his chains than sinners would be to emancipate themselves from the sore bondage in which they are held. Realize then, brethren, that I am authorized in the name of Jesus Christ to "preach deliverance to the captives and the opening of the prison to them that are bruised" (Luke 4:18, 19). The jubilee trumpet now sounds in your ears. It proclaims to you a restoration to all that you have ever lost and forfeited. Do you not think that the poor slave when he was given his freedom and inheritance did not see the trumpet to be a joyful sound? Let the gospel then be such a sound to you. Instead of regarding God's service as a heavy bondage, take up the language of the Psalmist: "I will walk at liberty; for I seek thy precepts." "Take upon you the yoke of Christ, and I pledge myself that you will find it light and easy; and you will obtain everlasting rest to your souls" (Matthew 11:28, 29).

Scripture Index

(References in bold type refer to sermon texts)

Subject Index